TYPOGRAPHY 35

HARPER
DESIGN

An Imprint of HarperCollins Publishers

CONTENTS

TYPOGRAPHY 35
Copyright © 2014 by
the Type Directors Club

For information, address:
Harper Design, 195 Broadway,
New York, NY 10007

HarperCollins books may be purchased for educational, business,
or sales promotional use.

For information, please write:
Special Markets Department
HarperCollins*Publishers*
195 Broadway, New York,
NY 10007

FIRST EDITION
First published in 2014 by:
Harper Design
An Imprint of
HarperCollins*Publishers*
195 Broadway,
New York, NY 10007
Tel / 212.207.7000
Fax / 212.207.7654
harperdesign@harpercollins.com
www.harpercollins.com

*Distributed throughout
the world by*:
HarperCollins*Publishers*
195 Broadway,
New York, NY 10007
Fax.212.207.7654

ISBN: 978-0-06-211289-7
Library of Congress
Control Number: 2014941854

Carol Wahler
Executive Director
Type Directors Club
347 West 36 Street
Suite 603
New York, NY 10018
Tel / 212.633.8943
E / director@tdc.org
W / tdc.org

ACKNOWLEDGMENTS
The Type Directors Club
gratefully acknowledges
the following for their
support and contributions
to the success of TDC60
and TDC2014.

DESIGN
Thomas Wilder
Leland Maschmeyer
Collins
collins1.com

EDITING
Dave Baker,
supercopyeditors.com

JUDGING FACILITIES
Pratt Institute,
Manhattan Campus

EXHIBITION FACILITIES
The Cooper Union

CHAIRPERSONS' & JUDGES' PHOTOS
Catalina Kulczer-Marin

**ONLINE SUBMISSION
APPLICATION DEVELOPMENT**

adcStudio

**TDC60 COMPETITION
CALL FOR ENTRIES DESIGN**
Thomas Wilder
Chris McCaddon
Leland Maschmeyer
Collins
collins1.com

BOOK DESIGN
Thomas Wilder
Leland Maschmeyer
Collins
collins1.com

The principal typefaces
used in the composition
of TYPOGRAPHY 35 are
Prestige Bold designed by
Clayton Smith, and Neuzeit,
designed by Wilhelm Pischner.

°*Signifies TDC Member*

Dutch typographer, type designer, author, lettering artist, and influential teacher Gerrit Noordzij was born in 1931 in Rotterdam and began teaching type design in 1960 at the Royal Academy of Art in The Hague. From 1970 until his retirement in 1990, he was an authoritative force in the writing and lettering program of the department of graphic design. Noordzij's influence is passed on to the international type community through the work of his former students — Petr van Blokland, Erik van Blokland, Just van Rossum, and Luc de Groot among them. He also continues to influence new generations of designers, as the method of teaching type design at the Academy is still largely based on his theoretical models, and his writings are still published in a variety of languages.

Although Noordzij has designed a number of typefaces, not many of them are available to the public. Instead, he has focused on type for his own projects, including his book design work for Van Oorschot publishers. He continues to refine, redraw, and add to many of his works. Ruse, Noordzij's first publicly distributed typeface, was issued by The Enschedé Font Foundry in 2000 when he was 68.

Noordzij is perhaps best known for *The Stroke: Theory of Writing* (the first incarnation of which was published in Dutch as *The Stroke of the Pen* in 1985), reissued by Hyphen Press in 2005. Noordzij's theory is that type is in its very essence calligraphic — although Noordzij would never use that word. He asserts that type is inextricably tied to writing, his preferred term, and defines typography as "writing with prefabricated letters." He proposes that handwriting reveals the logical construction of letters, through the dynamic translation, expansion, and rotation that occur when one is writing with a pen. With his "cube" theory, Noordzij can be seen as a progenitor of digital type development, in which typefaces have distinct axes of design variables that can be smoothly interpolated.

TDC board member Matteo Bologna pinpoints Noordzij's pivotal influence on type design software such as Superpolator — itself developed by Noordzij's student Erik van Blokland — which helps type designers generate type families with multiple axes of weight, width, contrast, et cetera.

Noordzij also wrote and edited *LetterLetter*, a journal in English for ATypI in which he published a series of meditations on typography, lettering, and typeface design. Noordzij's wit and irreverence are particularly evident in this series, where he spars with his "most faithful opponent" Nicolete Gray.

The Gerrit Noordzij Prize, an initiative of the Type and Media masters program of the Royal Academy, is bestowed upon typographic designers for extraordinary contributions to the field. The award, given every three years, recognizes writing and teaching as essential qualifications. Past recipients include Erik Spiekermann, Tobias Frere-Jones, and Wim Crouwel. Noordzij was the first person to receive this prize, in 1996.

TDC60
COMMUNICATION
DESIGN
CHAIRWOMAN'S STATEMENT

I've done everything in my power to avoid writing this statement, other than balancing my checkbook or getting my teeth cleaned. It shouldn't be that hard. I love type — everything about it, from ascender to descender, from initial cap to final punctuation. Good type makes getting through difficult text easier, even painless, and the shame of it all is that most people don't even realize it.

But not us — we're special. As type aficionados, we revel in each new font release, cherish weathered and worn ghost signs, and collect crazy things like old bottle caps because of the typography (okay, that one may just be me). We bookmark, we hoard. Few people get us, but we soldier on undeterred. We attend lectures. We join TDC. We have passion and a desire to share with our colleagues, and we crave more, more. More type blogs. More apps. More attention to letterspacing. We obsess.

Welcome to *Typography 35*, the place where we type folks can feel safe in our obsessions. Pore through the smartly designed pages from the folks at Collins and feel free to linger. You know you want to. You'll see familiar faces from annuals past, and hot new talent that makes your head explode. My thanks are extended to our fabulous jury for being so generous with their time and wisdom. Much gratitude goes to everyone who volunteered valuable weekend hours to help out, whether it was hanging posters or herding cats. And of course, without TDC Executive Director Carol Wahler, we'd just be printing a blank book.

Enjoy *Typography 35*, absorb it, and revisit it often for inspiration. That's the end of my statement; it's time to turn the page.

— Gail Anderson

Gail Anderson° is a New York-based designer, writer, educator, and partner at Anderson Newton Design.

From 2002 to 2010, Gail served as creative director of design at SpotCo, a New York City advertising agency that creates artwork for Broadway and institutional theater. From 1987 to early 2002, she worked at *Rolling Stone*, serving as designer, deputy art director, and finally as the magazine's senior art director.

Gail is co-author, with Steven Heller, of *The Typographic Universe*, as well as *New Modernist Type*, *New Ornamental Type*, and *New Vintage Type*. She teaches at the School of Visual Arts and serves on The Citizens Stamp Advisory Committee and the board of the Type Directors Club. Gail is the recipient of the 2008 Lifetime Achievement Medal from the American Institute of Graphic Arts.

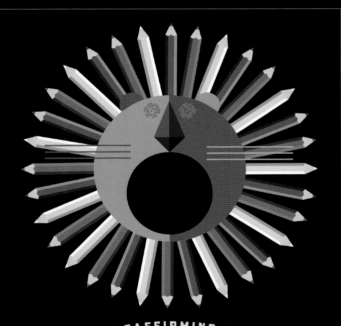

IN REAFFIRMING THE

greatness

OF OUR NATION,
WE UNDERSTAND THAT
GREATNESS IS NEVER A GIVEN.

IT MUST BE EARNED.

-PRESIDENT BARACK HUSSEIN OBAMA
INAUGURAL ADDRESS · JANUARY 20, 2009

School of VISUAL ARTS
SVA.EDU

MO'
META
BLUES

THE WORLD ACCORDING TO
QUESTLOVE

AHMIR "QUESTLOVE" THOMPSON
and BEN GREENMAN

TDC60 JUDGES

COMMUNICATION DESIGN

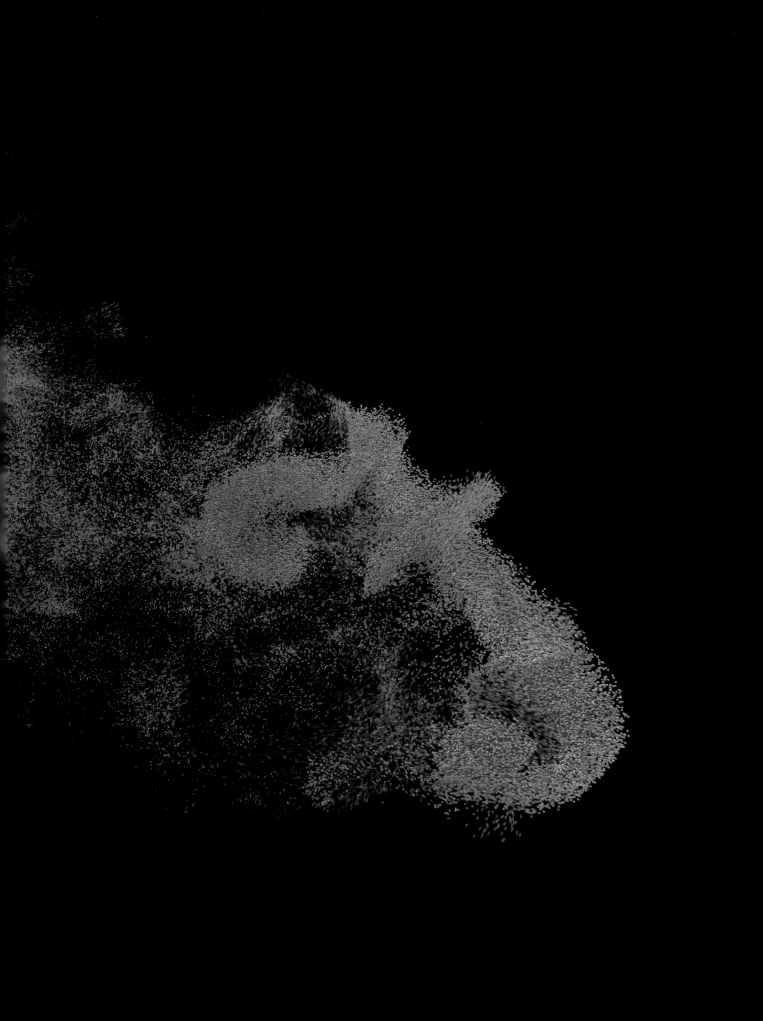

Debra Bishop° is creative director of *More* magazine. Previously she was vice president, design director, and initial brand creator of *Blueprint* magazine for Martha Stewart Living Omnimedia. During her twelve years at MSLO, Deb was in charge of branding several publications, including *Martha Stewart Baby*, *Kids: Fun Stuff to Do Together*, *Body&Soul*, and Martha's first catalog: *Martha by Mail*. Deb's early years were spent working for *House & Garden*, *Rolling Stone*, and Paula Scher.

Deb has been lauded by the Art Directors Club, the Type Directors Club, AIGA, and American Illustration and American Photography. *Kids: Fun Stuff to Do Together* won an ASME award for design in 2005. It was also named Magazine of the Year by the Society of Publication Designers in both 2004 and 2005, and *Blueprint* received that honor in 2008. *More* magazine was nominated for a General Excellence award by ASME in 2011 and was a finalist for Magazine of the Year by the Society of Publication Designers in 2010.

DESIGN YOUR LIFE

Blueprint

SEPTEMBER | OCTOBER 2007

issue Nᵒ **6**

GET THE BEDROOM
You Dream About

CUSTOMIZE A COCKTAIL Party

REVAMP Your ROOMS
15 Surprising
(and Simple) Projects

Fall Fashion
TAILOR-MADE
for You

❀ Plus
How to Buy a Rug
A Clip-and-Save Guide

Blueprint
HOLIDAYS

GLAM I AM

CALL OFF THE DOGS.
WE'VE TRACKED DOWN DAZZLING DRESSES AND
SMART SEPARATES FOR EVERY
SOIRÉE FROM NOW
UNTIL THE NEW YEAR.

TEXT BY *Alexa Valdenaia*
PHOTOGRAPHS BY *Wynn Robertson*

Blueprintmag.com

Chelsea
HANDLER'S
★ ★ **DIRTY** SECRETS ★ ★

VODKA ★ **SWILLING,**
INSULT-HURLING
Handler
HAS **BROKEN**
BARRIERS *For*
Female Comics.
BUT BEHIND THE
BLUSTER
IS A SURPRISINGLY
GROUNDED, THOUGHTFUL
Woman ♀
{ WHO MISSES HER MOM, CARES
ABOUT UNDERDOGS AND DOESN'T DRINK
NEARLY "AS MUCH AS I SHOULD" }

★ BY SANDRA TSING LOH ★

PHOTOGRAPHS BY **PEGGY SIROTA**

Ted Halbur has spent his career working on award-winning creative for the Target Corporation, where he is an associate creative director. At Target he has worked on a wide range of special projects, with a focus on gift cards. His work has been featured in *Print*, *HOW*, AIGA, and *Graphis*, and he has been awarded more than fifty U.S. patents for his gift card innovations.

In 2011, he co-founded the Heartwork poster series that raises money for art supplies for children staying at Target House while they are receiving treatment from St. Jude Children's Research Hospital. Ted lives in Minnesota with his wife and three boys.

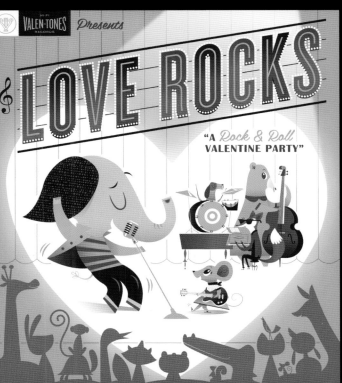

Named one of the most influential designers working today by GDUSA, Debbie Millman° is a designer, author, educator, and strategist. She is president of the design division at Sterling Brands, where she has worked on the redesign of more than 200 global brands. Debbie is also co-founder and chair of the world's first Masters in Branding program at the School of Visual Arts in New York City. She is president emeritus of AIGA, the largest professional association for design in the world, and a contributing editor at *Print* magazine. In 2005, she began hosting *Design Matters*, the first podcast about design on the Internet. In 2011, the show received a Cooper Hewitt National Design Award. She is the author of six books on design and branding.

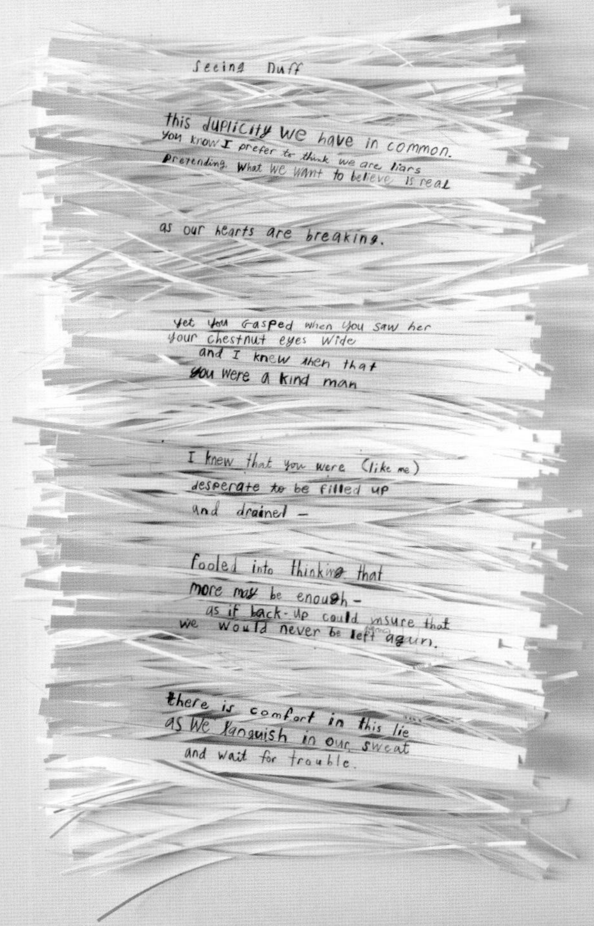

Seeing Duff

this duplicity we have in common.
you know I prefer to think we are liars
pretending what we want to believe is real

as our hearts are breaking.

Yet you Gasped when you saw her
your chestnut eyes wider
    and I knew then that
you were a kind man

I knew that you were (like me)
desperate to be filled up
and drained —

fooled into thinking that
more may be enough —
as if back-up could insure that
we would never be left again.

there is comfort in this lie
as we vanquish in our sweat
and wait for trouble.

Penelope

Penelope

Penelope

Oliver Reichenstein is the CEO and founder of Information Architects Inc., based in Tokyo and Zürich. He studied philosophy, before noticing that handling abstract concepts was essential for information architecture. After graduating, he worked as a brand consultant for Interbrand Zintzmeyer & Lux. In 2005, he founded IA in Tokyo, where he also held a position as lecturer at Keio University. IA's clients include Ringier, Die Zeit, Yandex, UBS, and NHK. IA also develops a bestselling text editor called Writer.

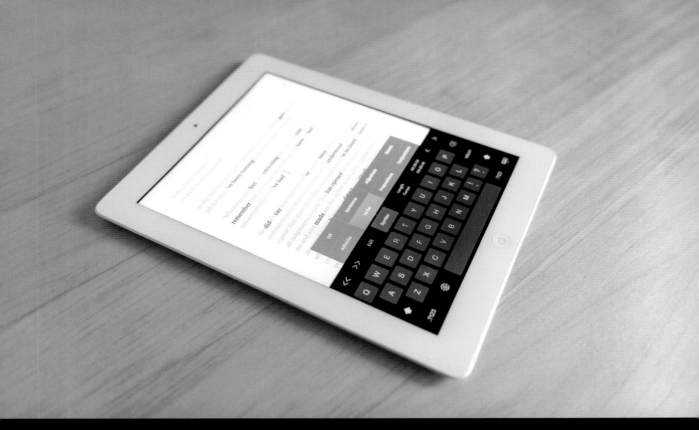

Jackie Seow is VP, executive art director of Simon & Schuster. Jackie has been an art director at the book publisher since 1994, art directing and designing book covers for the Simon & Schuster imprint and overseeing the Scribner, Atria, Touchstone, and Gallery imprints.

Jackie earned her BFA in graphic design at the School of Visual Arts in New York City. She joined S&S immediately upon graduating and has held various positions throughout the company.

Jackie has had the opportunity to design and art direct covers for many bestselling and celebrity authors. Her work has been featured in the New York Book Show, *Print*, AIGA, Communication Arts, and the Society of Illustrators.

A PRESIDENTIAL NOVEL

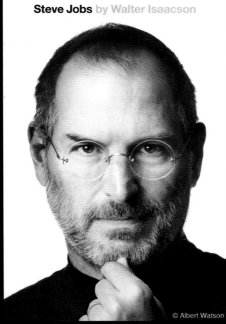

Steve Jobs by Walter Isaacson

© Albert Watson

Living History
Hillary Rodham Clinton

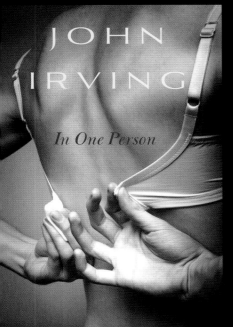

JOHN
IRVING

In One Person

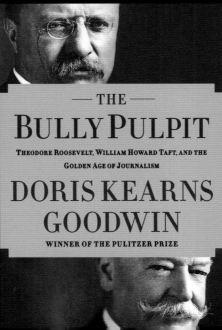

— THE —
BULLY PULPIT
THEODORE ROOSEVELT, WILLIAM HOWARD TAFT, AND THE
GOLDEN AGE OF JOURNALISM
**DORIS KEARNS
GOODWIN**
WINNER OF THE PULITZER PRIZE

BOB DYLAN

CHRONICLES
VOLUME ONE

Will Staehle grew up reading comics
and working summers at his parents' design
firm in Wisconsin. He was art director for
HarperCollins Publishers in New York and
design director at JibJab in Los Angeles.
Will was labeled by *Print* magazine as one
of the Top Twenty Under Thirty New Visual
Artists, an Art Directors Club Young Gun,
and has exhibited a solo show of work
at the Type Directors Club. His work has
appeared in various design annuals as well
as in the AIGA's *50 Books/50 Covers* exhibit.
Will now lives in sunny Seattle, where he
runs his own studio using his design and
illustration background to create book
jackets, stylized posters, and odd comics
to ensure that he gets as little sleep
as possible.

CHAMPION
BEE-BEARDER
&
WORLD-FAMOUS
HONEY-MAKER
&
AMATEUR
SLEUTH

Detective HONEY-JAW
AND HIS Queen

IN THE
SWEET-TOOTH
MURDERS
BY A CELEBRATED
AUTHOR

INCLUDES:
A HONEY-COOKIE RECIPE FROM THE DETECTIVE, HIMSELF!

SITKA   ALASKA

MICHAEL
CHABON
The YIDDISH
POLICEMEN'S UNION
A NOVEL

THE PULITZER PRIZE-
WINNING AUTHOR OF
THE AMAZING ADVENTURES
OF KAVALIER & CLAY

HI.

BYE.

Originally a jazz guitarist, Paul Sych° found himself in the creative field of graphic design in the late '70s to support his music studies and session and performance work. By 1990, Paul had founded his design practice, Faith, which focused on graphic design and served as the birthplace of Paul's curiosity for typography. From day one, his design practice grew to become a platform for unyielding creative imagination and unexpected discovery. In addition to maintaining his design practice, he teaches graphic design and typography at York University's Design Department in Toronto.

For more than two decades, Paul has collaborated with agencies, retailers, producers, and publishers to create specialty typography and provide creative direction in everything from magazines to broadcast design.

Today, Paul is fueled on a daily basis by conceiving designs that are rooted in exploration. By combining custom typography and the art of handlettering, he has created a number of books and magazines that have cemented his position in the design community. Paul's true talents lie in his ability to manipulate the way one reads, looks, and understands concepts and ideas.

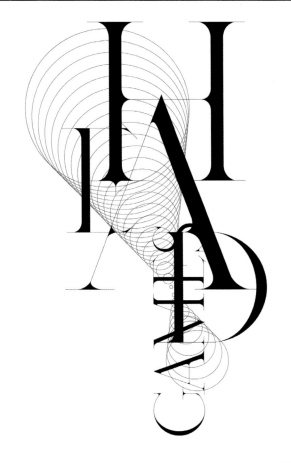

Make a Ga-Ga worthy entrance
to any party with bold headpieces and hats.
With all eyes up top, who needs pants?

Photography by Lara Jade
Style by Jennie Jazeel
Make-up by Megumi Matsuno

MONTREAL RAISED PHOTOGRAPHER MIKE RUIZ
GETS THE GREEK MODEL MUSE MODEL
THE CAMERA

NY 88 PCT 20
1009957

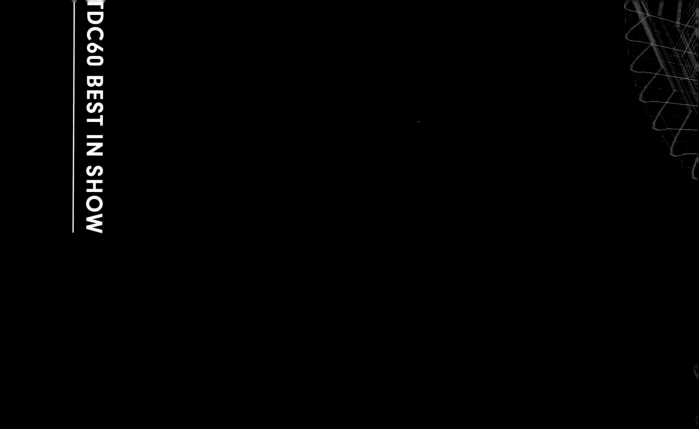

DESIGNER'S CONCEPT / Today's world is digital and interactive. However, we still often heavily rely on and use old-school forms of communication, even if it is not for a one-on-one conversation (mailers, letters, newspapers, etc.). We are pleasantly surprised and appreciative of something that is created for "real"—something physical that we can touch and feel.

Our continued use of old-school communications is what sparked my Type of Letters idea. Returning home every day, I would find myself inundated with letters in my mailbox (even though I did not sign up for any offers or memberships). I started to collect them. I also started to collect snail mail from my friends.

I set out to explore what it would look like when we merged the new school with the old. Arranging the mail in a vintage mail sorter, I created symbols and letters to provoke a conversation about digital versus physical—which is the better form of communication? I started the typography installations by creating the @ symbol and the *New York Times* symbol because they represent the two forms of communication: digital and physical. It was a tedious process because each piece of mail for each cubby hole had to be carefully planned for and then placed by mapping out each cubby hole like a single pixel. A process that could take just a few hours using digital software took days in the physical world and caused numerous paper cuts, unpaid bills (I lost them somewhere in the @ symbol, I think), and backaches!

TDC60 STUDENT DESIGN AWARDS

IF YOU HAD TO
SELECT FIVE
TYPEFACES TO PUT
IN A TIME CAPSULE
SO THAT YOU COULD
STILL USE THEM IN
100 YEARS,
WHAT WOULD YOU
CHOOSE?

JEONGHO PARK

DESIGN Jeongho Park, Seoul / URL jeonghopark.com / SCHOOL Minneapolis College of Art and Design / INSTRUCTOR Nandev Nairuiy / PRINCIPAL TYPE Akkurat / DIMENSIONS 12.2 × 12.6 in. (31 × 32 cm) / CONCEPT "Type Capsule" is an infographic book project about typefaces based on a personal survey. Some typefaces such as Garamond and Helvetica are more frequently used than others, considered "timeless" and impervious to passing trends, and I wanted to explore this issue through my project. One of the most important design concepts of this project is simplicity in the face of complicated survey data, and I used a number of typefaces as a design tool as well as the project's subject.

STUDENT AWARD
FIRST PLACE

35

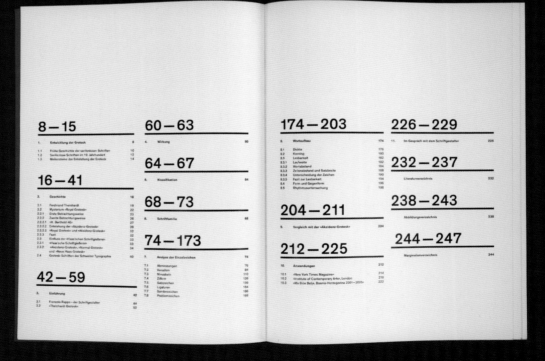

STUDENT AWARD
SECOND PLACE

DESIGN Kevin Kremer, Miriam Rieger, and Corinna Rusker, Munich / PROFESSOR Sybille Schmitz / PRINCIPAL TYPE Theinhardt Grotesk Font Family / DIMENSIONS 11 × 14.7 in. (28 × 37.4 cm) / SCHOOL Mediadesign Hochschule München / URL mediadesign.de / CONCEPT A simple outline of Theinhardt Grotesk would be too easy — this type was published in 2009 by Swiss typographer and graphic designer François Rappo. It strongly resembles the Akzidenz-Grotesk of the Berthold Type Foundry, but during our research, many more facts about this outstanding font came to light that stretch back to the beginning of the nineteenth century. The analysis contains a detailed overview of the individual glyphs of the font as well as interviews with graphic design professionals. Further, many current examples of typographic works using Theinhardt Grotesk are displayed in the book.

»Keine Schrift
wurde sooft
nachgeschnitten
wie die
Garamond«

DESIGN Benny Lämmel, Nadine Mayer, Lars Reiners, and Lea Roth, Münich / PROFESSOR Sybille Schmitz / SCHOOL Mediadesign Hochschule München / PRINCIPAL TYPE Stempel Garamond LT Std / DIMENSIONS 7 × 11 in. (18 × 28 cm) / CONCEPT The Garamond typefaces are the most famous in history. This work is a tribute to Claude Garamont. The first book shows the history of the typeface, the Stempel AG foundry, and the famous punch-cutter. At the end, we show some present designs using Garamond. The second book is a detailed analysis on Stempel Garamond LT Std Roman. The front side of the first book shows a portrait of Claude Garamont. The portrait was made by hand with a nyloprint in the hand composition. The spine of the second book is opened to show the analysis character. It was important for us to represent the beauty of the typeface in the book design.

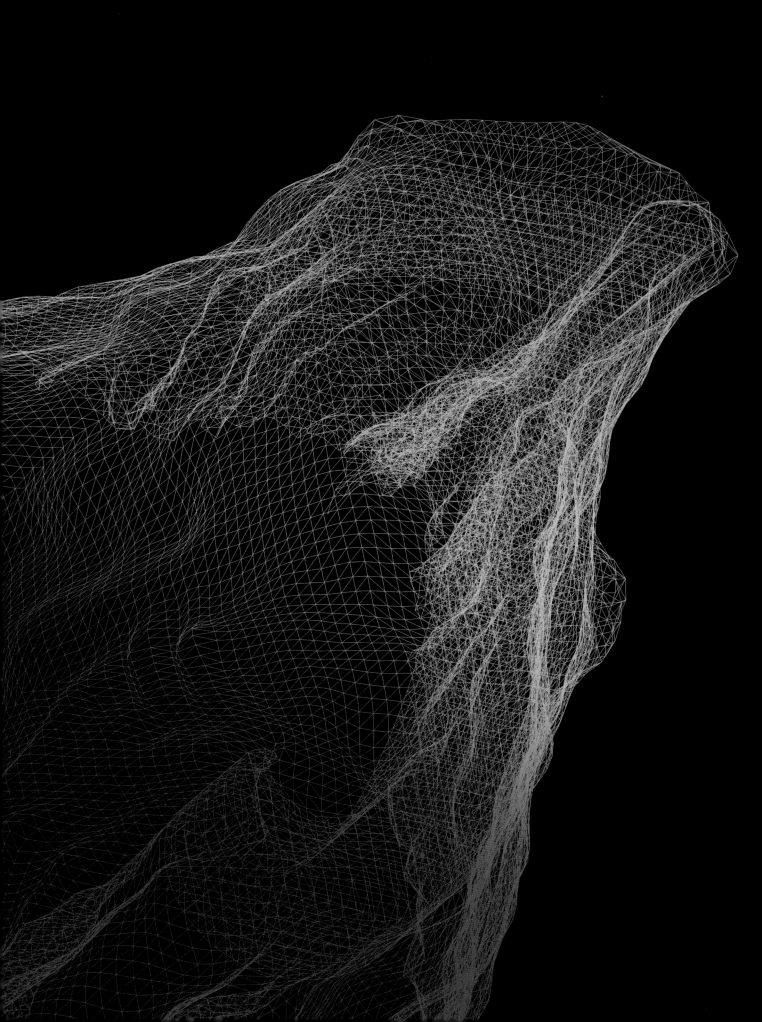

TDC60 JUDGES' CHOICES

COMMUNICATION DESIGN

DESIGN Susanne Hoerner, Berlin and Stuttgart / DESIGN FIRM Strichpunkt Design / CLIENT TYPE HYPE / PRINCIPAL TYPE Various /
DIMENSIONS 5.8 × 8.3 in. (14.8 × 21 cm)

NOTEBOOKS

DESIGNER'S CONCEPT / Each letter is individually designed, and each number is lovingly placed and playfully entwined with flourishes. The Luise collection notebooks, which have been produced for Berlin label Type Hype, portray the young Queen Luise of Prussia and the styles prevalent at the turn of the last century. The pages (the best paper from Lake Tegernsee-based paper manufacturer Gmund) are blank with a deep-embossed hot-foil cover, which is available in thirty-six varieties, from A to Z and 0 to 9. The endpaper protecting the brilliant-white pages features decorations to match the cover.

DEBRA BISHOP'S STATEMENT / It was love at first sight. These twenty-six notebooks are each adorned with an exquisite, carefully chosen initial. Each book is beautifully letter-pressed on soft cream cover stock with rounded corners—irresistible to the touch. The initials, a brilliant red, are embellished with lovely, intricate graphic details. Even the tiny logo at the bottom of each book is beautiful.

Is it the "N" book that I can't resist? Something about the juxtaposition of the bright slab serif letter mixed with those tiny dots gets me every time. Or is it the "S" book, a classic design with a cool, modern twist that any designer would envy? I can't decide which notebook is the most beautiful. Never mind that my name starts with a "D." I am seduced and incredibly jealous, and I want to gaze at each one individually and collectively. I'll have to buy them all.

JANE AUSTEN

PRIDE AND PREJUDICE

GUSTAVE FLAUBERT

MADAME BOVARY

DESIGNER'S CONCEPT / Penguin Drop Caps is a series of twenty-six collectible hardcover editions of fine works of literature, each featuring on its cover a specially commissioned illustrated letter. A collaboration between Jessica Hische and Penguin art director Paul Buckley — whose series design encompasses a rainbow-hued spectrum across all twenty-six books — Penguin Drop Caps debuted with an "A" for Jane Austen's *Pride and Prejudice*, a "B" for Charlotte Brontë's *Jane Eyre*, and a "C" for Willa Cather's *My Ántonia*, and continues with more perennial classics from Penguin. The project's initial inspiration came from Jessica's Daily Drop Caps, a project for which she illustrated the alphabet over and over, one letter at a time, for more than a year.

TED HALBUR'S STATEMENT / The best ideas are ones that, at their core, are simple and brilliantly executed. Penguin Drop Caps is exactly that. At first glance, you fall in love with the simplicity of an alphabetic system celebrating famous authors. As you study the series closer, the attention to detail and masterfully hidden symbols really bring the series to life. From start to finish, each cover is amazing on its own — yet, with an artfully coordinated color palette and thoughtfully crafted composition, the series tells the perfect story.

WILLA CATHER

MY ÁNTONIA

JAMES JOYCE

A PORTRAIT OF THE ARTIST
AS A YOUNG MAN

GEORGE ELIOT

MIDDLEMARCH

XINRAN

SKY BURIAL

©DESIGN Paul Buckley° and Jessica Hische° / ART DIRECTION Paul Buckley / PUBLISHER AND EDITORIAL DIRECTOR Elda Rotor / JRL jessicahische.is/awesome / TWITTER @jessicahische / DESIGN FIRM Jessica Hische and Paul Buckley / CLIENT Penguin Books /

DESIGNER'S CONCEPT / In the two decades since I first designed the
identity for the Public Theater, the graphics have become a familiar presence
in New York and a kind of visual shorthand for "theater" itself. For a major
revitalization of the Public's home in the historic Astor Library, we worked
with renovation architects Ennead to translate the identity into an environment
that celebrates the Public as a theater for the "public." The reconfigured
lobby centers on a circular front desk that doubles as a dimensional, large-
scale version of the logo, while the various theaters are identified with
typography inset into the building's distinctive arches. The box office has
been sniped with a collage of the posters we've designed for the Public over
the years.

DEBBIE MILLMAN'S STATEMENT / Paula Scher's new identity for the Public
Theater lobby is proof positive that after twenty-three years at Pentagram
she is still doing some of the best work of her life. The lobby has all of her
signature brilliance: It is simultaneously bold, beautiful, and mesmerizing.
The typographic LED signs crowning the circular front desk are not only
striking, they are surprising, fun, and uniquely original. Paula worked with
renovation architects Ennead to capture her Public identity into the physical
environment in seamless yet significant ways: The theaters use typography
directly inset into the building's arches while the box office is now a
veritable museum of Paula's award-winning, ground-breaking theater posters.
The overall impression of the refurbished lobby is grand, and allows the public

DESIGNER'S CONCEPT / In Japanese, peace is "heiwa," written as "へいわ."
OLIVER REICHENSTEIN'S STATEMENT / The world is expressing the wish
for peace. From afar, it is hard to comprehend the two posters from Hajime
Tsushima. I might be too close to them to explain them calmly.

You can probably imagine how visually striking they become when standing in
front of them. The white poster reads "へいわ," "heiwa," meaning peace. The red
poster reads "8.6," which is the intensity of the 2011 Tohoku earthquake that
led to the devastating tsunami and the Fukushima meltdown. "Peace" is drawn
in horizontal strokes forming an image that looks like a stormy sea in black
and white. "8.6" is drawn in red and black vertical strokes forming the image
of an intense fire. Peace is not illustrated as an opposite of the earthquake;
fire and water are drawn with the same strokes, turned ninety degrees. The
two posters tell the story of a fight that you cannot escape and that you will
inevitably lose.

If you haven't been in Japan on March 11, and if you cannot immediately
read and explore your own sentiments in the typographic flames and waves, the
posters transport their message in a formal knockout that easily earned its
typographic price despite being closer to art than design.

DESIGNER'S CONCEPT / "Uselessness Is Gorgeous" is a part of *The Happy Show*, filling the Institute of Contemporary Art's entire second-floor galleries and ramp, and activating the in-between spaces of the museum. The show offers visitors the experience of walking into Stefan Sagmeister's mind as he attempts to increase his happiness via meditation, cognitive therapy, and mood-altering pharmaceuticals.

DESIGN Jordan Amer, Santiago Carrasquilla, Simon Egli, Martin Gnat, Esther Li, Verena Michelitch, and Jessica Walsh, New York / ART DIRECTION Jessica Walsh / CREATIVE DIRECTION Stefan Sagmeister / AGENCY Sagmeister & Walsh / PRINCIPAL TYPE Custom / DIMENSIONS 76 × 12 ft. (23.2 × 3.7 m)

JACKIE SEOW'S STATEMENT / The digital submission of this piece did not do it justice. Regardless, it still managed to bowl me over. I was most impressed with the vast scale of the project. The typography takes on a whole other form as sculpture. The flow of the typography is enhanced by the fact that it is made up of sticky notes. I love the use of negative space and the white-on-white playing up the empty "uselessness." It's a beautiful marriage of idea and words. The addition of the fans blowing on the sticky notes creates a whimsical and ethereal feel that is enhanced by the slogan "Uselessness Is Gorgeous." And that it is.

DESIGNER'S CONCEPT / For this limited edition of *On Such a Full Sea*, by Chang Rae-Lee, we wanted to create an object that would celebrate the publication of the regular edition of the book by one of our most important authors and touch on the futuristic nature of the novel. The story takes place in a dystopian future, quite a departure for Lee from his previous work. Pursuing a forward-thinking approach to producing and designing the object, we partnered up with MakerBot Industries. This opened new ways to consider packaging a book; most exciting perhaps was thinking of type sculpturally. Together we created the slipcase, which is 3D-printed on a MakerBot Replicator using PLA filament, a bioplastic derived from corn.

WILL STAEHLE'S STATEMENT / Book covers have standards. Hardcovers are roughly six inches by nine inches. They're printed in four colors (or more, if you're lucky). If the publisher really loves you, you might get foil on your cover, or perhaps even an embossed effect.

It's safe to say that if you get all of the above, your name is generally accompanied by the term: New York Times Bestselling Author. Have I mentioned that book covers have standards? Sure, from time to time, there are covers with die cuts, or ones wrapped delicately in printed vellum.

But again, it's paper, and it's ink. The standards. And I think that's why I was so floored when I came across Helen Yentus's limited-edition slipcover for *On Such a Full Sea*. Here we have a package for a book that defies these traditional standards. First, the cover is built upon a simple structure. Stacked lettering creates the groundwork. But the lettering truly comes to life through the slipcover's dimensional extrusion. The real beauty of this project is Helen's decision to make only a partial slipcover. For me, the magic of this package is the tall seam where the two-dimensional letters meet their three-dimensional counterparts, and where the three-dimensional letters skew forward into space. The pairing of old technology (the book) and current technology (three-dimensional printing), guided under Helen's hand, has created something quite fresh and compelling. Although we've been taught to never judge a book by its cover, does that rule also apply to three-dimensionally printed slipcovers?

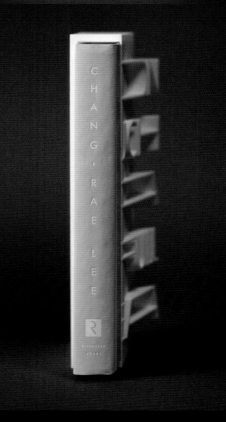

DESIGN Helen Yentus° and MakerBot®, Brooklyn, New York and New York / PROJECT MANAGER Lisa D'Agostino and Nicholas Joshi (MakerBot) / PRODUCTION MANAGER John Sharp / 3D CONSULTANT Leonid Yentus / MAKERBOT STUDIO DIRECTOR Lane Feuer / PUBLISHER Riverhead Books / PRINCIPAL TYPE Futura / DIMENSIONS 6.5 x 9.75 in. (16.5 x 24.7 cm)

BOOK JACKET

MENACE by Chris Yee

Debuting as his first solo exhibition, Chris Yee invites you into his world of Misinterpreted Americana, parallel universes, rap royalty and bitter rivalries where everyone is a menace.

Including a year long collection of black and white ink work, Chris explores techniques familiar to stylings of 90's comics, punk, rap and gang aesthetics.

Opening reception:
6pm Wednesday
6 November 2013

Continues daily until:
11am–7pm Sunday
10 November 2013

Presented by:
kind of — gallery

Venue:
kind of — gallery
70 Oxford Street
Darlinghurst NSW

Sponsored by:
Magners Australia

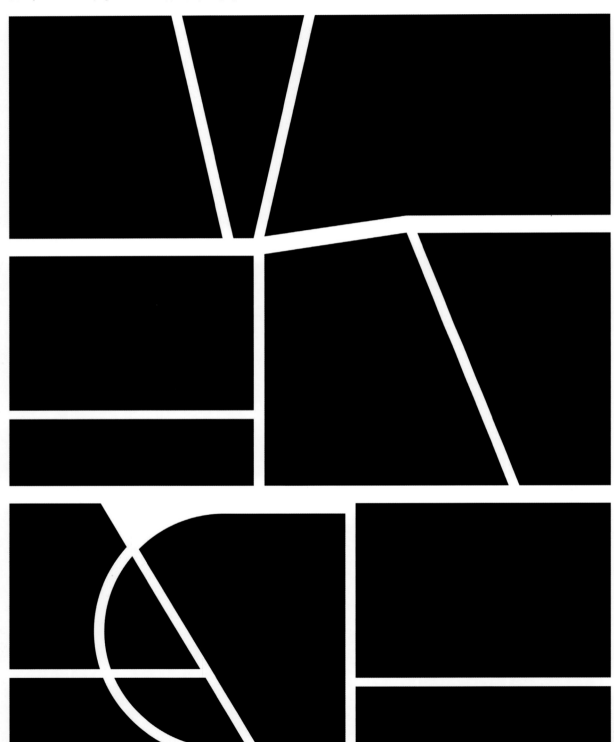

DESIGN Wing Lau, Sydney / CREATIVE DIRECTION Wing Lau / URL winglau.net / TWITTER @winglau.net / CLIENT Kind of Gallery / PRINCIPAL TYPE Custom / DIMENSIONS 23.4 × 33.1 in. (59.4 × 84.1 cm)

POSTER

DESIGNER'S CONCEPT / Kind of Gallery opened its doors in 2011, bringing to Sydney, Australia some of the best local talents as well as internationally renowned artists. It was with great pleasure that I was trusted to help build the graphic languages of the gallery since the beginning. *Menace* was the debut solo exhibition of the extremely talented and dedicated illustrator Chris Yee in 2013. Yee explored techniques reminiscent of '90s comics; his black-and-white drawings are crammed with detail and hypnotic textures familiar to the stylings of punk, rap, and gang aesthetics. Yee said he wanted to invite us into "his world of misinterpreted Americana, parallel universes, rap royalty, and bitter rivalries where everyone is a menace." Instead of filling in the poster with selected pieces of the artist's work, we left them out completely. Spatial arrangement in the design resembles the grid structure of comic books, capturing the essence of how Yee wanted us to explore an epic world that is dangerous but exciting.

PAUL SYCH'S STATEMENT / Chris Yee's poster was simply my favorite piece in the show. It evokes a pureness of form, balance, and tone and conjures a perfect example of stylized simplicity. The playfulness, structure, and rhythm between the shapes made me question if they were actual letterforms at all. The abstract shapes merge into one another with such fluidity and abstraction that with a closer look, you are able to see the emergence of the word "Menace."

The custom letterforms also mimic Yee's striking black-and-white illustration work. Simplicity is paramount in the eyes of its designer, Wing Lau.

TDC60 WINNERS

COMMUNICATION DESIGN

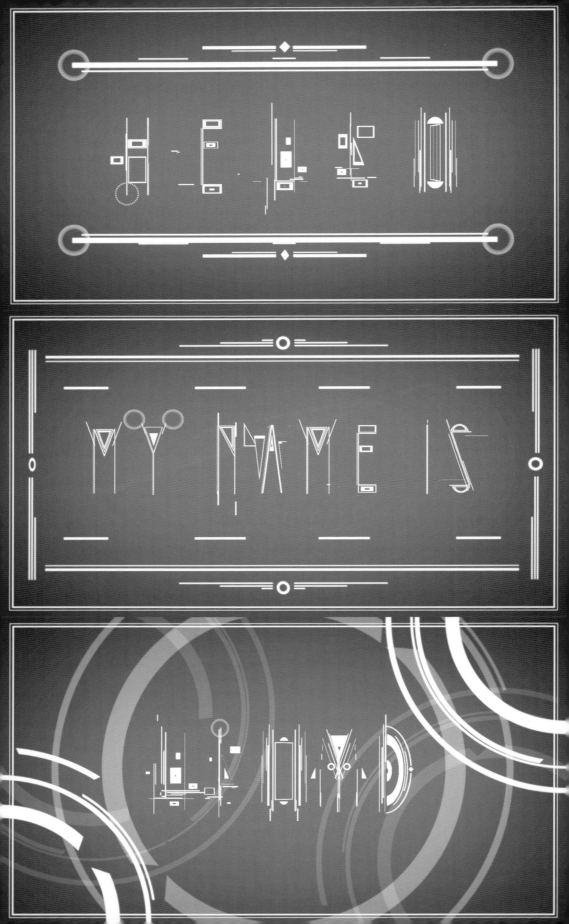

SANFRANCISCO

DESIGN Ina Bauer and Sascha Lobe⁰, Stuttgart / DESIGN FIRM L2M3 Kommunikationsdesign GmbH / CLIENT American Institute of Graphic Arts (AIGA), San Francisco / PRINCIPAL TYPE Akkurat / DIMENSIONS 33.1 × 46.8 in. (84.1 × 118.9 cm) / CONCEPT For the exhibition *InsideOut San Francisco*, designers from San Francisco and around the world were invited to capture their image of the city in a design. Ours is a typographical rendition of the special topography of San Francisco.

PEACE
&
JOY

2013

JOHN & DITI
JORDAN
BRAUNA
BRETT
JONATHON
CRISTIAN
BRADLY
ALISON
CLAIRE VICE
MATTHEW
SANDRA
MARIA
AURORA
LUCIA
BRANDY

DESIGN Matthew Boyd, Toronto / CREATIVE DIRECTION Diti Katona° and John Pylypczak / URL concrete.ca /
DESIGN FIRM Concrete Design Communication / PRINCIPAL TYPE Neue Haas Grotesk / DIMENSIONS 14 × 4 × 4 in. (35.6 × 10.2 × 10.2 cm) /
CONCEPT At holiday time, Concrete sends wine and chocolate to clients, suppliers, colleagues, and friends. For the 2013 season we
created a gift box made of plain corrugated cardboard silkscreened with opaque white type. The bottles of wine are wrapped in tissue
that doubles as the greeting card. The tissue is bible paper that is foil-stamped with the names of everyone in the office.

DESIGN Julia Ochsenhirt, Berlin and Stuttgart / DESIGN FIRM Strichpunkt Design / CLIENT TYPE HYPE / URL strichpunkt-design.de /
PRINCIPAL TYPE Bodoni Classic and Chancery / DIMENSIONS 15.75 x 15.75 in. (40 x 40 cm) / CONCEPT Love letters for letter lovers:
Berlin's Mitte district is synonymous with bustling, urban energy and high acceptance of the new bohemians, who have settled there in
large numbers since German reunification. Their individual form of expression and unconventional style is reflected in the black-and-
white illustrations and letters printed on the cushions in the Made in Mitte black-and-white design line, which was produced for Berlin
label TYPE HYPE. There is a choice from among the twenty-six letters of the alphabet, ten numbers, and the ampersand, which must never
be left out in today's reunified Berlin. This work features sustainable production from German textile manufacturers.

/ ABCDEFGHIJKLMNOPQRSTUVWXYZ
0123456789 &
PATTERN

40 X 40 CM

Manche Rätsel des Lebens lassen sich nicht so leicht lösen.
Einige nie. Wer solches aushält oder gar liebt, dem seien unsere
40 x 40 cm großen, schwarzweiß bedruckten Baumwollkissenhüllen
der Linie 'Made in Mitte' empfohlen. In den 26 Varianten –
allen Zeichen des Alphabets – gibt es Strichmännchen mit explo-
dierenden Köpfen, Bären mit Singvögeln im Arm, mit Topfpflanzen
flirtende Diven oder Libellen mit Melonen, die über Quitten
tanzen. Baby, it's a wild world.
Größe: 40 x 40 cm
Material: 100% Baumwolle

DESIGN Rodrigo Corral, New York / CREATIVE DIRECTION Rodrigo Corral / ILLUSTRATION Erik Jones / PUBLISHER Farrar, Straus and Giroux / URL fsgbooks.com / PRINCIPAL TYPE Gill Sans Regular and custom / DIMENSIONS *The Whispering Muse* (hardcover): 5.1 × 7.6 in. (13 × 19.2 cm); *The Blue Fox* (paperback): 5 × 7.5 in. (12.7 × 19.1 cm); *From the Mouth of the Whale* (paperback): 5 × 7.5 in. (12.7 × 19.1 cm) / CONCEPT The author is Icelandic, which was a huge factor. The language, the myth, and philosophy and abstraction infused into his writing all inspired me. It was important to include the fantastical nature of his world. I wanted to focus on mood and tone because this book is such a layered experience. I wanted to treat the type uniquely. It's not often that you get an author with one name that's only four letters, so I just started to explore and have fun with the possibilities. Digital type seemed too restricting. Instead, I started ripping up paper and thinking about the most basic letterforms and letters that didn't have to fit into a whole typeface.

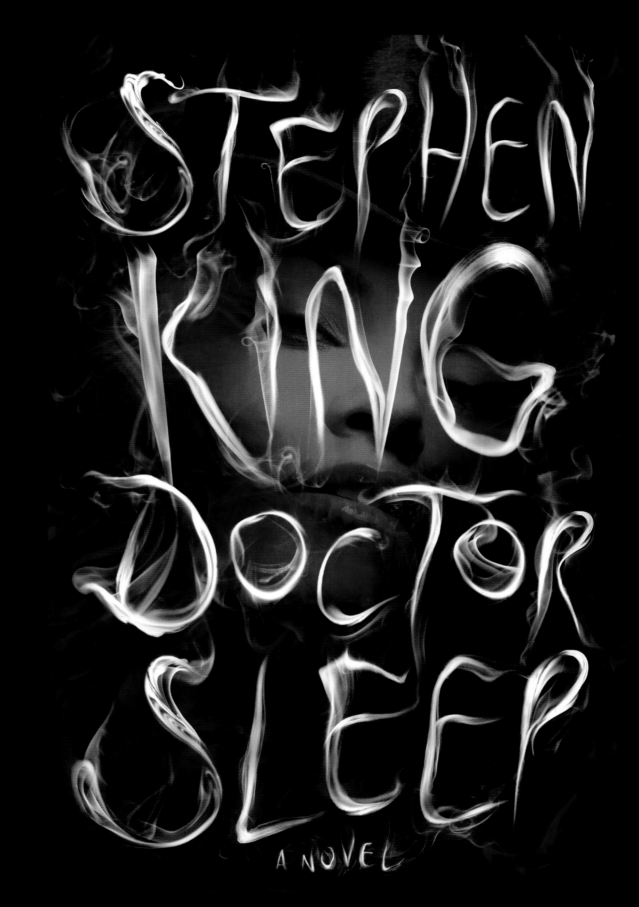

ART DIRECTION Tal Goretsky, New York / ILLUSTRATION Sean Freeman / PUBLISHER Scribner / PRINCIPAL TYPE Custom (illustrated) / DIMENSIONS 6.25 x 9.5 in. (15.9 x 24.1 cm) / CONCEPT *Doctor Sleep,* Stephen King's sequel to *The Shining,* takes place decades later, in our time. A gang of human-looking supernatural beings called the True Knot travels around the United States in RVs, hunting for children who possess the psychic powers known as The Shining. The True Knot lives off the "steam" these children release when they are tortured and killed. The type on this cover is made of "steam," and the evil, beautiful leader of the True Knot, Rose the Hat, is seen in the background inhaling it.

ANS COMINTERN ENEMY WITHIN KU KLUX KLAN MIND CON
N ASSASSINS 9/11 ANGELS THE MATRIX ENEMY ABOVE O
HOST DANCE "BOB" MYSTIC CLAN ENEMY OUTSIDE BACKM
OF THE QUEST HIDDEN PERSUADERS FREEMASONRY TRYS
CHIEFS JONESTOWN DANITES ILLUMINATI CIA ZOMBIES GE
TROL FEMA COINTELPRO BENEVOLENT CONSPIRACY DISC
PERATION CHAOS MEN IN BLACK ELDERS OF ZION POD PE
KING NIGHT DOCTORS WATERGATE CULTS MANCHURIAN C
O SLAVE POWER MKULTRA ENEMY BELOW VATICAN FLYING
EVA CLUB **THE UNITED STATES OF PARANOIA** ROSICRU
LPRO BENEVOLENT CONSPIRACY DISCORDIAN SOCIETY S
N IN BLACK ELDERS OF ZION POD PEOPLE HOMINTERN G
RS WATERGATE CULTS MANCHURIAN CANDIDATE ORDER O
LTRA ENEMY BELOW VATICAN FLYING SAUCERS SECRET CH
ANS COMINTERN ENEMY WITHIN KU KLUX KLAN MIND CON
N ASSASSINS 9/11 ANGELS THE MATRIX ENEMY ABOVE O
HOST DANCE "BOB" MYSTIC CLAN ENEMY OUTSIDE BACKM
OF THE QUEST HIDDEN PERSUADERS FREEMASONRY TRYS
CRET CHIEFS **A CONSPIRACY THEORY** JONESTOWN
ENEMY WITHIN KU KLUX KLAN MIND CONTROL FEMA COI
11 ANGELS THE MATRIX ENEMY ABOVE OPERATION CHAOS
MYSTIC CLAN ENEMY OUTSIDE BACKMASKING NIGHT DOC
N PERSUADERS FREEMASONRY TRYSTERO SLAVE POWER M
N DANITES ILLUMINATI CIA ZOMBIES GENEVA CLUB ROS
COINTELPRO BENEVOLENT CONSPIRACY DISCORDIAN SO
AOS MEN IN BLACK ELDERS OF ZION POD PEOPLE HOMIN
DOCTORS WATERGATE CULTS MANCHURIAN CANDIDATE O
OWER MKULTRA ENEMY BELOW VATICAN FLYING SAUCER
UB ROSICRUCIANS COMINTERN ENEMY WITHIN KU KLUX
AN SOCIETY SATAN **JESSE WALKER** ASSASSINS 9/11 A
F ZION POD PEOPLE HOMINTERN GHOST DANCE "BOB"
ULTS MANCHURIAN CANDIDATE ORDER OF THE QUEST HI
ELOW VATICAN FLYING SAUCERS SECRET CHIEFS JONES
RN ENEMY WITHIN KU KLUX KLAN MIND CONTROL FEMA
S 9/11 ANGELS THE MATRIX ENEMY ABOVE OPERATION C
OB" MYSTIC CLAN ENEMY OUTSIDE BACKMASKING NIGHT
HIDDEN PERSUADERS FREEMASONRY TRYSTERO SLAVE P

SENIOR DESIGN Jarrod Taylor, New York / PUBLISHER HarperCollins Publishers / PRINCIPAL TYPE Akzidenz Grotesk / DIMENSIONS 6.2 x 9.25 in. (15.6 x 23.5 cm) / CONCEPT The idea was to illustrate the deep-rooted paranoia behind the various conspiracy theories discussed in the book by repeating them multiple times on a shredded (and then reassembled) document. The image of Masonic symbols on the reverse side of the jacket was an attempt to add another layer by alluding to the hidden powers at work.

Brave Genius

A Scientist, a Philosopher, and Their Daring Adventures from the French Resistance to the Nobel Prize

Sean B. Carroll

DESIGN Elena Giavaldi, New York / ART DIRECTION Christopher Brand / PUBLISHER Crown Publishing Group / URL crownpublishing.com / PRINCIPAL TYPE Lettera and handwriting / DIMENSIONS 6.25 × 9.25 in. (15.9 × 23.5 cm) / CONCEPT Brave Genius tells the story of two of the twentieth century's great minds, scientist Jacques Monod and writer and philosopher Albert Camus. They met in Paris during the French Resistance and became friends after the war. My first instinct was to walk away from the complexity of the story and focus on their faces. But still, the story had to be told in some way. That's why I added the red and blue colors, which are meant to hint at the French flag; Camus's signature for the writing aspect; Monod's equation for the scientific one; and an old paper texture for the historical part of the book.

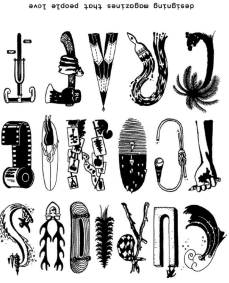

designing magazines that people love

Ü

\i/\/\i\t\t\l\e\/\w\h\i\t\e\/\l\i\e\s

ü

CURIOUS
ICONIC
CRAFT

designing magazines that people love

CREATIVE Fabrizio Festa, Evan Lelliot, and Angus MacPherson, London / CEO Danny Miller / CREATIVE DEVELOPMENT MANAGER Liz Haycroft / CREATIVE DIRECTION Rob Longworth and Paul Willoughby / ILLUSTRATION Anna Dunn and Eve Lloyd Knight / URL humanafterall.co.uk / TWITTER @HumanAfterAll / DESIGN FIRM Human After All / PRINCIPAL TYPE Hand-drawn / DIMENSIONS 7.9 × 9.6 in. (20 × 24.5 cm) / CONCEPT Curious Iconic Craft: Designing Magazines That People Love is a limited-edition book on the creative processes and principle behind the award-winning Little White Lies and Huck magazines, available exclusively through Kickstarter. A dual cover introduces each magazine: Typography provides clues to the Little White Lies film content found within, while flipping the book reveals surf/ skate/snow iconography representing Huck's youth culture. To unite the concept, we designed a spine that marries the two sides with equal precedence.

DESIGN Yong Joon Cho, New York / ASSOCIATE CREATIVE DIRECTOR Ryan Adair / CHIEF CREATIVE DIRECTOR Stewart Devlin / PRODUCTION MANAGER Steve Lipman / TYPOGRAPHER Yong Joon Cho / COPYWRITER Stewart Devlin and Nate Dwyer / URL redpeakgroup.com / TWITTER @RedPeak_Group / AGENCY Red Peak / CLIENT Lisa Sanders Public Relations / PRINCIPAL TYPE Gotham / DIMENSIONS 7.25 x 7.25 in. (18.5 x 18.5 cm) / CONCEPT Lisa Sanders PR needed to create a promotional mailer that would not get lost in the daily deluge of unwanted mail and that informed clients not only of the issues LSPR deals with, but also the solutions the agency provides.

DESIGN Roberto de Vicq de Cumptich°, New York / CREATIVE DIRECTION Randi Sirkin, Philadelphia / URL devicq.com / TWITTER @rdevicq / DESIGN FIRM de Vicq design / PRINCIPAL TYPE Little Cecily, Modesto, Sina, and others / DIMENSIONS Various / CONCEPT Le Diplomate pays homage to French café culture by recreating it in the heart of Washington, D.C. The branding involved designing the logo, symbol, outdoor signage, a variety of menus, postcards, matches, and more.

GREETING CARDS

DESIGN Julia Ochsenhirt, Berlin and Stuttgart / URL strichpunkt-design.de / DESIGN OFFICE Strichpunkt Design / CLIENT Type Hype / PRINCIPAL TYPE Bodoni Classic and Chancery / DIMENSIONS 4.3 × 5.9 in. (11 × 15 cm) / CONCEPT Berlin label Type Hype has great fun with letters, characters, and numbers, and shares this passion for the alphabet with discerning, like-minded people. The Made in Mitte collection, which was produced for Type Hype, pays homage to Berlin's artist scene — after all, more artists work in Berlin than anywhere else in Europe. The collection is full of artistic diversity and *joie de vivre*. The stamped and hand-drawn illustrations combine to form unique collages and are just as unconventional and spontaneous as the center of Berlin.

ART DIRECTION Sven Quadflieg, Cologne, Germany / PHOTOGRAPHY Sebastian Hoppe / CLIENT Düsseldorfer Schauspielhaus / PRINCIPAL TYPE Replica / DIMENSIONS 5.8 × 8.3 in. (14.8 × 21 cm) / CONCEPT The seasonal program lists the company's premieres and gives additional service information for the upcoming year in three volumes. The choice of different types of paper creates a haptic experience and hierarchy. The design establishes a contrast between the austere typographical look of the layout and the creative freedom of the headings and pictures — while at the same time color reduction and the absence of paper finishing reduce the printing costs compared to the previous year.

DESIGN Patrick Märki, Münich / SENIOR DESIGNER Robert Börsting / PROJECT MANAGER Marc Schergel /
TEAM MANAGER Patrick Märki / MANAGING DIRECTOR Knut Maierhofer / FINAL ARTWORK Angela Keesman / PRODUCTION Matthias Karpf /
DESIGN FIRM KMS TEAM GmbH / URL kms-team.com / CLIENT Museum Villa Stuck / PRINCIPAL TYPE Gill Sans Regular / DIMENSIONS 9.6 × 12.2 in.
(24.5 × 31 cm) / CONCEPT The magazine marking the twentieth anniversary of Villa Stuck is playfully inspired by the building's design,
which makes it fresh and easy to read. The magazine format makes this commemorative publication seem less serious. All of the graphic
elements are taken from the geometric details of the villa (tiles, ceiling panels, reliefs, etc.). The accents are reminiscent of Art
Nouveau and Art Deco, but still have a contemporary look. A detachable poster with miniatures of all the exhibition posters is included
as a template, with registration marks and a color chart for the printer — work in progress.

DESIGN Daniel Kuhlmann, Thomas Langanki, Martina Morth, and Tobias Nusser, Berlin and Stuttgart / DESIGN FIRM Strichpunkt Design / URL strichpunkt-design.de / CLIENT Takkt / PRINCIPAL TYPE Simple and Univers / DIMENSIONS 8.3 × 11.7 in. (21 × 29.6 cm) / CONCEPT The first sustainability report by Takkt AG takes the reader into the world of mail order. The envelope is from recycled corrugated cardboard, a parcel sticker is the title theme, parcel icons serve as chapter dividers, and graphics that look like forms show the information. In order to save on packaging, we sealed the report at the side with an easy-open sticker; it can be franked and shipped without any further envelopes. The natural paper used is certified with the Blue Angel and conforms to the highest

MATERIAL WORLD

The rigors of outer space, the artforms of of Galactic Empire, the rituals of planetary wildlife. Costume design and materials more key to creating the feel of their rich amultitude of cultures inside a vast galactic consistent.

BY	BY
DROID TC-120	CLONE ET-831

Lace

SARTORIAL SENATE

Photography by
DROID TC-17RX

SLY MOORE	MAS AMEDDA	MON MOTHMA
"Fabulous, the movement of the material is sending shivers through my Servo Processor."	"Sonic really mysterious materials here, not sure if that is Rejannski leather or what. But whatever it is, it's working."	"Elegant and healthy. Sells but timeless. It says 'you will take orders from me, but that's ok.'"

CHANCELLOR PALPATINE	BAIL ORGANA	SENATOR AMIDALA
"Red is the power color, whether you're telling lies or traditional senatorial vestige. He's owning it."	"A really sleek and refined palette. A polished outfit. I wouldn't change a thing."	"A royal triumph. Padmé is revealing her noble roots in that purple brocade and crown-like headpiece."

ROGUE

THE NEW SCENT FOR SCOUNDRELS

Metal

Silk

장 소 : 서울특별시

시공자 : 미완성도시 프로젝트

시행처 : 서울시청

공사기간 period:

2017.03.17.-
2020.04.10

unfinished city

미완성도시

DESIGN Misu Kim, Ansung, Korea / URL misutery.com / SCHOOL Hankyoung National University / INSTRUCTOR Namoo Kim / PRINCIPAL TYPE Apple SD Gothic Neo Bold, Axel Bold, and Korean DREAM 5 Regular / DIMENSIONS 33.1 × 46.8 in. (84.1 × 118.9 cm) / CONCEPT The Unfinished City* is an initiative in which we create a city that revolves around our dissatisfaction with the current city. This is a project with all possibilities open, enabling each of us to address our ideals and suggestions. Inspired by the night landscape of the city, the poster illustrates that the project is in progress. The lights are neither fully off nor fully on, indicating it is in constant progress. The lights also reveal the Chinese letter 美, meaning beautiful, projecting our hopes for the beautiful city once completed. (*The original Korean title, "Miwanseong doshi," contains a pun — the prefix "mi" [un-] is homonymous to "beauty" [美].)

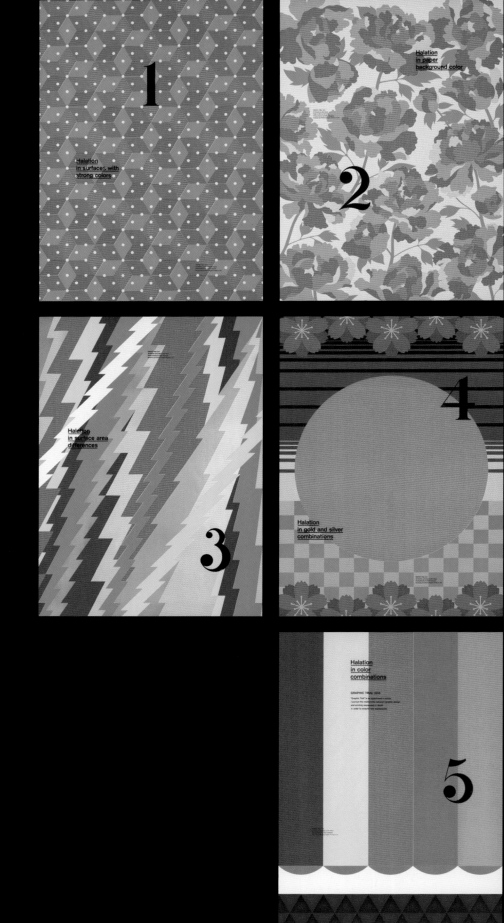

and custom / DIMENSIONS 28.7 × 40.6 in. (72.8 × 103 cm) / CONCEPT "Halation" is an experiment in which I pursue the relationship between graphic design and printing expression to acquire new expressions. The concept is "halation by the strength of the color."

DESIGN Claire Dawson, Toronto / CREATIVE DIRECTION Claire Dawson and Fidel Pena / URL underlinestudio.com / STUDIO Underline Studio / PRINCIPAL TYPE Engravers' Gothic / DIMENSIONS 5 x 4.5 in. (12.7 x 11.43 cm) / CONCEPT Underline Studio designed the packaging for a handcrafted, limited-edition set of sixty-five bottles of beer. The design and messaging are a play on words, capitalizing on the word "SIP," which is used as an acronym for the three types of beer included in the set: Stout, India Pale Ale, and Pumpkin Ale.

DESIGN Charles Calixto, Mariela Hsu, and Dave Kreibel, Washington, D.C. / ART DIRECTION Sucha Becky / SENIOR ART DIRECTION Tom Wright (Neenah) / CREATIVE DIRECTION Jake Lefebure and Pum Lefebure / COPYWRITER S.W. Smith / AGENCY Design Army, Washington, D.C. / CLIENT Neenah Paper / PRINCIPAL TYPE Custom / DIMENSIONS Various / CONCEPT "Love Me" is a new packaging promotion for Neenah Paper that features the company's most popular paper lines. Neatly tucked inside the blind embossed and foil-stamped carrier are several flat packaging samples that you fold and assemble yourself. Almost every finishing technique known to the industry is showcased, from laser cuts to spot UV varnishes. If it exists, it's in this promo. What's not to love?

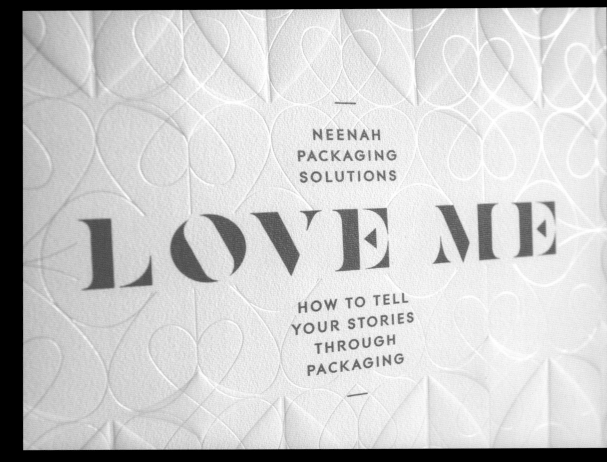

NEENAH
PACKAGING
SOLUTIONS

LOVE ME

HOW TO TELL
YOUR STORIES
THROUGH
PACKAGING

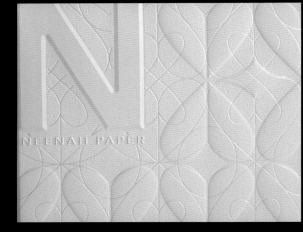

NEENAH PAPER

NEENAH
PACKAGING
SOLUTIONS

LOVE ME

HOW TO TELL
YOUR STORIES
THROUGH
PACKAGING

DESIGN Marie Jones, Bristol, England / SENIOR DESIGN Casey Blackmore / ACCOUNT DIRECTOR Kate Kew / CHIEF CREATIVE OFFICERS Spencer Buck and Ryan Wills / COPYWRITER Lindsay Camp / ILLUSTRATION Sam Hadley and Steve Noble / TYPOGRAPHER Rob Clarke / URL taxistudio.co.uk / TWITTER @taxistudio / DESIGN AGENCY Taxi Studio Ltd. / CLIENT Kate Hudnott / PRINCIPAL TYPE Bodoni, EcuyerDAX, Engravers MT, and Rockwell / DIMENSIONS 2.8 × 7.7 in. (7 × 19.5 cm) / CONCEPT Ms. Hudnott's pride, so well concealed in her daily life, pours unstoppably into her fine flavored spirits. However, her existing branding did not live up to the quality of her premium tipples — so she asked us to put that right. There are two sides to her character—the "darker" one emerging only in her drinks. So to tie the two together, we used the seven deadly sins to segment the range. Each sin relates to an aspect of the product and cleverly aligns with Ms. Hudnott's unswerving passion for concocting liquid perfection.

ART DIRECTION Richard Bélanger / CHIEF CREATIVE OFFICER Antoine Bécotte, Montréal / ASSOCIATED CREATIVE DIRECTOR Richard Bélanger /
CREATIVE DIRECTION Barbara Jacques / MOTION GRAPHIC Richard Bélanger and Hugo Brochard / STRATEGIC PLANNER Florence Girod /
DESIGN FIRM Cossette Infopresse / CONCEPT "OFF" is a gathering of the brightest in business, architecture, design, and human sciences.
Our mandate was to evolve the visual identity while attracting a new generation of leaders. To live up to the hype generated at launch,
we repositioned "OFF" in a new light, making it essential for anyone interested in creativity. The theme was based on five power types:
branches for math; snails for introverts; engines for trans-humanism; medusa for madness; and corncobs for local initiatives. Inkblots
represented how these powers stimulate the imagination and evoke the abstract.

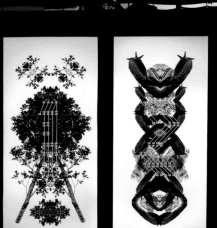

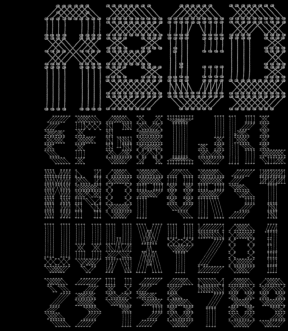

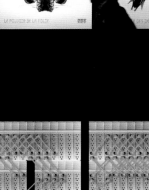

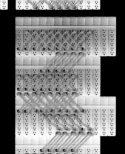

DESIGN Peter Großöhme, Jana Heidenreich, Sonja Marterner, and Isabell Zirbeck, Berlin / ART DIRECTION Peter Großöhme and Sonja Marterner / URL sonnenstaub.com / TWITTER @sonnenstaub / DESIGN FIRM Sonnenstaub-Büro für Gestaltung und Illustration / CLIENT P & T — Paper & Tea GmbH / PRINCIPAL TYPE National and Scotch Modern / DIMENSIONS Various / CONCEPT P & T offers ambitious tea drinkers rare teas and stationery. The packaging combines the key aspects of tea and paper as well as "Reuse & Recycle." For daily consumer packaging, resealable vacuum bags are furnished with a simple typographical label. For gifts, there is an additional paper-folded packaging, which by the means of its folding technique picks up the thought of a letter and a journey. Here, wrapping paper brown and natural white meet colored illustrations and plain typography. The different oxidation states of the tea are reflected in the concept of colors.

DESIGN Susanne Hoerner, Berlin and Stuttgart / URL strichpunkt-design.de / DESIGN OFFICE Strichpunkt Design / CLIENT Type Hype / PRINCIPAL TYPE Various / DIMENSIONS 4.3 × 5.9 in. (11 × 15 cm) / CONCEPT Love letters for letter lovers: Luise is the ultimate way to write one's declarations of love in early-twentieth-century style. The Luise collection, which was produced for Berlin label Type Hype, takes us back to the days when the popular Queen Luise of Prussia would stroll around the Tiergarten park with her son, who would later become Kaiser Wilhelm I. The product collection is bursting with retro romance for typography connoisseurs on the finest paper, handmade linens, and classical enamel.

DESIGN Chris Duchaine, Toronto / TWITTER @LeoBurnett / AGENCY Leo Burnett, Toronto / PRINCIPAL TYPE Akkurat and Pop / DIMENSIONS 5.5 × 5.5 in. (14 × 14 cm) / CONCEPT We needed a standardized card that would make it easy, and still special, to celebrate all the occasions people around the office commemorate. We discovered that all occasions can be tied back to numbers, so we created "The One Card," a single card (in five colors) that allows people to easily punch out the special number and circle a reason. Now, spreading a good feeling is easier than ever.

DESIGN Stefan Guzy and Björn Wiede, Berlin / URL zwoelf.net/portfolio / DESIGN FIRM Zwölf / CLIENT Helmut (Band) / PRINCIPAL TYPE Custom / DIMENSIONS 28 × 40 in. (72 × 102 cm) / CONCEPT The poster artwork (made with a marker) calls to mind the multiple sound-effects units used by Helmut, a Berlin band.

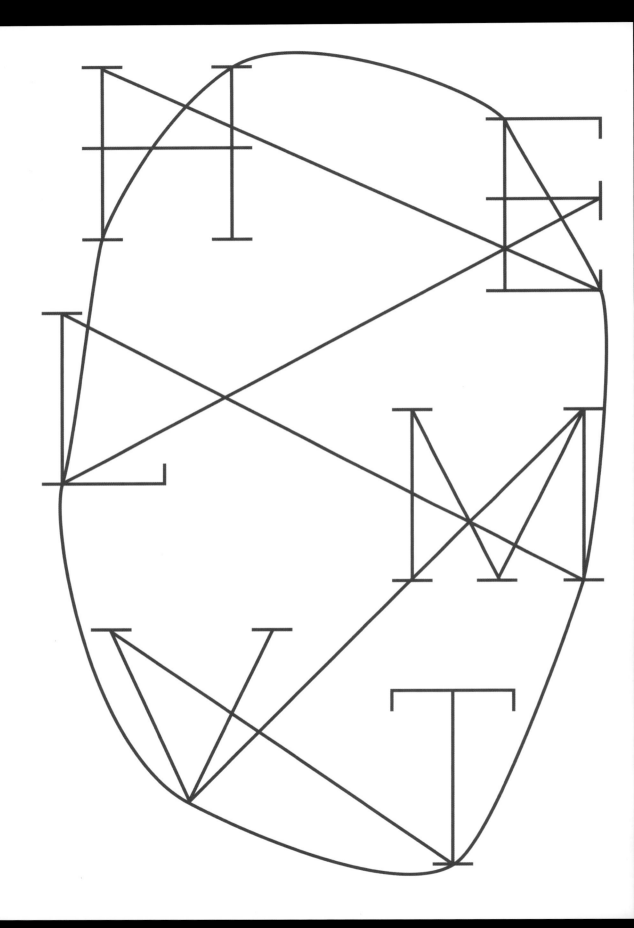

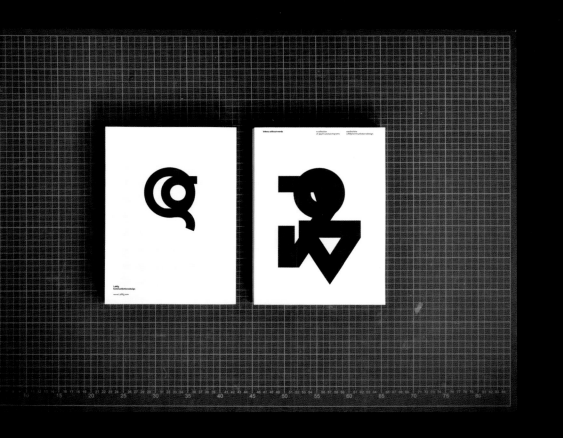

DESIGN Ina Bauer, Sascha Lobe°, and Yvonne Kümmel, Stuttgart / URL L2M3.com / STUDIO L2M3 Kommunikationsdesign GmbH / PRINCIPAL TYPE Bayer Next / DIMENSIONS 7.9 × 10.8 in. (20 × 27.5 cm) / CONCEPT "Letters Without Words" showcases a selection of glyphs. fonts, pictograms, and symbols created at L2M3 in various projects between 2005 and 2013. Some involved creating new fonts, others reworking or refining existing fonts. Within the various projects, they help form an image, develop a theme for a poster, or lend

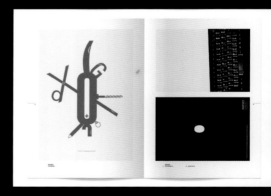

DESIGN Andreas Barden, Sebastian Berns, Jonas Bolzenius, Marie Bourgeret, Nicolai Diekmann, Sandra Eikel, Philip Erpenbeck, Dennis Galle, Nadine Gerloff, Robert Goesch, Gerrit O. Graff, Philipp Hammel, Jan Herkens, Hannah Honnef, Clara Hüsch, Patrick Kämmerling, Andreas Koch, Lena Konopka, Nicole Körfer, Alexandra Lazinski, Till Lenecke, Anika Lohse, Katarina Lueth, Rebekka Lynders, Matthias Mettenbörger, Nora Miebach, Carolin Nebgen, Romina Patt, Anja Rauenbusch, Lisa Roffmann, Julian Schlitter, Timo Schmitz, Julia Schöneweiß, Carolin Stiller, Judith Strich, Paul Trienekens, Christoph Vanwersch, Marie Voge, Sven von Osten, Jann de Vries, Artur Wied, Simon Wolf, and Stefan Zimmermann, Aachen, Germany / ART DIRECTION Alexandra Lazinski / PROFESSOR Ralf Weissmantel / URL cd-labor.de / DESIGN FIRM FH Aachen, FB Gestaltung, Corporate Design Labor / CLIENT FH Aachen University of Applied Sciences / PRINCIPAL TYPE FF Clan / DIMENSIONS 11.7 × 16.5 in. (29.7 × 42 cm) / CONCEPT Plakatzeichen is a collection of fifty typographic posters about type. Each poster represents one typeface. Together they form an experimental font catalog.

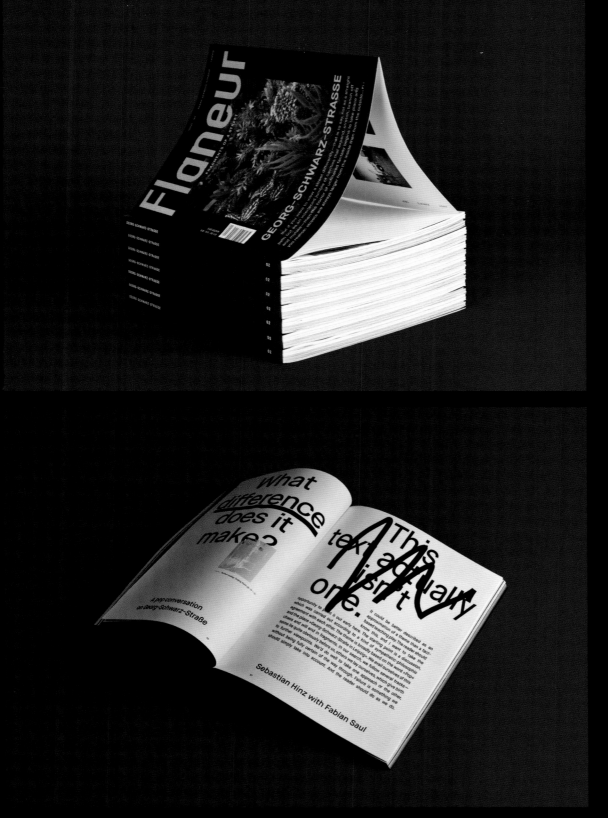

DESIGN Johannes Conrad, James Lunn, and Michelle Phillips, Berlin / URL y-u-k-i-k-o.com / TWITTER @studio_yukiko / STUDIO YUKIKO / CLIENT *Flaneur Magazine* / PRINCIPAL TYPE Hadriano, Maison Neue, and MilieuGrotesque / DIMENSIONS 9.1 × 11.8 in. (23.7 × 30.8 cm) / CONCEPT *Flaneur* presents one street per issue, embracing the street's complexity, its layers and stories, through a multi-disciplinary exchange between artists and writers. As art directors, we were required to build a clear framework that acts as a pillar to help suspend various elements of the magazine and continuously bring the reader back to a fixed point. We attempted to combine and cross-reference the involved artists/writers within this bound journal. The street's layers are deepened through the use of different papers, French fold, and street corners as chapters. We aim to conceptually push the boundaries of what a print magazine should be.

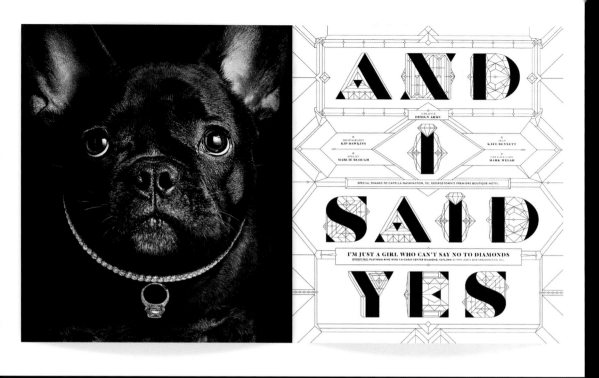

Mariela Hsu, Washington, D.C. / ART DIRECTION Mariela Hsu / CREATIVE DIRECTION Jake Lefebure and Pum Lefebure° / ...TER Mark Welsh / AGENCY Design Army / CLIENT *Washingtonian Bride & Groom* / PRINCIPAL TYPE Custom / DIMENSIONS 9 x 10.25 in. ...26 cm) / CONCEPT Every groom has a strategy for asking the "big question," and this feature editorial for *Washingtonian Bride* ...takes a look at some of the most popular ways to pop the question. Custom type is highlighted throughout, using faceted

CREATIVE DIRECTION Nejc Prah (2011–September 2013); Biba Košmerl (September 2013–present), Ljubljana, Slovenia / EDITORS Izidor Barši, Simon Belak, Lana Durjava, Jasmina Šepetavc, and Jurij Smrke / ILLUSTRATION Aljaž Košir-Fejzo / CONTRIBUTING ARTISTS Aljaž Celarc, Istvan David, Anna Ehrlemark, Nika Erjavec, Nejc Franetič, Klemen Ilovar, Nemanja Knežević, Miha Kosmač, Nataša Košmerl, Andrej Lamut, Matija Medved, Katra Petriček, Adrijan Praznik, Ajda Schmidt, Jure Kastelic, Sara Vrbinc, Dijana Vukojević, and Jon Žagar / URL tribuna.si / TWITTER @trobilo / CLIENT ŠOU Ljubljana / PRINCIPAL TYPE Tribunal / DIMENSIONS 11.8 × 16.5 in. (30 × 42 cm) / CONCEPT *Tribuna* is a student newspaper from Ljubljana, first published in 1951. During the time of the "death of the newspaper," we were thinking about a better understanding of what a newspaper is. Its activity should exceed publishing, and the list of those who create it should exceed the regular crew. Shy moves in the direction of a tactical understanding of the media and minor experiments with a horizontal editorial process inevitably led to different structures of content and of the newspaper as a whole, as well as various relations between written and visual. The newspaper is dead, long live the newspaper.

DESIGN Niklaus Troxler°, Willisau, Switzerland / ART DIRECTION Niklaus Troxler / DESIGN STUDIO Niklaus Troxler Design /
CLIENT Jazz in Willisau / PRINCIPAL TYPE VAG Rounded Bold and VAG Rounded Light / DIMENSIONS 35.4 × 50.4 in. (90 × 128 cm) /
CONCEPT This poster was designed for a jazz duo concert with a singer and a bass player. The red stripes stand for the bass lines:
the blue dots stand for the voice. The contrast between the warm and the cold color expresses the dialogue between the two characters.
Dots and stripes are an extreme contrast. The concrete design is based on a strong grid.

SYMPOSIUM 07III2013
TENTOONSTELLING 07III2013 — 18IV2013

DE MIJLPAAL HEUSDEN-ZOLDER
I.S.M. MAD-FACULTY

De Mijlpaal / PRINCIPAL TYPE BigVesta Black and Cooper Black / DIMENSIONS Unfolded: 18.9 × 28.4 in. (48 × 72 cm); Folded: 4.7 × 7.1 in. (12 × 18 cm) / CONCEPT "Beyond Art & Design" critically reflects on the relevance of recent Ph.D.'s in the arts through a conference and exposition. These Ph.D.'s are more than a pure creation of art and/or design, and are therefore "beyond art and design." The poster/ invitation illustrates the diversity and the dynamic working process of the design researcher. It consists of a typographic image in which letters and words are constructed through manifold lines, reflecting the individual and dynamic working process and reasoning of an artistic researcher. The explosion of lines, flanked by two power fields on the top and bottom, illustrates the researcher's balancing of theoretical insights, self-reflection, and the design process. At the back of the poster, more information about the event may be revealed by unfolding the poster. The paper, with its rough and soft sides, adds a tactile aspect to the invitation.

WEAVE CLOTH ORIMONO KOUBOU LE POILU

織物工房　le poilu
http://orimoyou.com/
OPEN ■ 11:00-19:00
REGULAR HOLIDAY ■ TUESDAY
TRIAL CLASS ■ AT ANY TIME ■ ¥3800
東京都台東区谷中 2-3-3

DESIGN Shinnoske Sugisaki, Osaka, Japan / ART DIRECTION Shinnoske Sugisaki / URL shinn.co.jp / TWITTER @shinnoske_s / DESIGN FIRM Shinnoske Design / CLIENT Osaka University of Arts / PRINCIPAL TYPE Gill Sans UltraBold (English) and Gothic MB101 (Japanese) / DIMENSIONS 28.7 × 40.6 in. (72.8 × 103 cm) / CONCEPT This was an experimental program for students. Each student used a three-dimensional object as the media that communicated a message. Students then represented the relation between the plane and the space through ambient typography in the two posters.

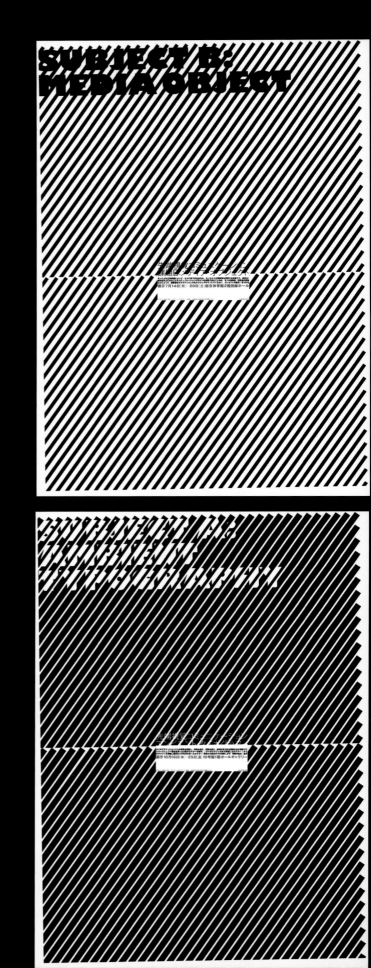

Todd

Brüsseler Straße 72
50672 Köln
www.temporary-todd.com

**Vernissage
22.3.13 18⁰⁰
Exhibition
23.3.13 & 24.3.13
14⁰⁰–21⁰⁰
Screening
24.3.13 19⁰⁰**

PHILIP EMDE INVITES

**WALTER DAHN
HAMED ESHRAT
DENNIS FREISCHLAD
STEFAN GOLZ
SIMON HEMMER
HUGO HOPPMANN
BELA JANSEN
SEBASTIAN KARBOWIAK
STEFAN MARX
ANDREAS SCHULZE
TIMOTHY SHEARER
TIM/TBOOKS
UNDENK
BJÖRN WIEDE
MARCO ZUMBÉ**

POSTER

DESIGN Stefan Guzy and Björn Wiede, Berlin / URL zwoelf.net/portfolio / STUDIO Studio Zwoelf / CLIENT Temporary Todd Gallery, Köln / PRINCIPAL TYPE Akzidenz Grotesk, Gothic 821, and Memphis / DIMENSIONS 28 × 40 in. (72 × 102 cm) / CONCEPT This is the poster for an exhibition, curated by Philip Emde, of several T-shirt designs from different designers and artists.

FRENCH&
MOROCCO&
YOU.

WE ARE
OPEN !!

TAMEALS IN PORTA

TAMEALS
CAFÉ & BAR

TAMEALS IN PORTA

TAMEALS
CAFÉ & BAR

TAMEALS IN PORTA

MORNING,
LUNCH, CAFÉ,
DINNER,
BAR,
WE ARE
OPEN !!

TAMEALS IN PORTA

DESIGN Momoyo Hosoya, Ren Takaya, and Syunryo Yamanaka, Tokyo / ART DIRECTION Ren Takaya / PHOTOGRAPHY Masayoshi Harabuchi / CHIEF EXECUTIVE PRODUCER Katsutoshi Kayaba / PRINTING DIRECTOR Daijiro Hasegawa / MANAGEMENT DIRECTOR Kentaro Ikeda / URL ad-and-d.jp / TWITTER @Rentakaya / DESIGN OFFICE AD&D / CLIENT Conception Co., Ltd. / PRINCIPAL TYPE Custom / DIMENSIONS 28.7 × 40.6 in. (72.8 × 103 cm) / CONCEPT "Tameals Yokohama" is a poster for the opening campaign and branding of a new restaurant. The stylized flower emblem of Morocco and France was used to develop the arabesque "French Morocco," which is the main concept of the restaurant. Also, we created a typeface with a tile motif to unify the image.

05.07
06.07
07.07

Exposituren: HfG-Campus, Schlossstraße 31 /
HfG-Atelierhaus, Geleitsstraße 103 / Hauptbahnhof,
Bismarckstraße 146 / Ölhalle, Hafen 6 / WohnBüro,
Platz der Deutschen Einheit 5 / City Passage Offenbach,
Frankfurter Straße 39 – 45

Mit freundlicher Unterstützung von: satis&fy AG Deutschland / Kulturstiftung der Städtischen Sparkasse Offenbach /
Stiftung der Frankfurter Sparkasse / FAZIT Stiftung / Wöhner GmbH & Co. KG / Dr. Marschner-Stiftung / Deutsche Börse AG /
freunde der hfg e.v. / Frankfurter Verein für Künstlerhilfe e.V. / Deutsch-Chinesischer Kulturaustausch für Kunst und Design (DCKD) e.V /
Ernst & Young AG / b·22 architekten + stadtplaner gbr / Eduard Geisheimer KG / Jugendkunstschule Offenbach am Main e.V.
Medienpartner: Frankfurter Allgemeine Zeitung / Journal Frankfurt

hfgOF_MAIN

small things - hundred and one rings

08.03. to 09.06.13

schmuckmuseum pforzheim im reuchlinhaus

jahnstraße 42 d-75173 pforzheim www.schmuckmuseum.de tel +49(0)7231|39 21 26

öffnungszeiten: di-so und feiertags 10.00-17.00 uhr außer heiligabend und silvester

DESIGN Raffinerie AG für Gestaltung, Zurich / URL raffinerie.com / CLIENT House of Electronic Arts Basel / PRINCIPAL TYPE Interstate / DIMENSIONS 35.6 × 50.4 in. (90.5 × 128 cm) / CONCEPT In its complex video works and installations, British artist duo Semiconductor explores the material nature of our world and the underlying forces and processes behind the world's physical appearance. The poster adopts this attitude by using a simple black-and-white binary code and a rough pattern. In a dirty and imperfect way, the two levels — typography and image — affect each other. The screen printing reinforces this atmospheric noise.

DESIGN Raffinerie AG für Gestaltung, Zurich / URL raffinerie.com / CLIENT House of Electronic Arts Basel / PRINCIPAL TYPE Interstate / DIMENSIONS 35.6 × 50.4 in. (90.5 × 128 cm) / CONCEPT The sound of European, African, or Asian cities is marked by the complex matrix of their social practices. Cities have a characteristic acoustic pattern. To demonstrate sounds in a three-dimensional context, we used a very simple visual language based on a black-and-white binary code. The use of typography and image makes you feel the noises; the screen printing reinforces this.

GRAPHIC DESIGN Michael Bierut, Tracey Cameron, Tamara McKenna, Jesse Reed, and Hamish Smyth, New York /
WAYFINDING SPECIALISTS Rachel Abrams, Sam Coultrip, David Gillam, Harriet Hand, Jenny Janssen, Matt Jephcote, Mike Rawlinson,
and Jason Smith / INDUSTRIAL DESIGNERS Eoin Billings, Duncan Jackson, Aidan Jamison, Simon Kristak, Paul Leonard, and Dale Newton
(Billings Jackson Design) / CARTOGRAPHERS Matthew Archer, Wendy Bell, David Figueroa, Thilda Garö, Kathryn Green, Charu Kukreja, Hanna
Lindahl, Rich Perkins, and Jeff Vonderheide (T-Kartor) / ENGINEERS Kevin Ballantyne, Chris Lucas, Jackson Wandres, and Klaus Weidemann
(RBA Group) / URL pentacitygroup / DESIGN FIRM PentaCityGroup, New York / CLIENT New York City Department of Transportation /
PRINCIPAL TYPE Helvetica DOT (customized version of Helvetica) / DIMENSIONS Various / CONCEPT WalkNYC is a new program of pedestrian
maps introduced by the New York City Department of Transportation that makes it easier to navigate the city streets. Placed on a system
of dedicated kiosks throughout the city, the maps are designed to encourage people to walk, bike, and use public transit. The maps were
developed in collaboration by a special consortium of designers and use an innovative "heads up" orientation that corresponds with
the direction the user is facing. The graphic language uses a customized version of Helvetica and features iconic New York landmarks
rendered as detailed, evocative line drawings.

DESIGN Ina Bauer and Sascha Lobe°, Stuttgart / URL L2M3.com / DESIGN FIRM L2M3 Kommunikationsdesign / CLIENT das programm / PRINCIPAL TYPE Akzidenz Grotesk / DIMENSIONS 33.1 × 46.8 in. (84.1 × 118.9 cm) / CONCEPT For an exhibition on Braun products of the 1960s at the Walter Knoll Showroom in London, designers from around the globe were invited to develop a poster that would serve both to announce the show and form part of the exhibition itself. The only requirement was that the design must incorporate the system idea of Braun design. Our design emphasizes the aspect of everyday use. Rotated 180 degrees, it becomes a unisex poster, mischievously breaking with the system.

NATIONAL THEATRE

DESIGN Giorgio Pesce©, Lausanne, Switzerland / ART DIRECTION Giorgio Pesce / URL atelierpoisson.ch / DESIGN STUDIO Atelier Poisson / CLIENT Musée de la Main, Lausanne, Switzerland / PRINCIPAL TYPE Akkurat, B-Dot, Pradell, and Sentinel / DIMENSIONS Various / CONCEPT For an exhibition on all aspects of salt (medical, cultural, gastronomical, artistic etc.), this scientific/cultural museum sought a visual concept that would translate the subject in a sensitive, "tasting" way. We came up with this simple idea: the tongue and its sensors (an old found illustration), with salt grains forming the word SALT. For the catalog/brochure, the museum was thinking about a few texts from different authors. What we proposed instead was a collection of many little notices and information, an alphabetical guide that you can consult as a mini-source. It's a funny way to give a lot of interesting facts and generate interest. It proved very very efficient.

DESIGN Anthony De Leo. Adelaide. Australia / ART DIRECTION Scott Carslake and Anthony De Leo / CREATIVE DIRECTION Scott Carslake and Anthony De Leo / CHALK BOARDS Sam Barratt / URL voicedesign.net / TWITTER @voice_of_design / DESIGN STUDIO Voice / CLIENT Hither & Yon / PRINCIPAL TYPE Brandon Grotesque / DIMENSIONS Various / CONCEPT The ampersand is the fundamental element of the Hither & Yon brand. It adorns each wine as a visual interpretation of its tasting notes, each time crafted specifically for that vintage and never reused. For use across generic applications, a bold ampersand is reversed out of the distinctive Hither & Yon bottle shape to reference the iconic packaging range.

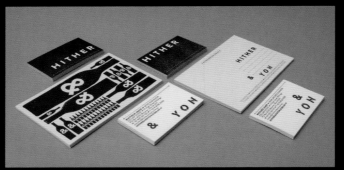

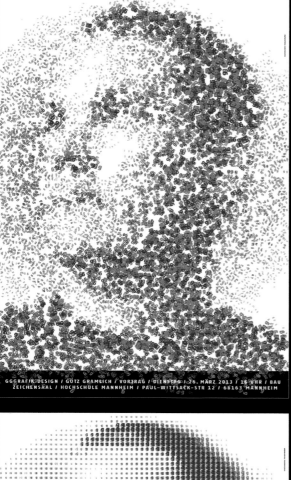

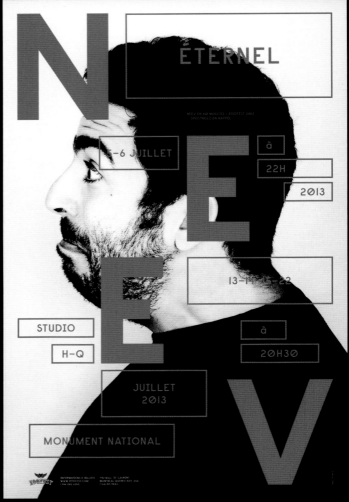

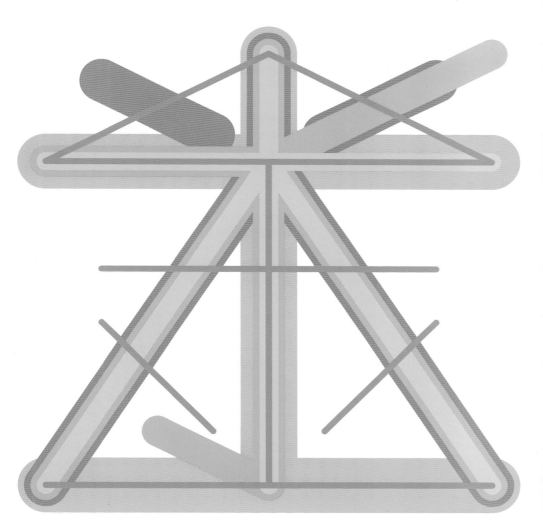

金木水火土

自然無為，
以小化大，
以無法為有法，
以無限為有限。

DESIGN Benny Leung Tsz Fung. Hong Kong / TWITTER @studio_m.hk / DESIGN FIRM Studio M / CLIENT Black Bird Theatre / PRINCIPAL TYPE Custom / DIMENSIONS 27.6 × 39.4 in. (70 × 100 cm) / CONCEPT This poster is an exploration of Taoism and

DESIGN

JAN TOMAS

...on Jan Tomas, Prague / Twirlex Jantomasdesign / Design Studio / Jan Tomas Studio / TRINCIAL life Future Typo, Future Typo 1, Future Typo 2, Future Typo 3, Future Typo 4, and Helvetica / DIMENSIONS 8.5 × 11.8 in. (21.5 × 30 cm) / CONCEPT This publication contains examples of 3D characters, texts, and words in the first 3D font series and points to new possibilities in the perception and importance of typography in touch technologies. Future Typo 2D and 3D typefaces can be ordered only through the author's website. This printed publication can also be purchased at the author's website. The designer, Jan Tomas, is the author as well.

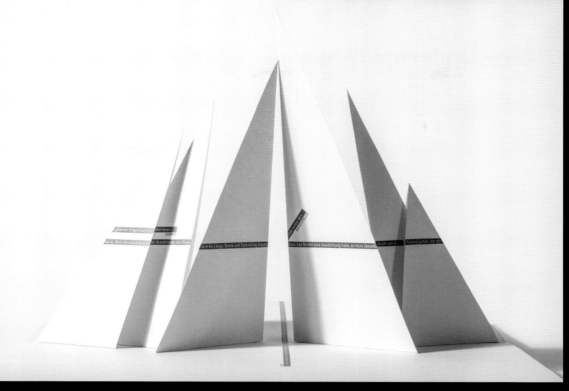

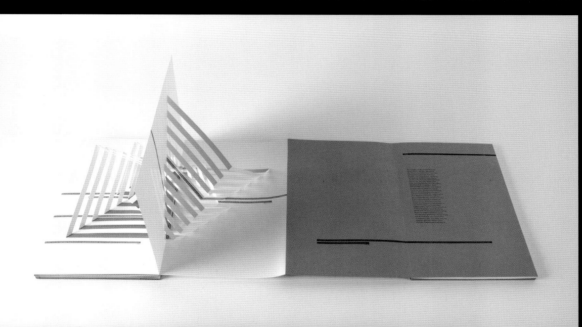

DESIGN Jochen Klaus and Marcel Menke, Münich / TWITTER @kjoko80 / SCHOOL Mediadesign Hochschule München / PROFESSOR Tobias Wuehr / PRINCIPAL TYPE Univers Condensed 57 and Walbaum Roman / DIMENSIONS 7.2 × 11.6 in. (18.2 × 29.5 cm) / CONCEPT This is an experimental typographic university project.

STUDENT PROJECT

DESIGN Lizá Ramalho and Artur Rebelo, Porto, Portugal / ASSISTANT DESIGN Artur Faria / ART DIRECTION Lizá Ramalho and Artur Rebelo / CREATIVE DIRECTION Lizá Ramalho and Artur Rebelo / TYPEFACE Photo Illustration: Lizá Defossez Ramalho and Artur Rebelo, assisted by Peter Chmela, Artur Faria, and Daniel Jacinto / URL r2design.pt / DESIGN STUDIO R2 Design / CLIENT Dados Favoritos–Associação (Dados Favoritos–Cultural Association) / PRINCIPAL TYPE Antwerp and Ordinaire / DIMENSIONS 6.9 × 7.9 in. (17.5 × 19 cm) / CONCEPT "Letters on Landscape" is a self-initiated project. In this visual essay, the starting point was an industrial machine abandoned on the Portuguese countryside. We read this piece near the road as a gigantic lowercase "a." On this basis, we created the whole uppercase alphabet as well as spaces and punctuation signs. The letterforms were based on the two-dimensional font Ordinaire, designed by David Poullard.

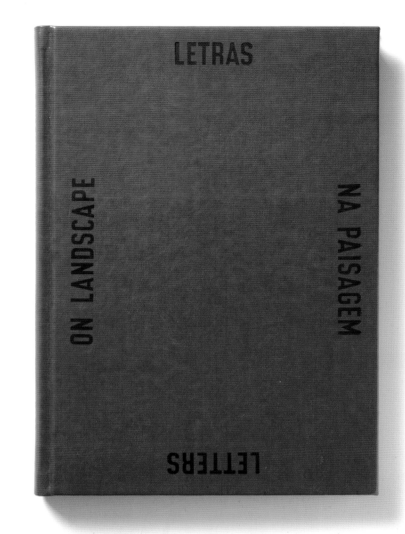

LETRAS

ON LANDSCAPE

NA PAISAGEM

LETTERS

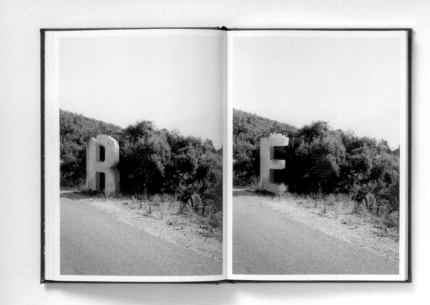

DESIGN Kristina Valiunas and Jeff Watkins, Toronto, Toronto / AGENCY Leo Burnett, Toronto / TWITTER @LeoBurnettTor / CLIENT Rooster Post Production / PRINCIPAL TYPE Miller Display Roman Bold, Miller Display Roman, and Tungsten Medium / DIMENSIONS 22.75 x 34 in. (57.8 x 86.4 cm) / CONCEPT To wish partners and clients a happy new year, the "Rooster — Don't Be a Large Cock" calendar was born. It's a lighthearted reminder that despite the stresses, pressures, and frustrations that we face in the advertising industry, we shouldn't be cocks (rude or mean) around the office. The calendar contained twelve rooster portraits and individual rooster bios that highlighted the types of characteristics we shouldn't adopt in 2013 if we truly wanted to make the year a happy one for all.

CALENDAR

CREATIVE DIRECTION Yomar Augusto / PRINCIPAL Yomar Augusto°, Rotterdam and New York / URL yomaraugusto.com / DESIGN OFFICE The Office of Yomar Augusto / PRINCIPAL TYPE Tampom Type System / DIMENSIONS 19.6 × 27.5 in. (50 × 70 cm) / CONCEPT This silk-printed poster announcement informed friends and clients of my decision to move the studio to New York City.

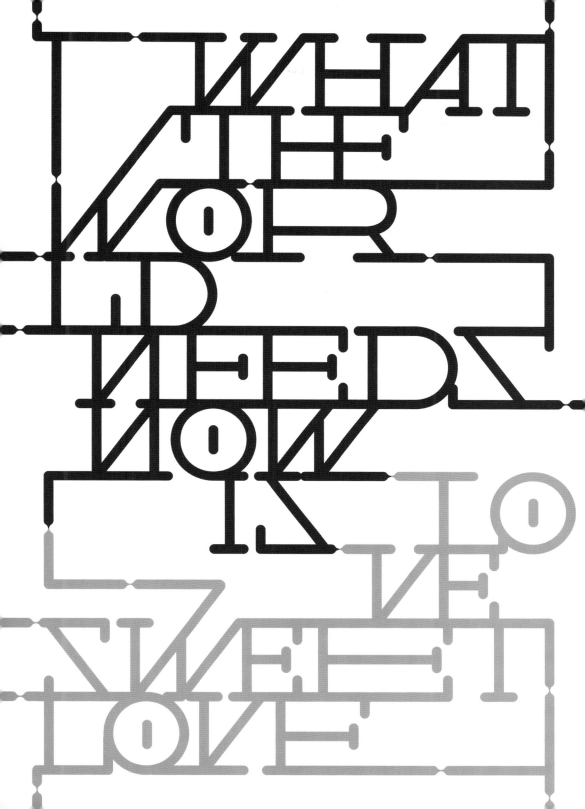

WHAT THE WORLD NEEDS NOW IS TO LOVE WHAT I LOVE

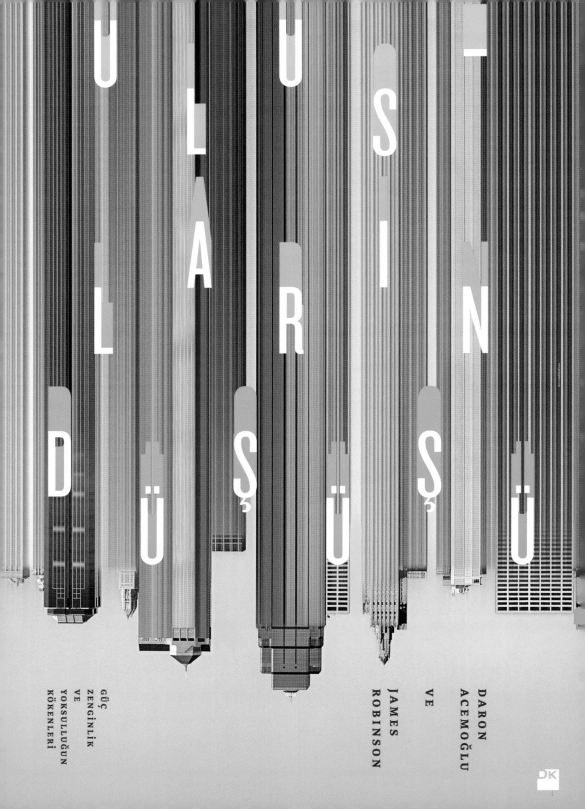

ULUSLARIN DÜŞÜŞÜ

GÜÇ, ZENGİNLİK VE YOKSULLUĞUN KÖKENLERİ

JAMES ROBINSON VE DARON ACEMOĞLU

DK

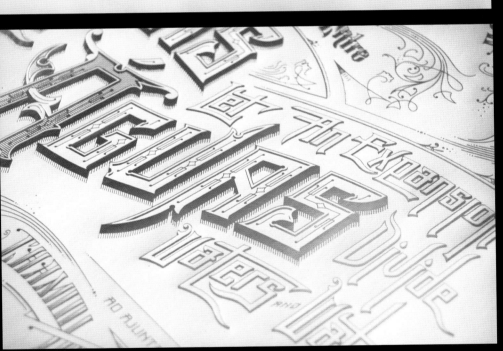

ART DIRECTION Kevin Cantrell, Salt Lake City, Utah / LETTERING Kevin Cantrell and Arlo Vance / URL hintcreative.com and kevincantrell.com / TWITTER @hintcreative and @kevincantrell / DESIGN FIRMS Hint Creative and Kevin Cantrell Design / CLIENT Gruppo Cordenons / PRINCIPAL TYPE Custom / DIMENSIONS 16 × 20 in. (40.6 × 50.8 cm) / CONCEPT "Águas," the second installment in the 7 Days series, is inspired by map insurance lettering. The text is taken from the first few verses in Genesis, about the Creation, suggesting the infinite possibilities to create using Gruppo Cordenons paper. The artwork is printed in six foil options on various Plike colors by Gruppo, each interpreting the concept of water.

DESIGN Kathleen Fitzgerald, Matt Kay, Jennifer Kinon, Jonathan Lee, and Bobby C. Martin Jr., New York /
DESIGN PARTNERS Jennifer Kinon and Bobby C. Martin Jr. / LETTERING Matt Kay / URL originalchampionsofdesign.com /
TWITTER @ocdagency / DESIGN FIRM OCD | The Original Champions of Design / CLIENT Image of the Studio / PRINCIPAL TYPE Custom /
DIMENSIONS 30 × 45 in. (76.2 × 114.3 cm) / CONCEPT The Free Manifesto: Small business owners are the new American revolutionaries.
Willing to lay down our lives, our fortunes, and our honor, we strike out for freedom. We lead a movement toward a stronger, more
stable union that functions on a more human scale. All heart and guts and grit, we find a way to do what we love, our way, every day.

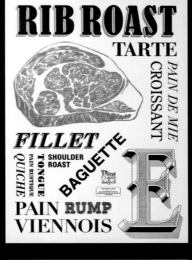

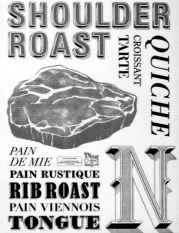

BODY
LAN-
GUAGE

BODY
LANGUAGE

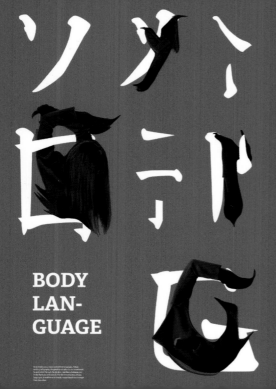

BODY
LAN-
GUAGE

BODY
LAN-
GUAGE

EINGHT
PRING-
CIPLE
OF YONG

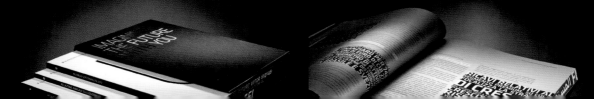

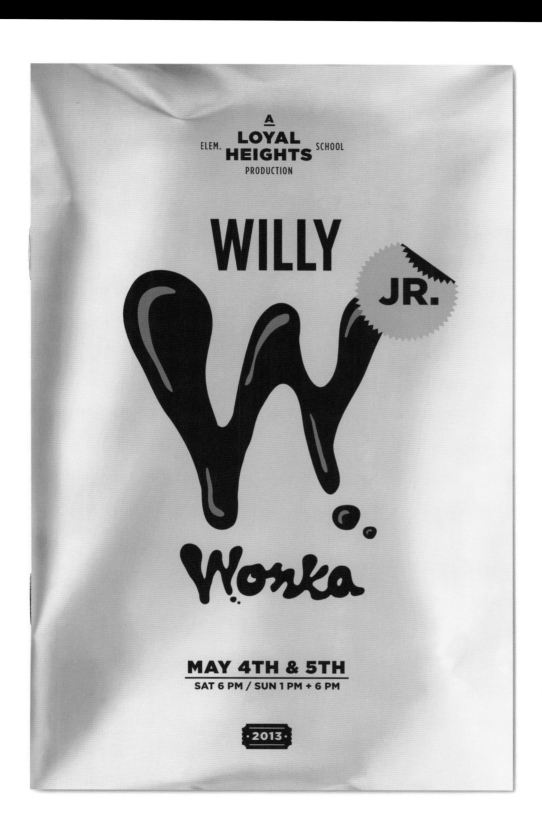

DESIGN Steven Watson, Seattle / CREATIVE DIRECTION Steven Watson / PHOTOGRAPHY Paul Edmondson / URL turnstylestudio.com / TWITTER @turnstylestudio / DESIGN FIRM Turnstyle / CLIENT The Loyal Heights Elementary School PTA / PRINCIPAL TYPE Gotham and custom / DIMENSIONS 5.5 × 8.5 in. (14 × 21.6 cm) / CONCEPT Turnstyle donated graphic design services for the Loyal Heights Elementary School stage production of *Willy Wonka Junior*. The graphic identity for the show was based on a reinterpretation of Willy Wonka candy packaging. Branded items produced by Turnstyle included a show logo, playbill, posters, candy bar wrappers, Golden Tickets, cast T-shirts, and various other props. The collateral and promotional items generated immense excitement in the school community and helped make the kids and attendees feel that they were participating in a real Broadway production. The cast put on three shows, with total attendance topping 1,400.

DESIGN Dusty Summers, Philadelphia / URL theheadsofstate.com / TWITTER @theheadsofstate / DESIGN FIRM The Heads of State / CLIENT *The New York Times* / PRINCIPAL TYPE Found wood type / DIMENSIONS 10.6 × 6.6 in. (26.9 × 16.8 cm) / CONCEPT This spread was created for the President's Day weekend *Book Review*, which highlighted three books about the lasting legacies of Abraham Lincoln, Calvin Coolidge, Dwight Eisenhower, and Richard Nixon.

DESIGN Andre Jointe, New York / DESIGN DIRECTION Fred Woodward© / PHOTOGRAPHY Terry Richardson / DIRECTOR OF PHOTOGRAPHY Dora Somosi / PUBLICATION GQ / PRINCIPAL TYPE Knockout / DIMENSIONS 16 × 11 in. (40.6 × 27.9 cm) / CONCEPT For "The 40 Things Making Us Laugh Right Now," we were influenced by promotional event posters, hand-painted signage and pre-1920s printed material.

DESIGN Steven Bonner. Stirling. Scotland / URL stevenbonner.com / TWITTER @stevenbonner / CLIENT Penguin Books /
PRINCIPAL TYPE Langdon / DIMENSIONS 8.7 × 12.6 in. (21 × 32 cm) / CONCEPT *All That Is Solid Melts Into Air* is the first novel by Irish
writer Darragh McKeon. It's a tale of love and lives in Russia set against the backdrop of the Chernobyl disaster. I was commissioned
by Penguin to create a typographical image for the cover that would not only reflect the mood of the events told within, but also give
a visual interpretation for the destruction caused by the disaster itself through the title.

DESIGN Timothy Goodman, New York / ART DIRECTION Jordan Awan / CREATIVE DIRECTION Wyatt Mitchell / LETTERING Timothy Goodman / PHOTOGRAPHY Grant Cornett / PROP STYLING Shane Klein and Theo Vamvounakis / FILM EDITING Ivan Hurzele / LASER CUT SOFTlab / STUDIO Timothy Goodman, Inc. / CLIENT *The New Yorker* / PRINCIPAL TYPE Custom handlettering and laser-cut typography / CONCEPT Here are six pieces for *The New Yorker*'s annual Summer Fiction Issue, titled "Crimes & Misdemeanors." The theme was noir fiction, and I was asked to come up with "title cards" to represent each fiction piece. We tried to cover an array of styles, from Gothic to Western to '70s Bollywood, depending on the premise of stories. Two of the pieces were laser cut; all of them were shot.

DESIGN DIRECTOR Fred Woodward / DESIGN DIRECTOR Levon Biss / DIRECTOR OF PHOTOGRAPHY Dora Somosi /
PHOTO EDITOR Krista Prestek / PUBLICATION GQ / PRINCIPAL TYPE Futura and handlettering / DIMENSIONS 16 × 11 in. (40.6 × 27.9 cm) /
CONCEPT For this story titled "Boob Job," we got lucky. While feeling our way through the letterforms in the title, we excitedly
discovered that nearly all of them could be legibly illustrated using — yep, you guessed it — boobs. And that suited the photo just
fine. We hope Ricky Gervais (the subject) and Chris Heath (the writer) had a chuckle when they saw it.

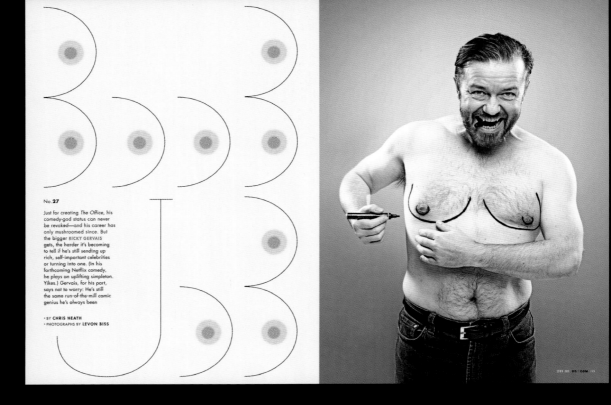

No. **27**

Just for creating *The Office*, his comedy-god status can never be revoked—and his career has only mushroomed since. But the bigger RICKY GERVAIS gets, the harder it's becoming to tell if he's still sending up rich, self-important celebrities or turning into one. (In his forthcoming Netflix comedy, he plays an uplifting simpleton. Yikes.) Gervais, for his part, says not to worry: He's still the same run-of-the-mill comic genius he's always been

• BY **CHRIS HEATH**
• PHOTOGRAPHS BY **LEVON BISS**

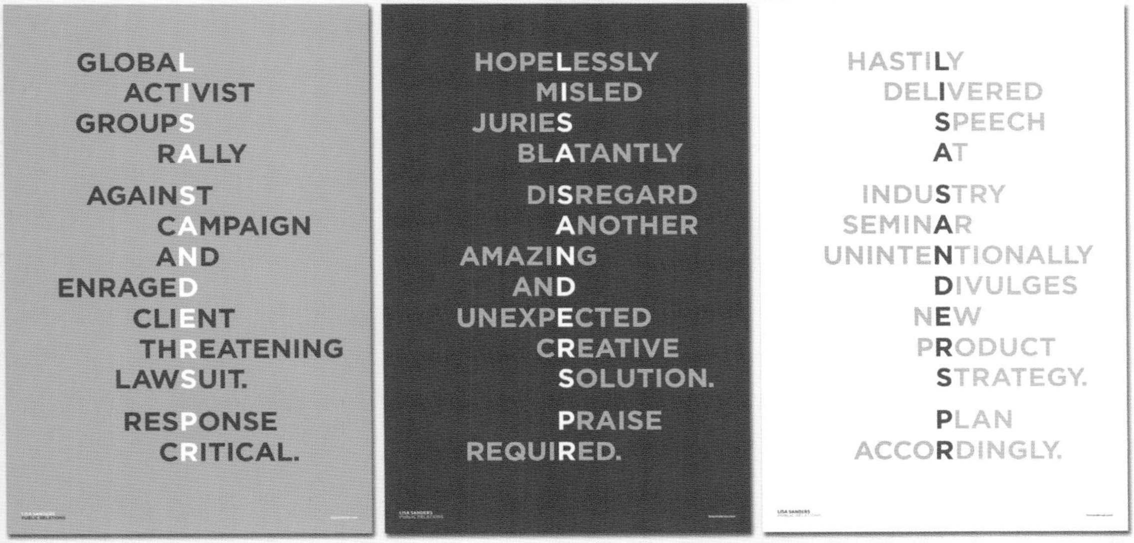

GLOBAL
ACTIVIST
GROUPS
RALLY

AGAINST
CAMPAIGN
AND
ENRAGED
CLIENT
THREATENING
LAWSUIT.

RESPONSE
CRITICAL.

HOPELESSLY
MISLED
JURIES
BLATANTLY

DISREGARD
ANOTHER
AMAZING
AND
UNEXPECTED
CREATIVE
SOLUTION.

PRAISE
REQUIRED.

HASTILY
DELIVERED
SPEECH
AT

INDUSTRY
SEMINAR
UNINTENTIONALLY
DIVULGES
NEW
PRODUCT
STRATEGY.

PLAN
ACCORDINGLY.

ISLAND

e Butzen and Mats Kubiak, Düsseldorf / CLIENT University of Applied Sciences / PRINCIPAL TYPE Aperçu / x 23.4 in. (84.1 x 59.4 cm) / CONCEPT The poster was designed for an exhibition of student works on the issue of re. The exhibition provided an overview of excursions from the past two years and presented the results of artistic extreme conditions. The poster's typographic construction visualizes the shape of the natural environment of Iceland.

Gestaltung: Stephanie Butzen und Mats Kubiak

...mm.com / SNYDER SNYDER NEW YORK (PRINCIPAL TYPE HANDLETTERING) DIMENSIONS 11.5 x 16.5 in. (29.2 x 41.9 cm)

...suggestion of Kristina at Snyder New York, I teamed up with the talented photographer Spencer Heyfron to showcase our forms. Printed on high-quality newsprint, the mailer includes twenty-seven portraits shot on the streets of New York. ...ts' quotes and occupations handlettered to reflect their unique personalities. To create the lettering I used pen. ...aphy, ink, and brushes.

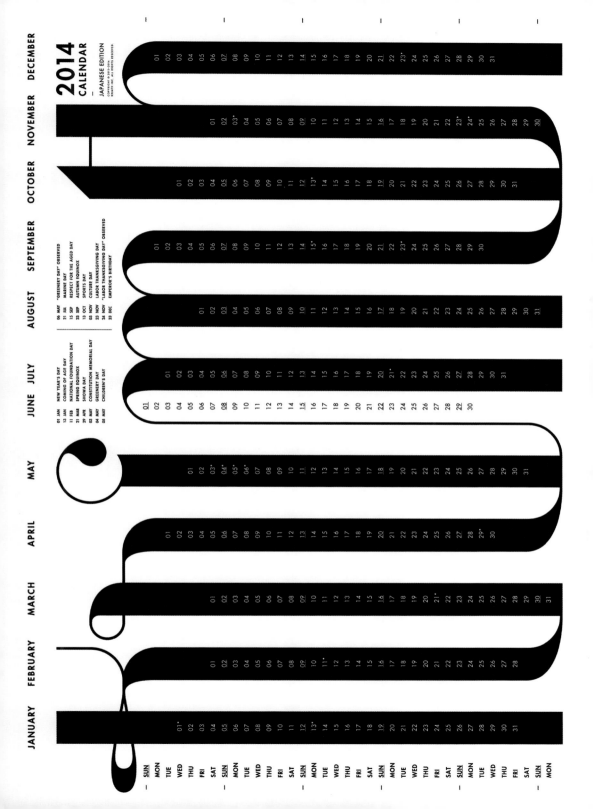

2014 CALENDAR

JAPANESE EDITION

01 JAN	NEW YEAR'S DAY	
13 JAN	COMING OF AGE DAY	
11 FEB	NATIONAL FOUNDATION DAY	
21 MAR	SPRING EQUINOX	
29 APR	SHOWA DAY	
03 MAY	CONSTITUTION MEMORIAL DAY	
04 MAY	GREENERY DAY	
05 MAY	CHILDREN'S DAY	
06 MAY	"GREENERY DAY" OBSERVED	
21 JUL	MARINE DAY	
15 SEP	RESPECT FOR THE AGED DAY	
23 SEP	AUTUMN EQUINOX	
13 OCT	SPORTS DAY	
03 NOV	CULTURE DAY	
23 NOV	LABOR THANKSGIVING DAY	
24 NOV	"LABOR THANKSGIVING DAY" OBSERVED	
23 DEC	EMPEROR'S BIRTHDAY	

WUNDERKIND
2014

Scheufelen

KIRSCH WASSER

SCHNAP[P]S
01

KIRSCH
WASSER

10

LEDERHOSE

8

AUTOBAHN

DESIGN Gloria Heik and Kit Hinrichs°, San Francisco / URL studio-hinrichs.com / STUDIO Studio Hinrichs / PRINCIPAL TYPE Various / DIMENSIONS Super Size: 23 × 33 in. (58.5 × 84 cm); Desk Size: 12 × 18 in. (30.5 × 45.75 cm) / CONCEPT The 365 Typography Calendar draws attention to the variety and aesthetic quality of type itself by making the typeface the primary graphic element on each page. It features twelve unique typefaces, includes descriptions of the type, shares a biography of each designer, and notes all major holidays and the birthdays of the type designers on the calendar. For the 2014 calendar, twelve world-renowned international members of the illustrious Alliance Graphique Internationale nominated some of their favorite typefaces. Their choices range from the traditional to

ART DIRECTION Flo Gaertner, Karlsruhe, Germany / URL magmabranddesign.de / DESIGN FIRM MAGMA Brand Design / CLIENT E&B engelhardt und bauer / PRINCIPAL TYPE Maison Neue / DIMENSIONS 27.6 × 39.4 in. (70 × 100 cm) / CONCEPT The E&B Art Calendar No. 62 is a colorful homage to Massimo Vignelli's iconic modernist design for the Stendig Calendar (1966). Day numbers refer to the days of the week in a diagonal, horizontal, or vertical system. Each of the seven days is linked to a specific graphic shape, bringing together letters and ciphers. The calendar sheets have each been printed in one run on a Heidelberg Speedmaster XL 106 in eight Pantone neon colors.

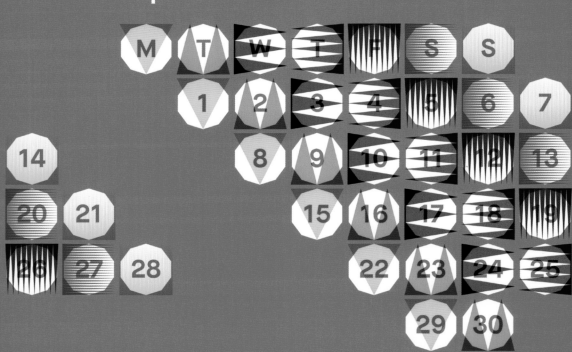

condolences

Childbirth should be a joyous
occasion. Sadly, in many countries
it's too often a tragedy.

congratulations

富山デザインウエーブ2013展

2013年10月2日（水）→7日（月）

ウイング・ウイング高岡1F交流スペース　入場無料

toyama
design
wave

富山で生まれる、次のデザイン。

遊び心をいつまでも

DESIGN Akira Miyamae, Tokyo / ART DIRECTION Akira Miyamae / URL kasugamaru-d.com / TWITTER @akiramiyamae / DESIGN FIRM KASUGAMARU / CLIENT YUTAU / PRINCIPAL TYPE Frutiger and custom / DIMENSIONS 28.7 × 40.6 in. (72.8 × 103 cm) / CONCEPT This poster commemorates the independence of the creative team at YUTAU. We took a trip to Okinawa to reaffirm YUTAU's motto: "To make something enjoying." I found coral reefs by chance during the trip and picked them up. To make this poster, I formed the alphabet from coral reefs. Unfortunately, the work was swallowed up by the waves as soon as I finished. Making things sometimes arouses fleetness. The activities of YUTAU will continue with the ideology "To remember to make something enjoying."

DESIGN Simon Brenner and Sascha Lobe . Stuttgart / DESIGN FIRM L2M3 Kommunikationsdesign / CLIENT Stiftung Kunstsammlung Nordrhein Westfalen / PRINCIPAL TYPE Akzidenz Grotesk and Akzidenz Grotesk Medium / DIMENSIONS 23.4 × 33.1 in. (59.4 × 84.1 cm) / CONCEPT Dissonance and distorted tones play a major role in the works of Susan Philipsz on show at the exhibition *The Missing String*. The exhibition materials use these themes in the typography, developing optical dissonances and distortions.

DESIGN Colin Christie, Atsuko Sasagawa, and Anzu Sato, Utsunomiya City, Tochigi Prefecture, Japan and London / URL tento10.tumblr.com / TWITTER @TENto10design / DESIGN FIRM TEN to 10 / CLIENT Utsunomiya City, Utsunomiya City Board of Education, Utsunomiya Museum of Art, and Kosugi Hoan Museum of Art, Nikko / PRINCIPAL TYPE Bell MT Regular (London), Braggadocio Regular (Nikko), and Impact Regular (Utsunomiya) / DIMENSIONS 24 × 36 in. (61 × 91 cm) / CONCEPT By engaging with unexpected elements of type, the workshops aim for participants to focus on their houses and their communities on a playful scale. Working with the shapes of the characters and letters from their hometown, participants build using painted card, scissors, and glue on typographic shapes recomposed from letters of the alphabet, Japanese kanji, hiragana, and katakana strokes.

ART DIRECTION Daniel Robitaille, Montréal / CREATIVE DIRECTION Louis Gagnon° / AGENCY Paprika / CLIENT Le Naturiste /
PRINCIPAL TYPE Executive / DIMENSIONS Various / CONCEPT The real challenge was to reinstate the identity of a brand that had been
neglected for more than twenty years. The new Canadian owners wanted to revive the brand. Therefore, we reviewed all the contact
points, all the communicational aspects of the business, in order to revitalize its image. The project was launched only recently,
so we hope it will have an impact on the organization.

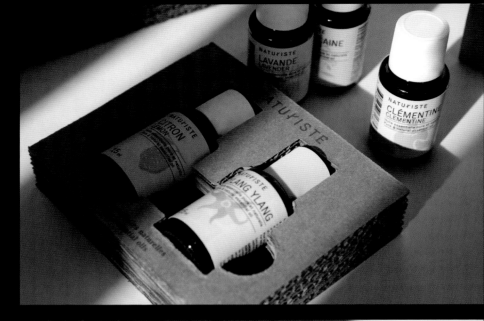

ART DIRECTION Daniel Robitaille, Montréal / CREATIVE DIRECTION Louis Gagnon° / AGENCY Paprika / CLIENT Slow Food Montréal / PRINCIPAL TYPE Handlettering / DIMENSIONS 15 × 26 in. (38.1 × 66 cm) / CONCEPT We created three clear visuals of a cow, a melon, and a chicken. Then we produced illustrations that could appeal to a wide range of clients with the use of colors that are close to nature. The challenge was that for each element, we had a large amount of information. We decided to integrate that information directly into the illustrations. Finally, to standardize the identity of the project, we created a sense of family between the three visuals.

DESIGN Tom Crosby, Adelaide, Australia / ART DIRECTION Tom Crosby and Anthony De Leo / CREATIVE DIRECTION Anthony De Leo / LETTERING Nate Williams / ILLUSTRATION Nate Williams / URL voicedesign.net / TWITTER @voice_of_design / DESIGN STUDIO Voice / CLIENT Casa Rio / PRINCIPAL TYPE Pluto and custom handlettering / DIMENSIONS 7.8 × 3.7 × 3 in. (19.7 × 9.5 × 7.7 cm) /

CONCEPT Rio Coffee has visited the four corners of the earth to source exceptional single-origin coffee beans. It is only fitting, then, that the packaging should convey the same excitement and enthusiasm with which the beans were sourced and locally roasted. Each box is adorned with captivating imagery of its homeland, telling a vivid tale of the landscape, people, coffee production, and, of course, enjoyment.

DESIGN Margo Graxeda, Los Angeles / DESIGN DIRECTOR Sharyn Belkin Locke° / ART DIRECTION Sharyn Belkin Locke° / CREATIVE DIRECTION Nanette Bercu / LETTERING Margo Graxeda / ILLUSTRATION Margo Graxeda / COPYWRITER Kaveri Nair / TWITTER @paulmitchellus / DESIGN OFFICE John Paul Mitchell Systems, In-House Creative Department / PRINCIPAL TYPE Custom / DIMENSIONS Various / CONCEPT In the sea of pink that appears every October, Paul Mitchell stands apart with a new, youthful breast cancer awareness campaign. Using irreverent language, handlettered type, and bold, colorful graphics, "The Girls Are Alright!" campaign features limited-edition products and messaging that supports early detection through breast self-exams, encouraging women to be their "own main squeeze" and make sure "the girls are alright." Every product purchase helps support the National Breast Cancer Foundation.

ART DIRECTION Oliver Munday, New York / URL omunday.tumblr.com / DESIGN FIRM Oliver Munday Group (OMG) / CLIENT Maurice Jackson and Wellfleet Library / PRINCIPAL TYPE Franklin Gothic and Adobe Garamond / DIMENSIONS 11 x 17 in. (27.9 x 43.2 cm) / CONCEPT The poster reflects a duality: a modern take on the story of Anthony Benezet and the piecing together of the history that led to American abolitionism.

A TALK

ABOUT

LET

ANTHONY BENEZET

THIS

FOUNDING FATHER of

ATLANTIC and AMERICAN ABOLITIONISM

by..

VOICE

MAURICE

JACKSON

BE

THURSDAY,
AUGUST 15

Wellfleet Public Library

55 West Main Street, Wellfleet, MA

HEARD

8-9
P M

DESIGN Hee Ra Kim / PHOTOGRAPHY Felix Nam Hoon Kim / URL heera-kim.com and behance.net/heerakim / TWITTER @heeraive /
SCHOOL School of Visual Arts, New York / INSTRUCTOR Barbara deWilde / PRINCIPAL TYPE Rita Smith, Scotch Roman MT, and handwritten
DIMENSIONS 13 × 17.5 in (33 × 44.5 cm) / CONCEPT I designed this book cover after the historical typeface of an old baseball ticket,
which was a perfect fit for the book cover I had in mind. I traced the font with pencil, trying many sketches until I had one I was
pleased with. I then finalized it using Illustrator.

DESIGN Anna Berkenbusch° and Christian Gralingen, Berlin / DESIGN FIRM Anna B. Design / CLIENT Professor Andrea Zaumseil / PRINCIPAL TYPE Letter Gothic and Zaumseil / DIMENSIONS 6.7 × 8.7 in. (17 × 22 cm) / CONCEPT The handlettered book cover with found objects taped on a studio wall in the background refers to the content of the book: the world of the sculptor Andrea Zaumseil with all her inspiration materials, photographs, and drawings.

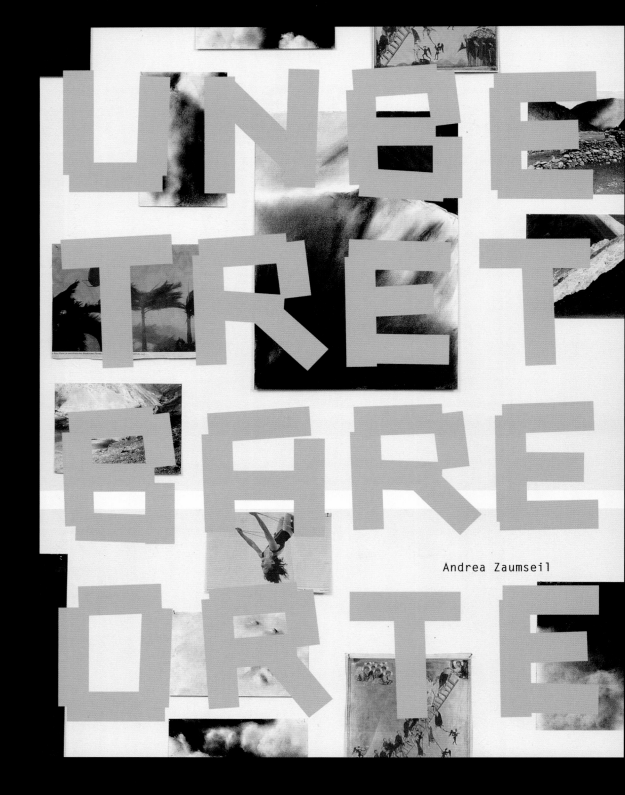

Andrea Zaumseil

Visionaries

Béhar helps startups—and legacy brands—grow
Interview by Brad Wieners

Category:	Industrial design, identity
Project:	Nivea
Designer:	Yves Béhar
Date completed:	2013

THE DESIGNER AS ENTREPRENEUR

In the middle of a former factory he's bought and is renovating for Fuseproject, his 60-person design firm, Yves Béhar has commissioned a plywood mountain. Roughly pyramidal, it has bleachers on one side (for presentations, impromptu meetings, naps) and is sheer on two others; the fourth slope merges with a side wall. It rises through a forest of unvarnished wooden trusses to an elevation of about 23 feet and culminates in a skylight, which will eventually function as an escape hatch, allowing a person to stand

at the summit, feet inside, head and body out, looking over San Francisco's China Basin as if on a surfaced submarine. "You can have a little respite," Béhar says, gesturing up. "Physically and metaphorically, you'll be above the activity of the office—above it all."

The mountain sits within an open workspace of about 22,000 square feet. Toward the front is a naturally lit loft divided in two, with one area dedicated to Jawbone, the wearable computing company in which Béhar has been a partner since 2002,

---

Reinventions

The familiar transformed

Category:	Transport
Project:	Double-decker bus
Designer:	Heatherwick Studio
Location:	London

"There had been a strong sense of dignity about taking the bus"

Edges have been rounded to give the appearance of a smaller bus and to ease sightlines for other drivers.

A second staircase facilitates movement. Glass cutaways bring in natural light and emphasize the window's most distinctive feature: the upper deck.

Heatherwick's redesign, made with bus manufacturer Wright Group, is 9 feet longer than the iconic Routemaster double-decker and 40 percent more fuel-efficient than existing buses.

It was a dream project. No design team had had a chance to design a bus for London for 50 years. There had been a strong sense of dignity about taking the bus. But the experience for the passenger had been degraded over time. The London Transport authority had just a single stipulation for bus manufacturers: The outside had to be red. Inside it was a hodgepodge of colors, patterns. If you panned your eye around the interior, like a sort of bus archaeologist, you could see all the regulations that had burst their way in. The hand poles were nuclear yellow, because of the directive that they had to stand out from the background. There was fluorescent lighting, which is the least flattering to people's skin. It's essential that cities use their infrastructure to keep reasserting their identities.
— Thomas Heatherwick, founder, Heatherwick Studio

Category:	Packaging
Project:	Ikea food
Designer:	Stockholm Design Lab
Location:	Stockholm

As with all Ikea merchandise, product names are in Swedish. Pictures do the work of telling non-Swedes what's inside.

For its marinated herring, Ikea whimsically turns a classic feature of tins, the pull tab, into the head and eye of a fish.

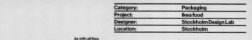

SKARPSILL

IKEA

100 g (65 g)

Ikea's private food label, introduced in 2006, now spans about 150 products, with uniformly simple packaging.

"simple and direct, humorous and smart"

Our relationship with Ikea is 20 years old. We've created packaging for their nonfurniture items and tweaked their logo. Then in 2005 we were approached to redesign the food line. At that point, Ikea stores were carrying iconic Swedish brands and fewer of their own brands. They wanted to promote the "Swedishness" of the brand. To us, that means it has to be simple and direct, humorous and smart. And to remove unnecessary information and merely decorative things. There was also a pedagogical problem that needed to be solved: The product name is in Swedish; sometimes people don't know how this product is meant to be consumed. So we have pictures to show that. This is a unique case. You are able to keep the packaging really simple because it's a private-label brand placed in stores where it has no competition at all. —Björn Kusoffsky, founder and CEO, Stockholm Design Lab

THURSDAY MAGAZINE

21 FEBRUARY 2013

Natural

The Healing Power of Food

SPRING CLEAN YOUR BODY

DESIGN Adonis Durado°, Muscat, Oman / URL timesofoman.com / PUBLICATION *Times of Oman's Thursday Magazine* / PRINCIPAL TYPE Farnham / DIMENSIONS 7.9 × 10.4 in. (20 × 26.5 cm) / CONCEPT This was the cover for a weekend supplement.

DESIGN Chelsea Cardinal, New York / DESIGN DIRECTION Fred Woodward© / DIRECTOR OF PHOTOGRAPHY Dora Somosi / PUBLICATION GQ / PRINCIPAL TYPE Flash, Futura, and Titling Gothic FB Skyline / DIMENSIONS 16 x 11 in. (40.6 x 27.9 cm) / CONCEPT This story about Bill Murray chronicles the actor's favorite pastime: spontaneously inserting himself into the lives and times of non-celebrities. Here, the attention-mongering deck crashes the party of the straight-laced headline, just as Bill Murray might crash your karaoke session or soccer game.

DESIGN Tom Brown, Port Moody, Canada / CREATIVE DIRECTION Tom Brown and Joshua Paul / PHOTOGRAPHY Joshua Paul / URL lollipop-gp.com / TWITTER @bealollipopper / PUBLISHER Lollipop Grand Prix Media / PRINCIPAL TYPE OL Headline Gothic and Regular / DIMENSIONS 8.25 x 10.75 in. (21 x 27.3 cm) / CONCEPT *Lollipop* magazine is a historical document showcasing each race weekend of the Formula 1 season. Named after an often-forgotten piece of racing equipment used by team mechanics during a pit stop. *Lollipop* is pure F1 candy.

DESIGN Ana Gomez Bernaus° Venice, California / URL anenocena.com / TWITTER @Anenocena / DESIGN FIRM Anenocena / PRINCIPAL TYPE ITC Avant Garde Bold, ITC Avant Garde Extra Light, and ITC Avant Garde Medium / DIMENSIONS 22.5 × 12 in. (57.2 × 30.5 cm) / CONCEPT The poem "First Fig" by Edna St. Vincent Millay made me think about the variety of approaches toward life. Her words touch the fatal destiny that life itself entails, with a passionate love for it. "The Love for Life" is an experimental project that focuses on using letterforms, composition, and lighting to express the intensity of St. Vincent Millay's lines.

INSPIRED BY:

FIRST FIG, EDNA ST. VINCENT MILLAY

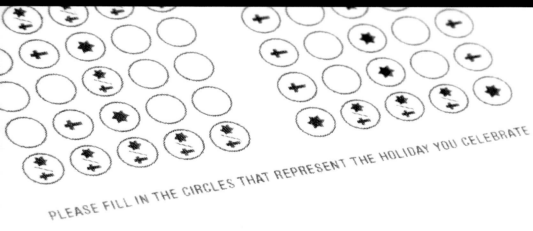

PLEASE FILL IN THE CIRCLES THAT REPRESENT THE HOLIDAY YOU CELEBRATE

YOU'RE INVITED TO

The CAA
FRIDAY
NIGHT
PARTY

FEBRUARY ◆ 22ND 2013

Greystone Mansion

BEVERLY HILLS

ART DIRECTION Thao Nguyen, San Francisco / URL jessicahische.is/awesome / TWITTER @jessicahische / DESIGN FIRM Jessica Hische° / CLIENT Creative Artists Agency (CAA) / PRINCIPAL TYPE Handlettering / CONCEPT Every year, talent agency CAA throws its Friday Night Party — an event for its A-list clients, friends, and colleagues the Friday before the Oscars. Thao Nguyen wanted something deco/ flapper-inspired as the party itself was influenced by this era because of the theatrical release of *The Great Gatsby* that year. The invitation would only exist online, so to give it a more tactile and special feel, a bit of jQuery was used (borrowing a save-the-date designed by Jennie Hallman) to make the invitation flip over when "moused" over, and textures were used in a subtle way to simulate

chran, Gilbert Ford, Jason Kernevich of The Heads of State, Chris Buzelli, Grady McFerrin, Alex Eben Meyer, Neil Swaab, , Gina & Matt, James Gulliver Hancock, and Jillian Tamaki / PRINTING Studio on Fire / URL jessicahische.is/awesome / cahische / DESIGN FIRM Jessica Hische / PRINCIPAL TYPE Sentinel and handlettering / DIMENSIONS 5 × 5 in. (12.5 × 12.5cm) / ss and I announced we were getting married, the pressure was on to do something awesome for our invitations. Instead of invite, we created a crazy parallax website and enlisted the help of our friends to create artwork for it. We decided ake to give out to wedding guests that included all the artwork from the site on one side (offset and gold foil) and the f how we got together on the back (two-color letterpress and gold foil). The fronts and backs were duplexed with gold

circle circle

take a

berry cascade
on a standard wreath

A tail of evergreens with bright pops of color replaces the usual big red bow.

Why settle for a standard wreath when you can make holiday magic?

Whether you want to spend 15 minutes jazzing up a bought model or an hour crafting one from scratch, these expert how-tos (from the authors of *The Flower Recipe Book*) deliver beauty to your own front door. All the materials are easy to find (see below), and you can watch helpful step-by-step videos at **realsimple.com/wreaths**.

CREATED BY **Studio Choo** | PHOTOGRAPHS BY **Nigel Cox** | WRITTEN BY **Danielle Claro**

WHERE TO GET SUPPLIES: *Find evergreen branches in a Christmas-tree lot, supermarket, or your own backyard. Buy flowers, berries, and specialized greenery, like olive and Berzelia branches, at a flower shop or a farmers' market. Get wreath frames, floral wire, and dried berries (like the white berries opposite) at a local craft store or at save-on-crafts.com.*

WHAT YOU'LL NEED

■ Evergreen wreath (any variety)

■ 8 additional evergreen branches (4 each of 2 varieties); if the wreath has short needles, use long-needled branches for contrast (and vice versa)

■ 5 bunches of berries (2 bright red, 2 dried white tallow, 1 dark red); for both the bright and dark red berries, choose from viburnum, winterberry, holly, Hypericum, crab apple, rose hip, or any other varieties you find and like

■ Garden gloves, shears, and 1 spool of medium-gauge floral wire

WHAT TO DO

1. Lay the wreath on a table. Set aside 3 long (12- to 18-inch) evergreen branches to create the drapey cascade. Trim the stems of the remaining 5 branches to 8 inches each. Trim the stems of 1 bunch or bright red berries and 1 bunch of white berries to about 6 inches each.

2. In your hand, make a loose bunch of 1 short (6-inch) evergreen stem, 2 short (6-inch) stems of bright red berries, and 1 short stem of white berries. Attach the bunch with wire at 10 o'clock on the wreath. Repeat, laying each bunch over the stems of the previous one, counterclockwise, until you've "berried" almost half the wreath.

3. At the center of the berried part of the wreath (about 8 o'clock), poke in the 3 long evergreen branches so that they arc down. Use 1 long piece of wire to bind all 3 branches together in the back.

4. Attach the remaining berries to the cascade: 2 or 3 long stems of dark red, 2 or 3 long stems of bright red, and 1 or 2 long stems of white

berries. Attach the bunch with wire at 10 o'clock on the wreath. Repeat, laying each bunch over the stems of the previous one, counterclockwise, until you've "berried" almost half the wreath.

5. Tuck the remaining evergreen stems into the unberried part of the wreath.

6. Tuck in extra berries as desired.

HOW LONG IT WILL LAST

This wreath could last for weeks outside. The berries might shrivel a bit, but that can look pretty. If the extra greenery doesn't age well, just pull it out and replace it.

take a

COMMAND
AND
CONTROL

NUCLEAR WEAPONS,
the DAMASCUS ACCIDENT, and the
ILLUSION OF SAFETY

DCAH-G

ERIC SCHLOSSER

TS-A94-0434
CLASSIFIED BY: ATSD(AE) AND CG-W-4

Copy 11

RESTRICTED DATA

#306

12-10-250

8 950611A

Ruggero LEONCAVALLO + ルッジェーロ・レオンカヴァッロ

PAGLIACCI
パリアッチ（道化師）

Pietro MASCAGNI + ピエトロ・マスカーニ

CAVALLERIA RUSTICANA
カヴァレリア・ルスティカーナ

東京二期会オペラ劇場
Tokyo Nikikai Opera Theatre

…wa, Tokyo. / ART DIRECTION Osamu Misawa / CREATIVE DIRECTION Osamu Misawa / URL omdr.co.jp / TWITTER @omdr.nakahashi / Co., Ltd. / CLIENT Tokyo Nikikai Opera Foundation / PRINCIPAL TYPE AW Conqueror Didot Light / DIMENSIONS 7.2 × 10.2 in / CONCEPT Cavalleria Rusticana and Pagliacci are love-and-hatred dramas with pastoral themes. The two Italian classica… performed together as a so-called Cav/Pag double bill. Expressing the drama of a couple trying to keep a secret from a… tional village bubbling up with both love and hate, using the elegant typeface Conqueror Didot, the letters conjure the …s of gazes at once with their scattered, chiseled look, with silver on four colors emphasizing the various gaps therein … programs were connected with Christianity, so we used a plus symbol to create a Christian cross motif …

公益財団法人 東京二期会
2012年二期会は創立60周年を迎えます

Anniversary
60th

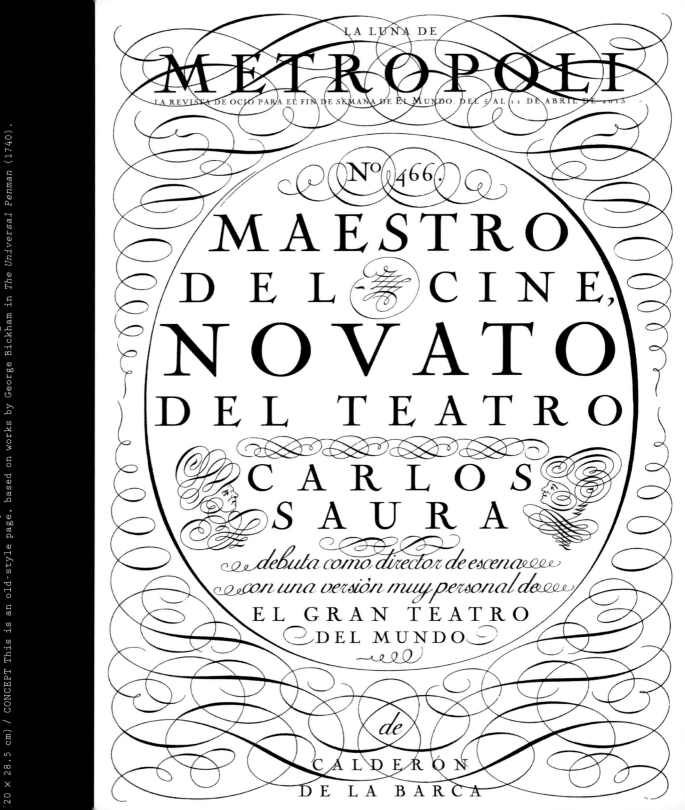

LA LUNA DE

METROPOLI

LA REVISTA DE OCIO PARA EL FIN DE SEMANA DE EL MUNDO. DEL 5 AL 11 DE ABRIL DE 2015

Nº 466.

MAESTRO
DEL CINE,
NOVATO
DEL TEATRO

CARLOS
SAURA

*debuta como director de escena
con una versión muy personal de*

EL GRAN TEATRO
DEL MUNDO

de

CALDERÓN
DE LA BARCA

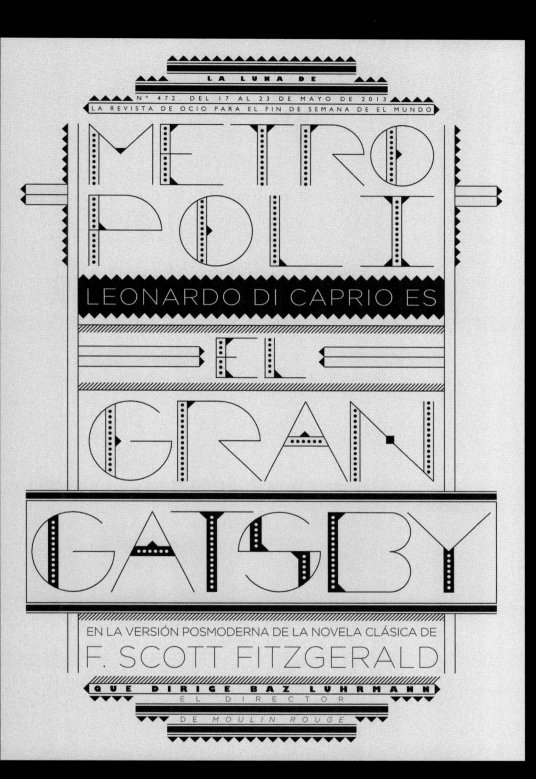

DESIGN Rodrigo Sanchez°, Madrid / ART DIRECTION Rodrigo Sanchez / CALLIGRAPHY Rodrigo Sanchez / URL facebook.com/ColeccionMetropoli /
DESIGN FIRM Unidad Editorial, El Mundo / PUBLICATION Metropoli / PRINCIPAL TYPE Gill Sans, Gotham, and handlettering /
DIMENSIONS 7.9 × 11.2 in. (20 × 28.5 cm) / CONCEPT This is an Art Deco-style cover.

DESIGN Yon Joo Choi○, Jeeyoon Rhee, Kathleen Scudder, and Luke Wilhelmi○, New York / ART DIRECTION Andrea Brown / CREATIVE DIRECTION Matteo Bologna○ / STRATEGIST Roberta Ronsivalle / INTERACTIVE DIRECTORS Josh Eriksen and Courtney Heffernan / URL mucca.com / TWITTER @muccadesign / DESIGN FIRM Mucca Design / CLIENT Shinsegae, Seoul, Korea / PRINCIPAL TYPE Dapifer and Dapifer Stencil (English), SD Book-L and SM JGothic (Korean) / DIMENSIONS Various / CONCEPT Shinsegae is South Korea's premier luxury department store. With SSG Food Market, it planned on opening the nation's leading supermarket devoted to locally sourced foods. Our goal was to engage and entertain customers by celebrating authentic Korean culinary culture. Inspired by Seoul's open-air farmers' markets, the Mucca team developed a brand system rooted in the connection between eating well and living well. A focus on local suppliers and their stories evokes the world of the farm, while custom stencil typography, natural materials, and hand-applied graphics convey a spontaneous energy and artisanal spirit. We covered a lot of ground to bring SSG Food Market to life by creating a brand identity, departmental signage, wayfinding, iconography, uniforms, retail packaging, private label packaging, and a website.

THE NATIONAL MAGAZINE OF TEXAS

TexasMonthly
THE 50 BEST BBQ JOINTS ~~IN TEXAS~~ in the WORLD!

BRISKET, RIBS, AND SAUSAGE FROM FRANKLIN BARBECUE, IN AUSTIN.

CREATIVE DIRECTION T.J. Tucker. Austin / PHOTOGRAPHY Wyatt McSpadden / FOOD STYLING Aaron Franklin / URL texasmonthly.com / TWITTER @TexasMonthly / PUBLICATION Texas Monthly / PRINCIPAL TYPE Handlettering / DIMENSIONS 8.1 × 10.5 in. (20.6 × 26.7 cm) / CONCEPT Every five years, we are tasked with not only ranking the top fifty barbecue joints in the state, but also creating a cover to make our readers drool. To help with the latter, Aaron Franklin, the owner of our number-one joint, arranged a heaping tray of his finest meats. Creative director T.J. Tucker painstakingly handlettered typography drawn by Jon Contino in Franklin's own Espresso barbecue sauce. The rest was left to photographer Wyatt McSpadden, who captured the full scene in all its glory and brought to life a next-level food cover.

DESIGN Brad Simon, Portland, Oregon / URL WKstudio.com / DESIGN STUDIO W+K Studio / CLIENT Wieden+Kennedy / PRINCIPAL TYPE Decoro and Public Gothic Square / CONCEPT We were tasked with designing a save-the-date invite for our agency's holiday party. The theme of the party was Russian opulence. We took inspiration from Fabergé eggs, Russian textiles, and ornate typography to create an invite that would introduce the theme as well as create anticipation and excitement for the upcoming party.

Привет

W+K HOLIDAY PARTY

11.26.13

8PM / FORMAL ATTIRE

до свидания

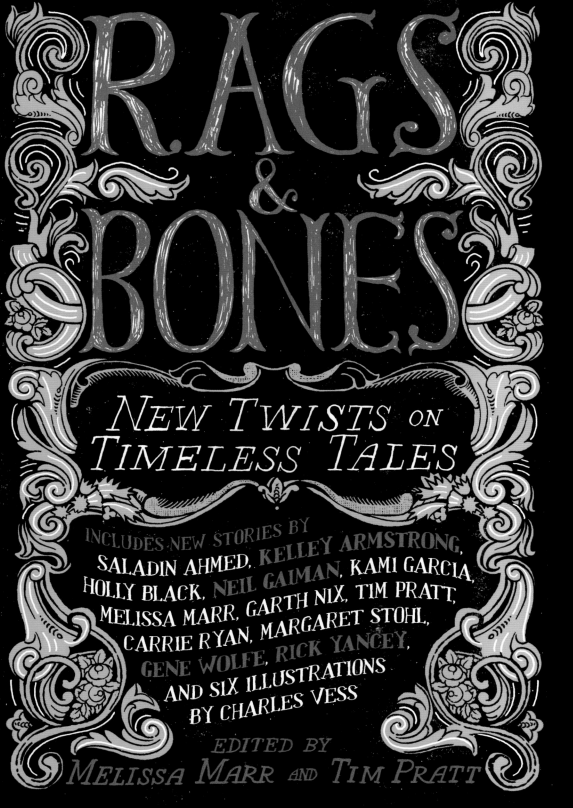

RAGS & BONES

NEW TWISTS ON TIMELESS TALES

INCLUDES NEW STORIES BY
SALADIN AHMED, KELLEY ARMSTRONG,
HOLLY BLACK, NEIL GAIMAN, KAMI GARCIA,
MELISSA MARR, GARTH NIX, TIM PRATT,
CARRIE RYAN, MARGARET STOHL,
GENE WOLFE, RICK YANCEY,
AND SIX ILLUSTRATIONS
BY CHARLES VESS

EDITED BY
MELISSA MARR AND TIM PRATT

DESIGN Neil Swaab, New York / CREATIVE DIRECTION David Caplan° / LETTERING Grady McFerrin / PUBLISHER Little, Brown Books for Young Readers / PRINCIPAL TYPE Handlettering and Paquita Pro / DIMENSIONS 5.5 × 8.25 in. (14 × 21 cm) / CONCEPT For the short story collection *Rags & Bones*, we wanted to have something that felt rich, exquisite, and like it could be a great gift book. The idea of an ornamental typographic treatment with lots of gold jumped out at us. I commissioned the amazing Grady McFerrin to illustrate a stylized typographic cover that incorporated some of the objects from the stories into a border. However, after a couple of rounds of sketches, it was clear that those objects were overwhelming his other beautiful work on the cover. So, we scrapped them in favor of letting his art and the feeling of the book shine through without getting too literal. Grady did a beautiful job rendering the illustrative elements and stylized typography; I used a font for the contributors' names to complement it and an additional font to set the flap and back panel copy. The result is an elegant, striking cover that feels rich and full of story—exactly what we were hoping for.

DESIGN Tracy Shaw and Sammy Yuen, New York / CREATIVE DIRECTION David Caplan© / LETTERING Gray318 / PUBLISHER Little, Brown Books for Young Readers / PRINCIPAL TYPE Handlettering / DIMENSIONS 5.5 × 8.25 in. (14 × 21 cm) / CONCEPT We were given the challenge of creating a cover for this raw, powerful novel about a suicidal teen boy. "Leonard" could exist in any town, and be anyone, so we stayed away from the specificity of photographic images, instead focusing on the striking title. After a few rounds of comps, we landed on a bold silhouette of a hand making the shape of a gun. Designer Tracy Shaw used a deep red, gray, and black color palette along with a gritty texture to convey the stark emotional depth of the story. Ultimately, the shape of the gun seemed too controversial, so we decided to strip away the hand silhouette and spotlight the book title. The project was handed over to the über-talented Gray318, who kept the grit and color palette we liked from the earlier comp and created an all-type cover treatment. Both concepts tried to reflect the mental state of a troubled teen who literally feels like he is up against a wall. The blown-out size of the title placed on the hard, intense background emphasizes the volume at which the main character is screaming his message, and his hopelessness at getting anyone to hear him.

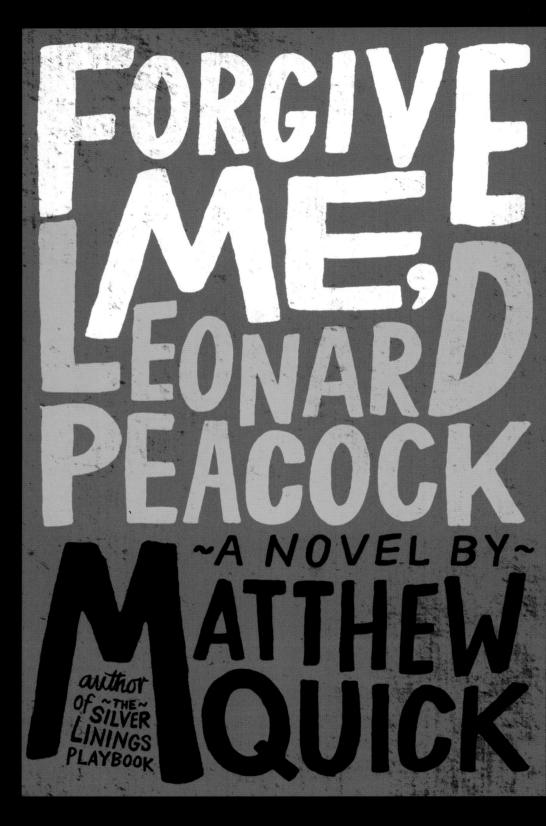

WASHINGTONIAN

MARCH 2013

GREAT

BARS

OUR FAVORITE PLACES TO DRINK

At Jack Rose Dining Saloon, Alex Strange whips up a Powerglove, with aquavit and egg whites.

MARYLAND   DC   VIRGINIA

GETTING ORGANIZED
Expert advice for an uncluttered home

JOHN WALL
Will the star's return lift the Wizards?

BEST OF BETHESDA
Shopping, fun outings, dining, and more

CREATIVE DIRECTION Michael Goesele, Washington, D.C. / TYPOGRAPHY Vault49 New York / PHOTOGRAPHY Jeff Elkins / URL washingtonian.com / TWITTER @washingtonian / PUBLICATION *Washingtonian* / PRINCIPAL TYPE BrightonTwo Gothika NBP and custom / DIMENSIONS 8.25 × 11 in. (21 × 27.6 cm) / CONCEPT The goal for our "Great Bars" cover was to create a Prohibition-era vibe with a contemporary twist. We started with a stellar photograph by Jeff Elkins to help create the tone. We then collaborated with Vault49, a multidisciplinary design collective in New York City, on creating the custom type. They did a fantastic job integrating the type and various elements into the photograph. The finishing touch was using a bronze metallic Pantone across various accents.

17

DESIGN Ty Wilkins, Austin / LETTERING Ty Wilkins / ILLUSTRATION Ty Wilkins / STUDIO TY / CLIENT Clay Ross, Matuto / PRINCIPAL TYPE School Script / DIMENSIONS 5.6 × 5 in. (14.2 × 12.4 cm) / CONCEPT *The Devil & the Diamond* is the second album by New York-based Matuto. Their music is an original fusion of Appalachian bluegrass and Brazilian folk music. In order to reflect this experimental hybrid, Ty Wilkins developed a new illustration technique that blends his bold and minimal style with influences from Appalachian and Brazilian folk art. The custom lettering crafted for the logotype and album title bridges the artistic traditions of these indigenous cultures and contemporary graphic design. The album artwork consists of illustration, custom lettering, and design for the packaging, disc, and sixteen-page booklet.

New Media Art Space
Media Façade & Social Networking Service

∩m∆Γ∆

DESIGN Namoo Kim, Anseong, Korea / LETTERING Namoo Kim / URL golden-tree.kr / AGENCY HKNU Design Lab, Hankyong National University /
CLIENT New Media Art Research Institute / PRINCIPAL TYPE Futura / DIMENSIONS 27.6 × 39.4 in. (70 × 100 cm) / CONCEPT This typographic
visualization represents time and space as uniform, continuous, and connected

DESIGN Olga Grlic, New York / ART DIRECTION Olga Grlic / ILLUSTRATION Harriet Russell / TWITTER @StMartinsPress / PUBLISHER St. Martin's Press / PRINCIPAL TYPE Handlettering / DIMENSIONS 5.5 × 8.25 in. (14 × 21 cm) / This is a coming-of-age novel about two misfits in love. I drew this out exactly as is for Harriet, and she redrew it in her own style. It shows the two main characters sitting on a school bus listening to music.

"This sexy, smart, tender romance thrums with punk rock and true love. Readers will swoon for Eleanor & Park"

- Gayle Forman, *New York Times* bestselling author of *If I stay* and *Where She Went*

eleanor & park

a novel

rainbow rowell

DESIGN Marc Clormann° and Michaela Vargas Coronado, Penzing, Germany / ART DIRECTION Michaela Vargas Coronado / CREATIVE DIRECTION Marc M. Clormann° / URL clormanndesign.de / TWITTER @clormanndesign / DESIGN FIRM Clormann Design / CLIENT *novum: World of Graphic Design*/Stiebner Verlag, Münich / PRINCIPAL TYPE Avant Garde, Baskerville, Clarendon, FF DIN, and Ultra / DIMENSIONS 9.1 × 11.7 in. (23 × 29.7 cm) / CONCEPT This cover of *novum*, one of the leading international design publications, presents its main theme of typography by showing an example of filigree type never before seen in magazine publishing. Clormann Design, a design agency located west of Münich, created the cover using laser technology to optically as well as haptically communicate the message: "Be bold, be light, be italic, but never be regular." The cover's inner page sparkles through the black letters' gaps in a copper tone with small letters, underlining the high-quality look.

CHILDREN ARE ALWAYS UNDER THE INFLUENCE. YOURS.

Talk now and avoid problems later.
Go to drinkaware.co.uk / parents

DESIGN Paul Belford, London / PHOTOGRAPHY Paul Belford and Nichole Dean / COPYWRITERS Sean Doyle and Dean Webb / DESIGN FIRM Paul Belford Ltd. / AGENCY TBWA London / CLIENT Drinkaware / PRINCIPAL TYPE Akzidenz-Grotesk Condensed Bold / DIMENSIONS 47.2 × 70.9 in. (120 × 180 cm) / CONCEPT For a message about the dangers of alcohol, we distorted the type by photographing it through liquid.

DESIGN Maude Lescarbeau, Montréal / CREATIVE DIRECTION Claude Auchu / INTERACTIVE ART DIRECTION Thibault Gehard / STRATEGIC PLANNER Pénélope Fournier / COPYWRITERS Éric Beaudin and Stuart McMillan / TYPOGRAPHER Maude Lescarbeau / PRINT & WEB PRODUCTION lg2fabrique / URL lg2boutique.com / TWITTER @lg2_tweets / DESIGN STUDIO lg2boutique / CLIENT Telefilm Canada / PRINCIPAL TYPE Akkurat Mono, Thienhardt Family, and custom / DIMENSIONS Various / CONCEPT The design was inspired by the country's distinctive geography, putting the focus on the immensity of Canadian talent that is equaled only by the breadth of the country. In a reference that links the size of the country and the depth of talent, the brand slogan "SEE BIG" was developed and will be the common thread of all the adaptations for visual identities. The color palette was centered on red, a natural and symbolic choice for Canada. The typography was conceived using the existing Telefilm Canada logo for greater visual unity. It's a complete visual language that puts the focus on the organization's roots.

DESIGN Maude Lescarbeau, Marilyn Marois, and Andrée Rouette, Montréal / CREATIVE DIRECTION Claude Auchu / PHOTOGRAPHY Luc Robitaille / COPYWRITERS Gabrielle Godbout and Pierre Lussier / CLIENT SERVICES Sara Caradec, Marion Haimon, and Catherine Lanctôt / STRATEGIC PLANNERS Pénélope Fournier and Cynthia Moreau / PRINT PRODUCTION lg2fabrique / URL lg2boutique.com / TWITTER @lg2_tweets / DESIGN STUDIO lg2boutique / CLIENT Johanne Demers (founder of La Vittoria) / PRINCIPAL TYPE Abolition, Arnhem Family, and Futura Bold / DIMENSIONS 8.5 × 7.5 in. (21.6 × 19.1 cm) / CONCEPT For its 2013 edition, La Vittoria teamed up with Cuisines collectives Hochelaga-Maisonneuve and Montérégie, grassroots organizations that promote food autonomy, notably by reintroducing their members to the basics of cooking. At the center of the evening's graphic universe was a return to the source. The elegant creative paid tribute to the earth and its flavors throughout the different pieces. The theme also served as a platform from which to celebrate chef Éric Gonzalez of Auberge Saint-Gabriel and his French roots now planted in Quebec soil, as well as his invited chefs, highlighting their story, origin, and inspirations.

DESIGN Katie Hatz and Mike Joyce, New York / ART DIRECTOR Mike Joyce / TWITTER @MikeJoyceNYC / DESIGN FIRM Stereotype Design / PUBLISHER Quirk Books / PRINCIPAL TYPE Akzidenz-Grotesk Medium / DIMENSIONS 11 x 14 in. (28 cm x 35.5 cm) / CONCEPT Drawing from my love of punk rock and Swiss modernism, I redesigned vintage punk, hardcore, and indie rock show fliers into International Typographic Style posters. I always liked that these two movements seemed at odds with each other in that punk has an anti-establishment ethos and Swiss modernism is very structured. At the same time, there's a common thread between the two—the Swiss modernists purged extraneous decoration to create clear communication, while punk rock took on self-indulgent rock 'n' roll and stripped it to its core. All 200 pages are micro-perforated so you can easily tear out your favorite poster.

DESIGN Andreas Enmensel, Goran Tomanovic, Felix Thomas, and Nina Thomas, Düsseldorf / CONCEPT Andreas Enmensel, Goran Tomanovic, Felix Thomas, and Nina Thomas / ILLUSTRATION Flavio Morais, Barcelona / PRODUCTION AND BOOKBINDING Silvia Stehle, brandbook.de / FINAL ARTWORK Achim Kubitsch / URL thomascorporate.com and die-gutgestalten.de / DESIGN STUDIOS die Gutgestalten and thomascorporate / CLIENT Paulinche—Initiative für brandverletzte Kinder e.V., Norderstedt, Germany / PRINCIPAL TYPE TheMix, RegularTheMix, MediumTheMix, BoldTheMix, BoldCapsTheMix, SemiLightTheMix, and SemiLightItalic / DIMENSIONS 5.1 x 8.2 in. (13 x 20.7 cm) / CONCEPT The guidebook Alex allows young victims of burn injuries to inform themselves about their injuries, their upcoming treatments, and the importance of each step of their physical and mental rehabilitation after the accident. Conceptualized as an agenda in an unobtrusive "Moleskine style," this guide is more than just a source of information; it also serves as a diary or personal notebook. Illustrations with positive content and text of clear, inspirational appearance convey the topic of the book with a high degree of lightness.

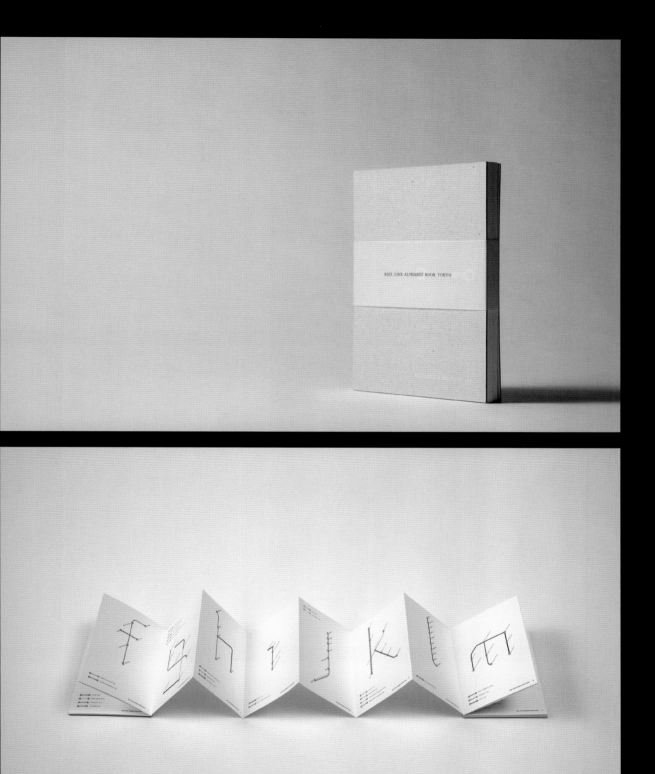

DESIGN Fuyuki Hashizume, Tokyo / ART DIRECTION Fuyuki Hashizume / COMPANY Toppan Printing Co., Ltd. / PRINCIPAL TYPE Bembo Small Caps and Oldstyle Figures, and Univers 55 Roman DIMENSIONS 4.1 × 5.8 in. (10.5 × 14.8 cm) / CONCEPT The type was inspired by railway maps of Tokyo.

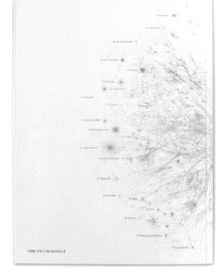

DESIGN Theresa Brandau, Stuttgart / CREATIVE DIRECTION Danijela Djokic and Martin Grothmaak / CONCEPT Herbert Arthen, Natalie Juraic, Jan Teunen, Bärbel Ulrich, and Simon Umbreit / COPYWRITERS Hajo Eickhoff, Cornelia Kurreck, Miriam Leypholdt, and Christoph Quarch / URL projekttriangle.com / DESIGN STUDIO Projekttriangle Design Studio / CLIENT dm-drogerie markt GmbH + Co. KG / PRINCIPAL TYPE Courier New: dmSoft Family: dmBrand, dmSupport, dmIntelligence; and Romain BP Text / DIMENSIONS 6.7 × 9.5 in. (17 × 24 cm) / CONCEPT Books are really nothing more than extremely long letters to friends, according to the poet Jean Paul. In this spirit, we have created the book Give Time a Value. It appears on the anniversary of four decades of dm — as a thank you for commitment, loyalty, constructive criticism, and encouragement. The thanks are expressed with philosophical concepts and inspiring ideas from various artists. The book is intended to incite its readers into further thinking, to inspire them to explore new potentials in themselves and in others. It is a sketchbook of ideas with plentiful free space for the reader's own thoughts, texts, and inspiring concepts.

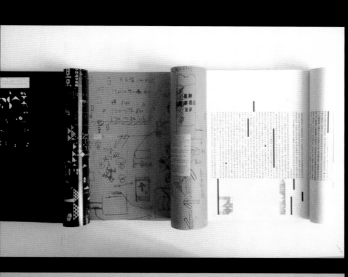

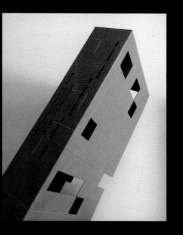

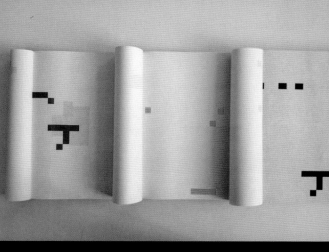

DESIGN Qing Zhao, Nanjing, China / URL www.hanqingtang.com / DESIGN FIRM Hanqingtang Ary Design Company / CLIENT Jiangsu Education Publishing House / PRINCIPAL TYPE Bauer Bodoni, Helvetica, and Shelley Allegro / DIMENSIONS 7.1 × 10.2 in. (18 × 26 cm);
7.1 × 10.2 in. (18 × 26 cm); 6.3 × 10.2 in. (16 × 26 cm) / CONCEPT These serial books, which are based on research of Chinese font design,
present an overview of a font design course. The main design concept comes from the square block of Chinese traditional movable type
printing; the block is shown on the front cover, the box set, and some separator pages. The whole series is divided into black, white,
and gray, and uses gradual improvement to show the relationship between each part. The black book, designed with blue color, contains
student design works. The gray book, designed with orange color, describes the font design course process. Finally, the white book,
designed with black color, offers examples of related master works. The text and images feature alternating layers of texture and color

DESIGN Billy Kiosoglou and Frank Philippin, London / AUTHORS Billy Kiosoglou and Frank Philippin / ART DIRECTION Billy Kiosoglou and Frank Philippin / EDITORS Billy Kiosoglou and Frank Philippin / URL brightenthecorners.com / DESIGN STUDIO Brighten the Corners / CLIENT Laurence King / PRINCIPAL TYPE Akzidenz-Grotesk Medium / DIMENSIONS 6.7 × 9.6 in. (17 × 24.5 cm) / CONCEPT The result of a research project about how designers find their voice, this book looks at the student and professional work of fifty individuals. The design splits the book in two: a left-hand student page and a right-hand professional page. This allows for comparisons throughout, as content is always mirrored. Project spreads were kept silent because the simple juxtaposition of student/professional work tells its own story. Responses relating to habits, inspirations, methodology, or more personal questions appear together, inviting individual as well as collective comparison.

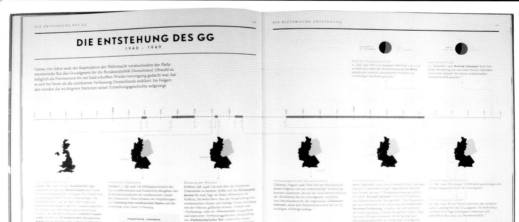

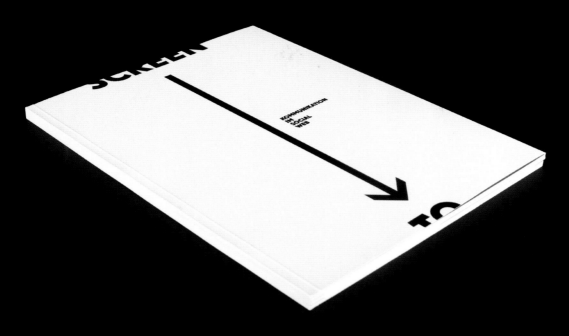

DESIGN Peter von Freyhold, Hamburg / URL vonfreyhold.com / SCHOOL Hochschule Mannheim, Fakultät für Gestaltung / PROFESSOR Veruschka Götz / PRINCIPAL TYPE Greta Text and FF Super Grotesk / DIMENSIONS 8.3 × 11 in. (21 × 28 cm) / CONCEPT The intention

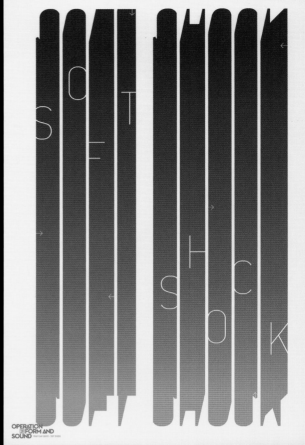

DESIGN Fabian Brunke, Bremen, Germany / SCHOOL Hochschule für Künste Bremen / PROFESSORS Andrea Rauschenbusch and Dirk Laucke / PRINCIPAL TYPE Adobe Caslon Pro, Futura LT Condensed, and ITC Tiffany LT Heavy / DIMENSIONS Tabloid: 3.5 × 15 in. (8.9 × 38 cm): Poster: 33.1 × 46.8 in. (84.1 × 119.8 cm): Laser-cut Posters: 26.8 × 18.9 in. (68 × 48 cm) / CONCEPT During a course at the University of the Arts Bremen, I developed a personal map of the cultural center Schlachthof. In the form of a travel guide, I tried to transmit a new meaning to signs there. In the first step, I extracted form and color from graffiti and transferred them, enlarged, onto posters. This was followed by cataloging the graffiti by name, dimensions, and color in the form of a tabloid. In the last step, I took objects from the skate park at the Schlachthof. These were transferred to posters using a laser cutter.

DESIGN Natalie Kennepohl, Laura Ostermeier, Hanna Rasper, and Sonja Schröder, Munich / PROFESSOR Sybille Schmitz / PRINCIPAL TYPE Trump Mediaeval / DIMENSIONS 67 × 94.5 in. (170 × 240 cm) / CONCEPT We wanted to give type designer Georg Trump of Munich the attention he deserves. During intensive discussion about him and his work during this type analysis, we came to regard him highly. In our research, we had access to shockingly little material. Literary sources served us, especially the memorial book for Trump's work, *Vita Activa*, by the Typografischen Gesellschaft München, from 1967, and the related new edition of 1997, titled *Grafischen Betrieb München*. Our type analysis consists of two parts: the main section of analysis as well as the book within the book, which introduces Trump. In design terms, our book should also be Georg Trump-appropriate. Because he was a classic typographer, our book features a classic format. However, Trump's type would be nothing special if it didn't break its classic form. Our analysis is therefore idiosyncratic by way of harmonious interaction between black, white, yellow, film, paper of different colors—and, of course, the book within the book.

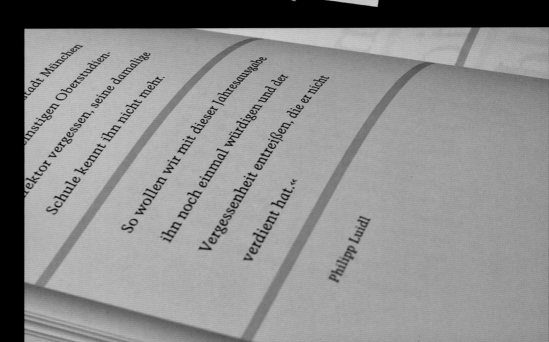

DESIGN Emily Oberman and Elliot Walker, New York / ART DIRECTION Emily Oberman / URL pentagram.com / TWITTER @pentagram /
DESIGN FIRM Pentagram, New York / CLIENT Jigsaw Productions / PRINCIPAL TYPE New Rail Alphabet / DIMENSIONS Various /
CONCEPT Jigsaw is the production company of Academy Award-winning documentary filmmaker Alex Gibney, the director of *Taxi to the
Dark Side*, *The Armstrong Lie*, and others. We used typography to create a strong identity that also captures the nuance of Gibney's
work. The system uses a lowercase, sans serif word mark and a journalistic black-and-white color palette. By removing sections of

VISUAL IDENTITY

LOGOTYPE — STANDARD

NAIL ART PRODUCTS
EST. 2013

LOGOTYPE — ALONE

TAGLINE

NAIL ART PRODUCTS
EST. 2013

SYMBOLIC PATTERN SYSTEM

PATTERNS

COLOURS

BLACK
C:0/M:0/Y:0/K:100
R:0/G:0/B:0

WHITE
C:0/M:0/Y:0/K:0
R:255/G:255/B:255

TYPOGRAPHY

FUTURA HEAVY
ABCDEFGHIJKLMNOPQRSTUVWXYZ
abcdefghijklmnopqrstuvwxyz
1234567890
?!(){}[]&""«»;:/-—

FUTURA MEDIUM
ABCDEFGHIJKLMNOPQRSTUVWXYZ
abcdefghijklmnopqrstuvwxyz
1234567890
?!(){}[]&""«»;:/-—

LOGOTYPE, PATTERNS, AND TYPOGRAPHY FOR NAIL ART PRODUCTS MANUFACTURER, KRIMTH INC. BASED IN JAPAN.
ART DIRECTION AND DESIGN: KEI TAKIMOTO / PRODUCE: YASUKO IMAI / CREATED: 2013

COPYRIGHT © 2013 KRIMTH INC. ALL RIGHTS RESERVED.

DESIGN Sookwung Lee, Seoul / SCHOOL Ewha Womans University / INSTRUCTOR Sujin Park / PRINCIPAL TYPE Custom / DIMENSIONS 16 × 23 in. (42 × 59.4 cm) / CONCEPT Seoul City has a long history, but more than seventy-five percent of its architecture has been built after 1980. These posters address this situation. Seoul is a typeface design that describes the change in architecture of five representative landmarks from 1980 to 2012. Each letter shows the style of architecture at a specific time. All letters have been selected for this design based on the connection between their shape and that of a specific building, and the architectural style it represents.

DESIGN Marie-Pier Gilbert and David Kessous, Montréal / CREATIVE DIRECTION Claude Auchu / COPYWRITER Stuart MacMillan /
STRATEGIC PLANNERS Pénélope Fournier and Cynthia Morea / CLIENT SERVICES Julie Bégin, Catherine Lanctôt, and Antoine Levasseur /
PRINT PRODUCTION lg2fabrique / URL lg2boutique.com / TWITTER @lg2_tweets / DESIGN STUDIO lg2boutique / CLIENT Segal Centre /
PRINCIPAL TYPE Handlettering / DIMENSIONS Various / CONCEPT The Segal Centre is a singular performing arts center, so it was important
to highlight this difference by developing a unique and relevant platform. Although the vast majority of theaters use photos, a graphic
and typographic approach was chosen that was both conceptual and simple. The main challenge was to anchor the graphic platform of the
new season in the center's current visual identity to increase awareness among the public. The artistic use of cutout forms bound the
season's platform to its visual identity.

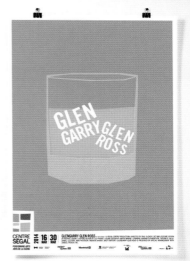

DESIGN Emi Tsukahara and Yoshiki Uchida, Tokyo / DESIGN FIRM cosmos / CLIENT Rittor Music, Inc. / PRINCIPAL TYPE Record Label Typo / DIMENSIONS 23 × 33 in. (59.4 × 84.1 cm) / CONCEPT This is an advertisement poster for the music guide *Rare Groove A to Z*. The typography of record labels hints that the book displays 1,000 records. The black on the back expresses the mood of records.

NO BAGGAGE FEES!

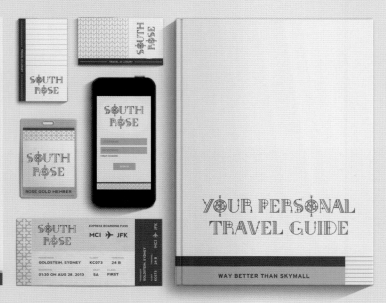

SOUTH ROSE

SOUTH ROSE

SOUTH ROSE

ROSE GOLD MEMBER

SOUTH ROSE

EXPRESS BOARDING PASS

MCI ✈ JFK

PASSENGER: GOLDSTEIN, SYDNEY
FLIGHT: KC073
SEAT: 24 B
01:30 ON AUG 28, 2013
GATE: 5A
FIRST

YOUR PERSONAL TRAVEL GUIDE

WAY BETTER THAN SKYMALL

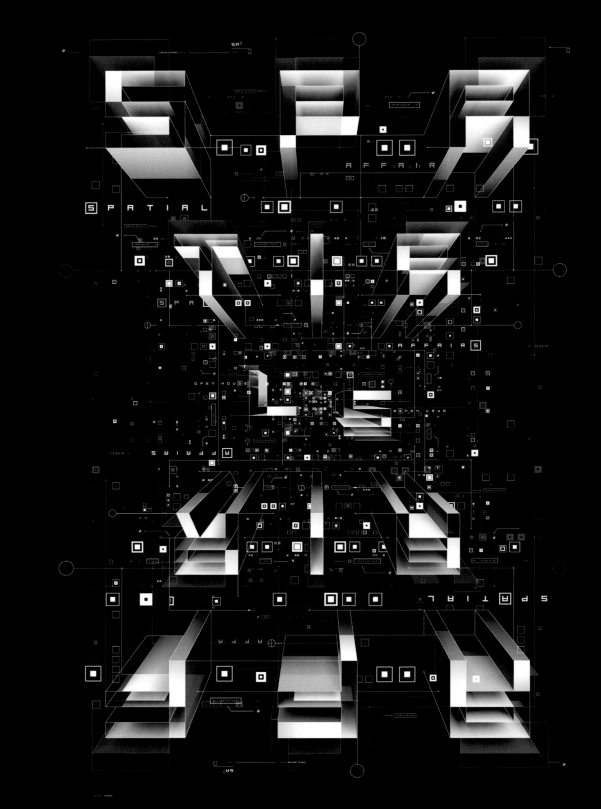

PRINCIPAL TYPE Custom / DIMENSIONS 26 × 38 in. (66 × 96.5 cm) / CONCEPT This poster was designed to announce an open house for Spatial Affairs Bureau, an architecture firm with offices in both the United States and the United Kingdom (and a name straight out of a science fiction movie). Taking inspiration from that reference, I thought it would be fun to illustrate a building being designed in outer space.

KEVIN
TYRIEK
COACH
BILLY
COLE
JUDAH

LITTLE BALLERS

★ EVERYBODY HAS A DREAM ★

DESIGN Matt Kay, Jennifer Kinon, Bobby C. Martin Jr.°, New York / DESIGN PARTNERS Jennifer Kinon and Bobby C. Martin Jr. / URL originalchampionsofdesign.com / TWITTER @ocdagency / DESIGN FIRM OCD | The Original Champions of Design / CLIENT *Little Ballers*, Crystal McCrary Productions / PRINCIPAL TYPE Custom / DIMENSIONS 30 x 45 in. (76.2 × 114.3 cm) / CONCEPT *Little Ballers* tells the story of four diverse eleven-year-old boys and their legendary coach as they set out to win an AAU National Championship. The handwritten typography speaks not only to the tradition of New York's basketball youth, but also to the heroes of the film and their passion for

CM PRODUCTIONS, FNF FILMS & STATOSPHERE present LITTLE BALLERS A FILM BY CRYSTAL McCRARY

EXECUTIVE PRODUCER LUPE FIASCO EXECUTIVE PRODUCER AMAR'E STOUDEMIRE PRODUCER LISA BONNER CO-PRODUCER TAMMY BROOK, ADRIENNE LOPEZ, BILLY COUNCIL & EVERTON McINTYRE

DIRECTOR OF PHOTOGRAPHY PHILIPPE ROC EDITOR BRIAN KAMERZEL PRODUCED & DIRECTED BY CRYSTAL McCRARY

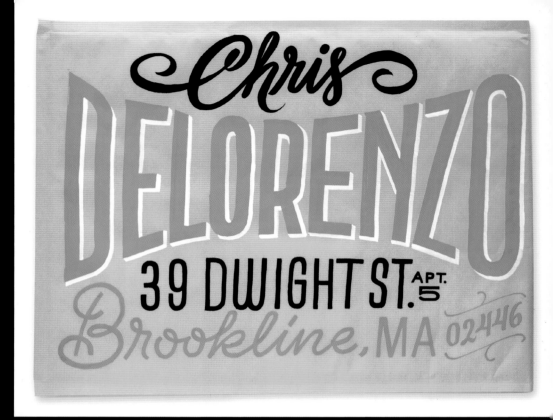

DESIGN BLTA MATINOVICH SAN FRANCISCO / OAK donotopen.it / TWITTER @ItaMatinovich / PRINCIPAL ITEM handlettering /
DIMENSIONS 14.25 × 19 in. (36 × 48.3 cm) / CONCEPT "Do Not Open" brings something (a hand-addressed envelope) that was specifically meant for friends and family to the general public. When an address is submitted to the project, a uniquely handlettered envelope will be carefully packaged and mailed to you. No two addresses will look the same. Each envelope is documented and placed online.

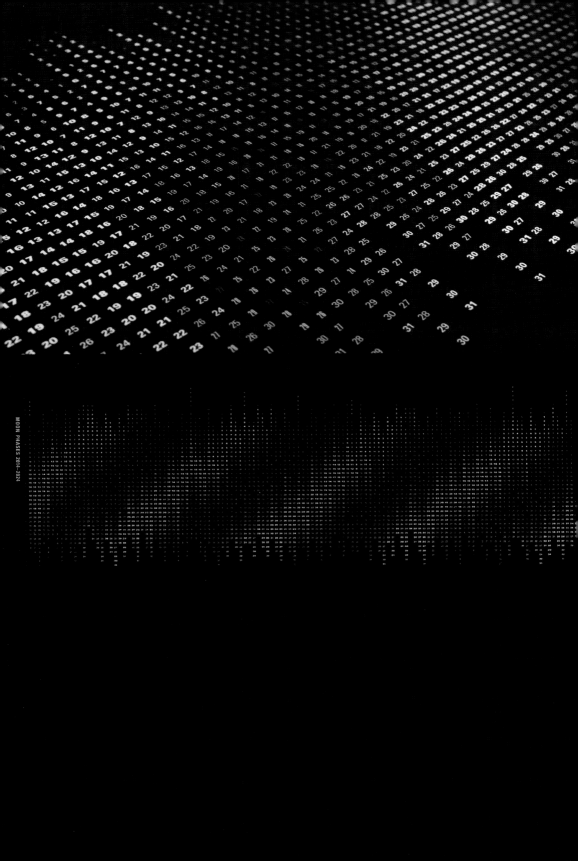

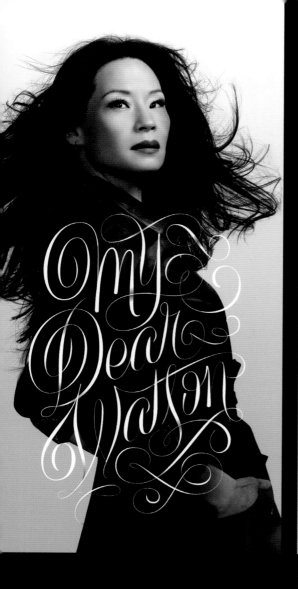

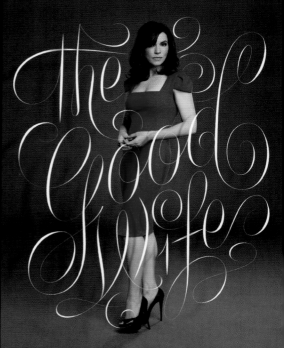

Redfern

DESIGN Gemma O'Brien°, Sydney / MC CREATIVE DIRECTION Chris Searl / MC PROJECTS DIRECTOR Kieran Burke / ARTIST REPRESENTATIVE The Jacky Winter Group / THE JACKY WINTER GROUP PRODUCER Bianca Bramham / FILM DIRECTION Lincoln Caplice / CINEMATOGRAPHER Campbell Brown / EDIT/ONLINE Miles Selwyn / URL jackywinter.com/artists/gemma-obrien / TWITTER @mrseaves / AGENCY MC Creative / CLIENT Kirin Cider / PRINCIPAL TYPE Helvetica Bold, Sarah Script, hand-painted, and custom / DIMENSIONS 15 × 10 ft. (4.6 × 3 m) / CONCEPT In 2013, Lion launched Kirin Cider, a range of ciders infused with Japanese-inspired flavors. They engaged typographer Gemma O'Brien to hand-paint thirty-seven bespoke advertising displays to be installed across Australia. The majority of the signs were painted off-site, with one painted on-site in Surry Hills. O'Brien says, "Hand painting thirty-seven billboards was an ambitious undertaking, but the results were effective. The typography was direct and spontaneous; each billboard was unique and retained the authenticity of the handcrafted strokes." The artist's creative process and the live event were documented in a short film, which became the online component of the "Inspired Creativity" campaign.

DESIGN Marc Damm, Carla Streckwall, Ulrike Zöllner, Berlin / SCHOOL Berlin University of the Arts / PROFESSORS Georg Barber, Fons Hickmann°, and Henning Wagenbreth / PRINCIPAL TYPE Chaparral Pro / DIMENSIONS 4.3 × 5.9 in. (11 × 15 cm) / CONCEPT Martin Conrads. Fons Hickmann, and Franziska Morlok. This is a story of three professors and forty-five students from Berlin who set out to learn what fear was. They spent five days and nights in an old farmhouse, surrounded by deep forests, in search of existing and imaginary fears. They then lexically defined and presented them in the form of expressive illustrations from the darkness of emotions to light the visual confrontation.

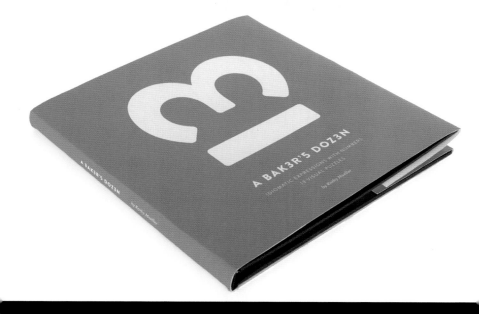

A BAK3R'5 DOZ3N
IDIOMATIC EXPRESSIONS WITH NUMBERS
13 VISUAL PUZZLES
by Kathy Mueller

A BAK3R'S DOZ3N
by Kathy Mueller

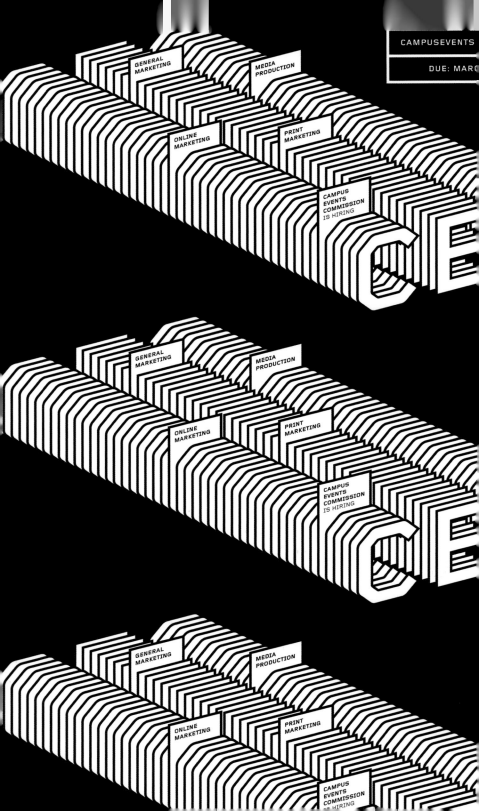

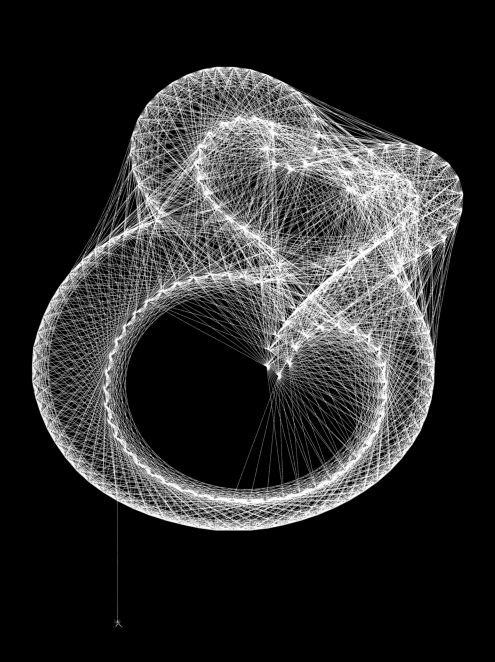

"

DOPE
ON *the*
DAMN
TABLE

—DANIELS

"

COME
AT *the*
KING,
YOU BEST *Not*
MISS

—OMAR

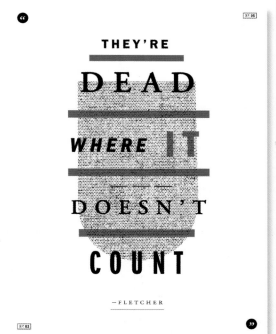

"

THEY'RE
DEAD
WHERE IT
DOESN'T
COUNT

—FLETCHER

DESIGN Sumayya Alsenan, New York / ART DIRECTION Sumayya Alsenan / CLIENT *Word on the Street* exhibit / PRINCIPAL TYPE Adobe Arabic, GE Asifa, and GE Jarida / DIMENSIONS 33.1 x 46.8 in. (84.1 x 118.9 cm) / CONCEPT What makes those headlines special is the obvious bias of the different authors of the articles. So the designer created a series of typographic posters to illustrate the exaggeration, irony, and sarcasm that lie between the lines of the headlines, which all come from prominent Middle Eastern news websites.

DESIGN Zhu Chao, Beijing / URL mintbrand.cn / TWITTER @superchao / DESIGN FIRM mintdesign / CLIENT 751 International Design Festival /
PRINCIPAL TYPE lantinghei / DIMENSIONS 27.6 × 39.4 in. (70 × 100 cm) / CONCEPT 751 is a park built from an old factory. The naked pipes
found everywhere inspired me to roll up the names of masters into the shape of pipes. The lecture was about construction, life, reading,
and fashion.

DER GOTT DES GEMETZELS

YASMINA REZA
SOLOTHURN AB 26|04|2013
BIEL AB 08|05|2013 THEATERTÄEHT
BIEL SOLOTHURN | BIENNE SOLEURE

Design: Stephan Bundi-Bonjour

DESIGN Stephan Bundi, Boll, Switzerland / ART DIRECTION Stephan Bundi / URL atelierbundi.ch / DESIGN FIRM Atelier Bundi AG / CLIENT Theater Biel Solothurn / PRINCIPAL TYPE Helvetica Neue LTD 95 Black / DIMENSIONS 50 × 35 in. (128 × 89.5 cm) / CONCEPT *Der Gott des Gemetzels* (God of Carnage) is a play by Yasmina Reza. Two pairs of parents discuss their children, and the discussion ends chaotically.

WOODY
GUTHRIE
CENTER | TULSA, OK

DESIGN Travis Brown and Eric Thoelke / CREATIVE DIRECTION Eric Thoelke / URL toky.com / TWITTER @tokybd / DESIGN FIRM TOKY / CLIENT Woody Guthrie Center, Tulsa, Oklahoma / PRINCIPAL TYPE Champion, Shelton Slab, and custom / CONCEPT The Woody Guthrie Center is a public museum and archive in Tulsa, Oklahoma that is dedicated to the life and legacy of American folk musician and songwriter Woody Guthrie. TOKY created the Woody Guthrie Center's logo, a mark inspired by the letterpress concert posters of the artist's time.

A FLEXIBLE TYPEFACE MADE FOR NEW YORK DJ CORY LASSER

CORY LASSER

MONDO LASSO

EPISODE #1 CORY LASSER

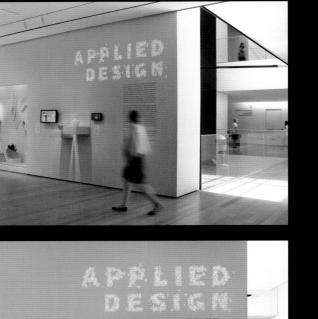

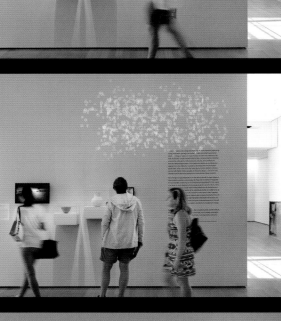

Make a gesture drawing

MoMA ART LAB: MOVEMENT

KNOW THIS!

Abstract Expressionist artists used
of gestures, or bod

MoMA ART LAB: MOVEMENT is an
interactive space where
you can explore, play,
and create as you discover
movement in art.

Alexander Calder balanced wire and
metal to create sculptures called mobiles.
Unlike most sculptures, mobiles move,
propelled by air and wind.
Make a mobile. Experiment with adding
wires and shapes to balance your mobile.

What types of movement do you see?

**MoMA ART LAB:
MOVEMENT** is an
interactive space where
you can explore, play,
and create as you discover
movement in art.

Alexander Calder balanced wire and
metal to create sculptures called mobiles.
Unlike most sculptures, mobiles move,
propelled by air and wind.

Make a mobile. Experiment with adding
wires and shapes to balance your mobile.

DESIGN Erik Marinovich, Dennis Payongayong, and Jason Wong, San Francisco / ART DIRECTION Dennis Payongayong /
WRITER Sarah Crawford / URL friendsoftype.com / TWITTER @friendsoftype / STUDIO Friends of Type / CLIENT BBDO New York /
PRINCIPAL TYPE Custom / DIMENSIONS 8 × 70 ft. (2.4 × 21.3 m) / CONCEPT Commissioned by the New York office of BBDO, Friends of Type,
working closely with writer Sarah Crawford, designed this mural as a series of dialogue-based panels illustrating the interactions

DESIGN Kevin Cantrell, Gloria Pak, and Arlo Vance, London / ART DIRECTION Kevin Cantrell, Laura Caudery (FP), and Christian Day (Knight Studios) / CREATIVE DIRECTION Christian Hansen / PHOTOGRAPHY Simon Upton / DEVELOPMENT Knight Studios, UK / LETTERING Kevin Cantrell / PROGRAMMERS Robert Kotecki, Luke Miler, and Filip Wróblewski / COPYWRITERS Tamryn Lawrence and Emma Woodhouse / URL hintcreative.com / TWITTER @hintcreative / DESIGN FIRM Hint Creative, SLC / CLIENT Fetcham Park House, UK / PRINCIPAL TYPE HTF Chronicle, HTF Forza, and custom lettering / DIMENSIONS Various / CONCEPT Fetcham Park, one of the top 100 wedding venues in the UK, contacted Hint to elevate its brand to a more premium market. The brand necessitated a customizable system to reflect the venue's seasonal appeal and personal experience offered to each client (corporate or private). Hint created a modular system with longevity, yet also contemporary appeal, inspired by FP. An extensive brand standard was created across multiple channels. The design focused on modularity with interchangeable patterns that integrate with the logotype, monogram, and patterns according to the seasons, allowing extravagance for the private clients and restraint for the corporate clients.

FUNCTION

DESIGN Wade Jeffree, New York / ANIMATION Joel Voelker / ART DIRECTION Jessica Walsh / CREATIVE DIRECTION Stefan Sagmeister / CLIENT Function Engineering / PRINCIPAL TYPE Custom / DIMENSIONS 16 × 30 in. (40.6 × 76.2 cm) / CONCEPT Function Engineering specializes in mechanical design and engineering for product development within, but not limited to, consumer electronics, computing and networking, mobile, medical, robotics, entertainment, commercial, and industrial equipment. Function approached us to create a new brand identity system. Narrowing in on the company's expertise in designing hinge and linkage mechanisms, we designed a typographic system based on a hinge/pivot system. We expanded it by creating a series of icons, illustrations, and patterns that can be used flexibly across various collaterals in print and online.

CREATIVE DIRECTION Jesper Bange, Toni Hurme, Mira Olsson, and James Zambra, Helsinki / STRATEGIC DESIGN Arttu Salovaara / PRODUCER Mirva Kaitila / CONTRIBUTOR Annika Järvinen / PHOTOGRAPHY Veikko Kähkönen, Paavo Lehtonen (case photography), and Mikko Ryhänen / DESIGN AGENCY Bond / CLIENT University of the Arts Helsinki / PRINCIPAL TYPE Benton Modern Display, Monosten, and FB Titling Gothic / DIMENSIONS Various / CONCEPT The Finnish Academy of Fine Arts, Sibelius Academy, and Theatre Academy Helsinki merged in the beginning of 2013 into the University of the Arts Helsinki. We created the complete branding solution for the new university. The strategy was to create a distinctive set of logotypes based on a common design language, and to introduce an anchor symbol that acts as a point of connection between the university mother brand and the three academy brands. The simple and bold "X" has plenty of meanings, just as art does, and the distorted text logos represent the rhythmic, dynamic, evolving nature of art.

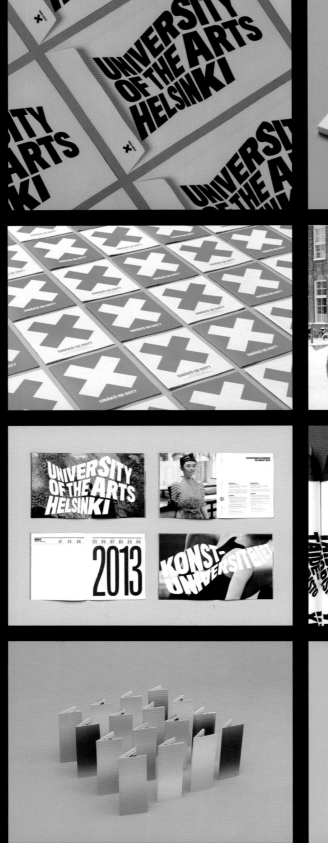

DESIGN Lynne Yun, San Francisco / URL lynneyun.com / TWITTER @Lynneyun / SCHOOL School of Visual Arts, New York / INSTRUCTOR Louise Fili° / PRINCIPAL TYPE The type was made by scanning an archive of old American wood type specimens from 1828 to 1900 / DIMENSIONS Various / CONCEPT Vercesi Hardware is a small hardware store that has a century-long history. It changed its name to 23rd Street Hardware Store in recent years, but the owner is still the same. This identity was made in an effort to revive the old name and history of the store. The wood type was individually scanned in and set in the characteristics of early-1900s ephemera. The business card features a mini

DESIGN Wael Morcos[©], Brooklyn, New York / URL waelmorcos.com / TWITTER @waelmorcos / SCHOOL Rhode Island School of Design / INSTRUCTORS Rafael Attias, Sulki Choi, Min Choi, and Bethany Johns / PRINCIPAL TYPE Bodoni / DIMENSIONS 50 × 50 in. (127 × 127 cm) / CONCEPT Bozoni is a typeface made of a system of three stacking fonts. It is based on the original well-known Bodoni font. The idea of the design considers what happens when a vector shape (with curves and obliques) is rasterized into an orthogonal pixel grid of a screen, and what happens when our expectations for beauty and elegance are processed through imperfect technologies.

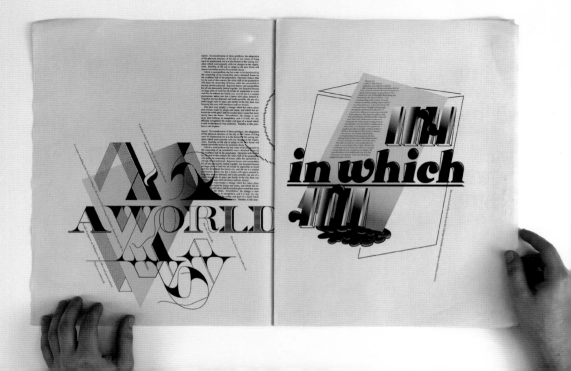

PHYSIKER UND PHILOSOPH

David Joseph Bohm wird 1917 in Wilkes-Barre,
Pennsylvania geboren. Er studiert zunächst Physik
am California Institute of Technology, später
an der University of California, Berkeley, bei dem
oft als »Vater der Atombombe« titulierten
Robert Oppenheimer. Oppenheimer arbeitet zu
dieser Zeit im Auftrag der Vereinigten Staaten
an der Entwicklung erster Nuklearwaffen
(dem sogenannten Manhattan-Projekt). Bohm ist
zunächst nicht direkt am Manhattan-Projekt
beschäftigt, engagiert sich stattdessen wie viele
andere Studenten von Oppenheimer in den
30er Jahren in pazifistischen und kommunistischen
Studentenorganisationen. 1943 promoviert
Bohm in Berkeley. Nach dem Zweiten Weltkrieg
unterrichtet er an der Princeton University
Quantenmechanik und Teilchenlehre und trifft
überdies auf Albert Einstein, mit dem ihn
später eine enge Freundschaft und Zusammen-
arbeit verbindet.

149

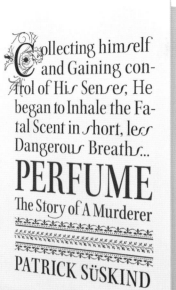

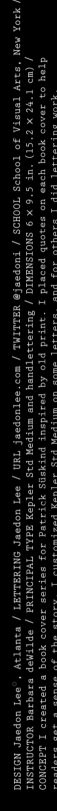

DESIGN Jaedon Lee°, Atlanta / LETTERING Jaedon Lee / URL jaedonlee.com / TWITTER @jaedoni / SCHOOL School of Visual Arts, New York / INSTRUCTOR Barbara deWilde / PRINCIPAL TYPE Kepler Std Medium and handlettering / DIMENSIONS 6 x 9.5 in. (15.2 x 24.1 cm) / CONCEPT I created a book cover series for Patrick Süskind inspired by old print. I placed quotes on each book cover to help readers get a sense of the story. I customized Kepler Std Medium on some letters, and for others I did lettering work.

DESIGN Marco Schmidt, Düsseldorf / SCHOOL University of Applied Sciences / PROFESSORS Holger Jacobs and Uwe J. Reinhardt / PRINCIPAL TYPE Fedra Serif and Univers Condensed / DIMENSIONS 11.8 × 15.7 in. (30 × 40 cm) / CONCEPT In my graduation project, I dealt with the visual interpretation of private myths by interviewing strangers from around the world about their religious worldviews and experiences with the supernatural. The outcome was five stories from five countries about mystic occurrences, rituals, and ideologies that serve as a base for my interpretation. In some cases, I used the whole story to create scenic setups, while in others I focused on the detail. Every visual approach was meant to be different and playful to represent the diversity of cultural backgrounds.

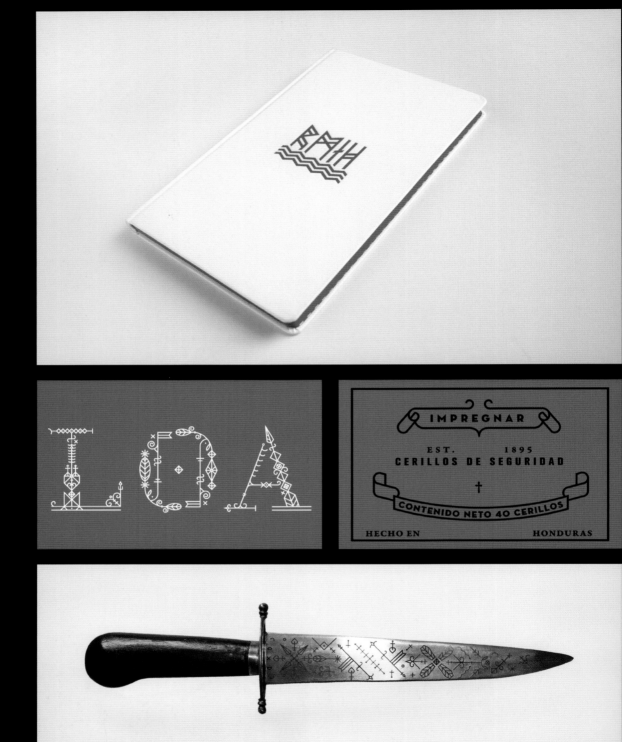

TO BE YOURSELF IN A **WORLD** THAT IS **CONSTANTLY TRYING TO MAKE YOU SOMETHING** Else is the greatest **ACHIEVEMENT**

@ /youbringfire

People Matter

@ youbringfire

TO BE YOURSELF IN A **WORLD** THAT IS **CONSTANTLY TRYING TO MAKE YOU SOMETHING** Else is the greatest **ACHIEVEMENT**

@ /youbringfire

DESIGN Kelly Shami, New York / URL kellyshami.com / TWITTER @kellyshami / SCHOOL School of Visual Arts, New York / INSTRUCTORS Gail Anderson° and Richard Mehl / PRINCIPAL TYPE Handlettering / CONCEPT This is a typeface first drawn by hand and then vectorized. It is completely original, with an emphasis on flourishes.

DESIGN Jeong-Woo Kim, New York City / URL jeongwookim.com / TWITTER @jeongtothewoo / SCHOOL School of Visual Arts, New York / INSTRUCTOR Carin Goldberg / PRINCIPAL TYPE Letter Gothic Std, Trade Gothic, and wood type / DIMENSIONS 5.25 × 8 in. (13.3 × 20.3 cm) / CONCEPT This book series is inspired by Ernest Hemingway, an avid traveler and expat novelist. Using the vernacular of letter-pressed airplane tickets from the 1920s to the 1960s, we see the influence on his novels from his years traveling abroad. The graphic elements of these travel documents became the vehicle to represent the most important of Hemingway's books. This book series cover merges typographies and stamps from various airplane tickets of the period.

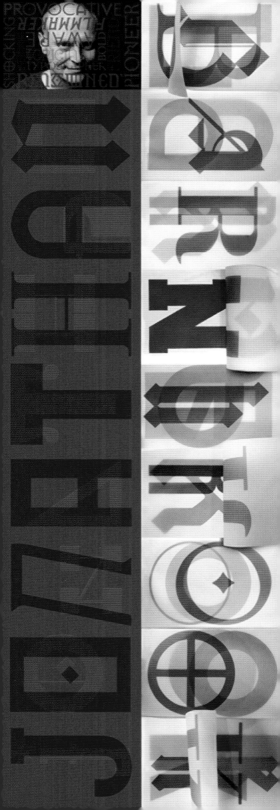

PROVOCATIVE
SHOCKING
WAR
FILMMAKER
RARE
BOLD
DEBATED
PIONEER
RENOWNED

Katherine:

Maria Grillo was an enormous inspiration for me. Not only a designer, she's a talented artist for me. Now to see her drawing and paintings. I'm also continually blow out of Plural Design

Katherine:

What makes your studio a co

Elaine:

We have an

Thurs

Nov ven

5.15

Dec 07, 2012 / 5:30p
NOVEMBER 2012

conference organized by the students of
and is now in its twelfth year. In the past,
widely recognized designers including Paula
Gyp Kidd, Jakob Trollbäck, Massimo Vignelli,

LeRo.
Neima
Cente
37 S.
Waba

Jennifer:

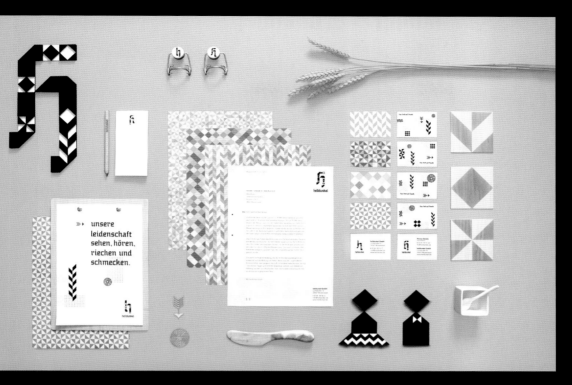

DESIGN Sung-Hi Leem, Dortmund, Germany / SCHOOL FH Dortmund, University of Applied Sciences and Arts / PROFESSORS Stefan Claudius and Lars Harmsen / PRINCIPAL TYPE Academy Engraved, Avenir, Pacifico, and custom / DIMENSIONS Various / CONCEPT The dynamic identity for the organic bakery and brewery helldunkel (lightdark) is based on different elements. It tells a story about cereal grains, which their homemade beer and bread both have in common. The three stages from seeds to grain ears and mill production are shown as icons and modules, which are variably combined as patterns based on simple triangles. The logo dynamically changes its form without changing its essence. The initial "h" as well as the lettering are part of a whole new custom-made corporate typeface for helldunkel, which is also based on triangles.

DESIGN Annie Jen / URL anniejen.com / TWITTER @annie76828 / SCHOOL School of Visual Arts, New York / INSTRUCTORS Shawn Hasto and Paul Sahre / PRINCIPAL TYPE Akzidenz-Grotesk BQ Bold / CONCEPT As graphic designers, we are very familiar with kerning, but if I were to explain to non-designers what kerning is, how could I relay it in a way that is easy to grasp and also captivating? To me, I often relate it as physical actions, as if the two letters were fighting to get it right. Therefore, I find there is no better way to visualize my idea than by having Bruce Lee headbutting bad guys to demonstrate exactly how kerning works.

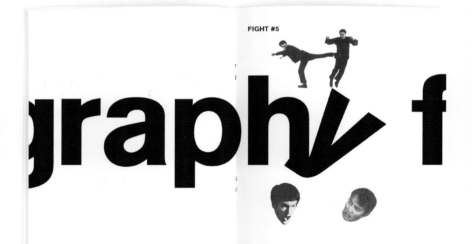

LE CORBUSIER
ARCHITECTURAL
POETRY IN THE
MACHINE AGE
BY JEAN LOUIS
COHEN

NEUTRA
1892-1970:
SURVIVAL
THROUGH
DESIGN BY
LAMPRECHT

WRIGHT
1867-1959:
BUILDING FOR
DEMOCRACY BY
BRUCE BROOKS
PFEIFFER,
PETER GOSSEL

HOFFMANN
1870-1956: IN
THE REALM OF
BEAUTY BY
AUGUST SARNITZ

Every period, if true to itself, must create its own cultural expression out of its specific place in history. – Herbert Bayer

SIGHTING! / Tiempos Headline in gorgeous use by Commodity

VILLAGE / New York / Monday — Friday 09:00 to 19:00 (GMT -5)

10:31:48

URTD	CONSTELLATION	MCKL	MCKL	CONSTELLATION	TYPESUPPLY
Doko	Apex New	Router	Shift	Brooklyn Stencil	Olen

FOUNDRIES / Village is the union of 10 foundries who have decided to go it alone together.

A2-TYPE / Outsiders

A2–Type

INCUBATOR / Ogg

Incubator

KLIM / Domaine Display

Klim

URTD / Odesta

Urtd

MCKL / Superior Title

MCKL

CONSTELLATION / Brooklyn Stencil

Constellation

TYPESUPPLY / Timonium

Type Supply

LUXTYPO / Colette

LuxTypo.

FELICIANO / Eudald News

Feliciano

SCHWARTZCO / Giorgio Sans

SCHWARTZCO

Second panel

Browse the collection by...
YEAR
ALPHABETICALLY
FOUNDRY

ABCDEF G HIJK L MN OPQRST U V W XY & Z!

Key

A	MCKL *Router*	O	A2-TYPE *Regular*
B	LUXTYPO *Colette*	P	SCHWARTZCO *Stag Stencil*
C	SCHWARTZCO *Giorgio Sans*	Q	INCUBATOR *Arbor*
D	TYPESUPPLY *Tiempos*	R	INCUBATOR *Sharp Sans*
E	KLIM *Feijoa*	S	MCKL *Shift*
F	TYPESUPPLY *Olen*	T	SCHWARTZCO *Giorgio*
G	CONSTELLATION *Aero*	U	URTD *Odesta*
H	FELICIANO *Flama*	V	TYPESUPPLY *Timonium*
I	SCHWARTZCO *Stag Dot*	W	INCUBATOR *Knox*
J	A2-TYPE *Typewriter*	X	LUXTYPO *Crush 8*
K	FELICIANO *Rongel*	Y	URTD *Benel*
L	CONSTELLATION *Galaxie C...*	&	KLIM *Pitch*
M	MCKL *Superior Title*	Z	TYPESUPPLY *Tiempos Headline*
N	CONSTELLATION *Brooklyn...*	!	FELICIANO *Eudald News*

Third panel

A2-Type
OUTSIDERS

Constellation
BROOKLYN STENCIL

Feliciano
EUDALD NEWS

NETS BKLYN JUMP POINTS DUNK

The Printing House West Village

Incubator
OGG

Klim
DOMAINE DISPLAY

LuxTypo.
COLETTE

Manuscript *inscriptions* LETTERING *calligraphic* Quixotically *alphabetize*

Francesco Franchi / Designn News

A

MCKL
SUPERIOR TITLE

Type Supply
TIMONIUM

SCHWARTZCO
GIORGIO SANS

C

EAST ROAD CITY WEST RAIL

101 ARTWORKS

Urtd
ODESTA

2013 *typeface* SCRIPT *lettering* DETACH *terminals* LINKED

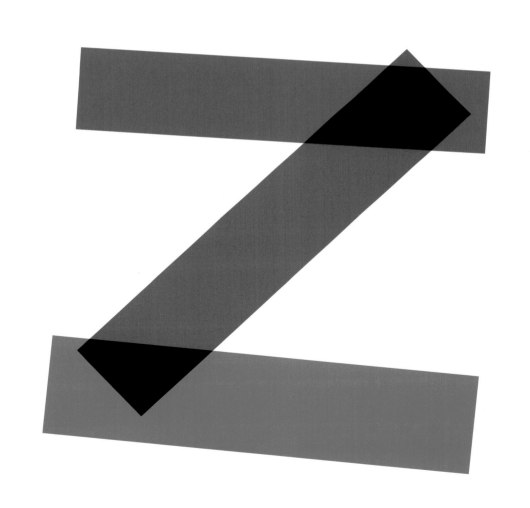

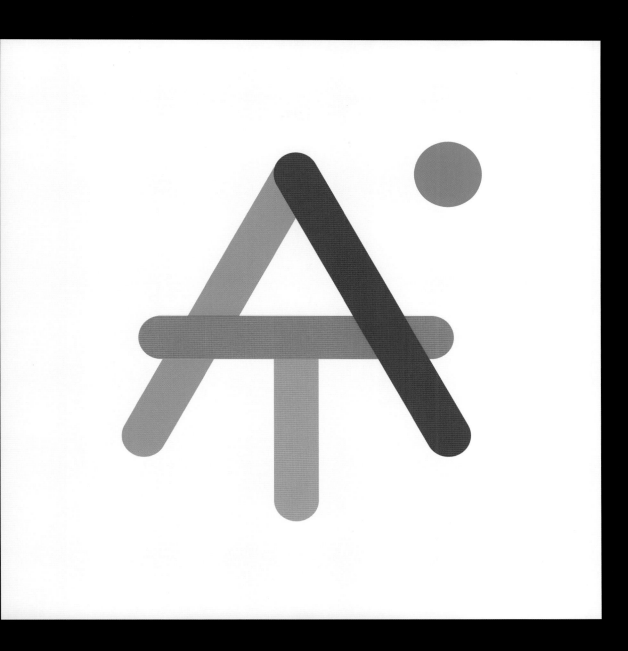

DESIGN Jono Brandel, San Francisco / URL anitype.com/entries / IN-HOUSE STUDIO Google Creative Lab / PRINCIPAL TYPE Anitype, based on Dosis / CONCEPT Anitype asks a simple question: What if letters could move? For thousands of years, letters have sat static on the page, but thanks to today's modern devices, they could do a lot more — they could dance and jump and wriggle their way across the screen. And you could help decide how they move. Anitype invites you to animate letters with JavaScript so we can begin to see what an animated typeface might look like on the web. The images are still frames from animations that people submitted on anitype.com.

DESIGN Yasmin Rose Malki / LETTERING Yasmin Rose Malki / SCHOOL School of Visual Arts, New York / INSTRUCTOR Ryan Moore / PRINCIPAL TYPE Custom / CONCEPT Inspired by the multifaceted spirit of Frida Kahlo, elements were extracted from various paintings to create a visual narrative. These elements often recede into the backdrop as her presence has a powerful impact on the viewer. A unique dialogue is created as the different rhythms of the graphics work in synergy. The growing tree highlights these while also carving the path to Frida's portrait. This video serves as an artist promo for the Museum of Modern Art.

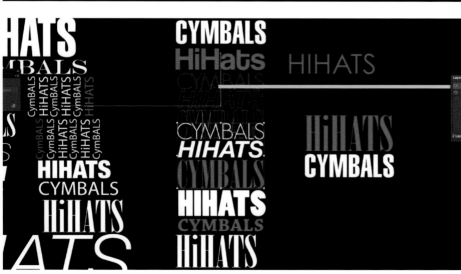

DESIGN Seoung Jun Lee, New York, New York / URL vimeo.com/junlee/dubsteptutorial and seoungjunlee.prosite.com / SCHOOL School of Visual Arts, New York / PRINCIPAL TYPE Various / CONCEPT This motion piece is a type-driven narrative explanation of a genre of music called Dubstep. The core concept is the balance between the music and typography while the music builds. The narration in the song explains the different sound-essential elements and then builds into Dubstep music. The narration and type design starts from simple design and beat and then gets more complex as the song progresses. I synchronized the beats to the visuals to have more sense of organization and rhythm because otherwise it might have seemed too hectic after "the drop."

DESIGN Agnetha Wohlert, Berlin and Stuttgart / DESIGN FIRM Strichpunkt Design / URL strichpunkt-design.de / CLIENT Type Hype /
PRINCIPAL TYPE Intro Black Caps, Intro Book Caps, and Intro Regular Caps / DIMENSIONS 4.3 × 5.9 in. (11 × 15 cm) / CONCEPT Cutting-edge
design meets GDR nostalgia: The Hauptstadt collection, which was produced for Berlin label Type Hype, features the twenty-six letters
of the alphabet in the form of twenty-six famous sights. The black-and-red illustrations each show a monument, a famous site, or a
cultural building in Berlin whose name matches the relevant letter. (A = Alexanderplatz, B = Brandenburger Tor, etc.) A clear design
language and smart abstraction are the right ingredients for a modern graphic design that truly does justice to the design tradition
of Bauhaus and the former capital city of the GDR.

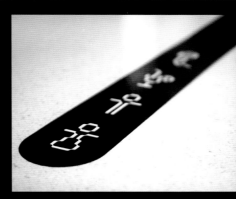

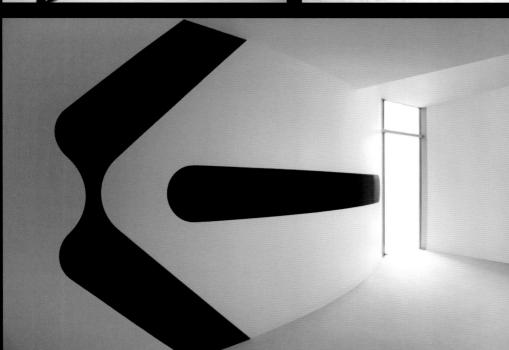

DESIGN Ken Deegan and Eddie Opara, New York / WAYFINDING DESIGN ASSISTANT Pedro Mendes / ART DIRECTION Eddie Opara /
DEVELOPERS Mark Lindsay and Chan Young Park / URL pentagram.com / TWITTER @pentagram / DESIGN FIRM Pentagram, New York /
CLIENT Platform / PRINCIPAL TYPE ThreeSix 11 / DIMENSIONS Various / CONCEPT Platform is a nonprofit organization and conference
that aims to increase the participation of underrepresented groups in technology and entrepreneurship, with a particular focus on
African-Americans, Latinos, and women. Our identity was designed with the goal of creating a memorable brand that could be expanded for
Platform's various initiatives. The logo uses the font ThreeSix 11, chosen for its futuristic, technological look. The wordmark has
been extended with a distinctive line that can be customized in an endless variety of forms and shapes. The segmented forms of the logo
also inspired the design of icons and the Platform website.

DESIGN Nick Adam, Greg Calvert, Ohn Ho, and Will Miller, Chicago / CREATIVE DIRECTION Nick Adam and Will Miller /
TWITTER @firebellydesign / DESIGN FIRM Firebelly Design / CLIENT Co-Prosperity Sphere / PRINCIPAL TYPE Absara and Hard Times /
DIMENSIONS 5.25 × 8 in. (13.3 × 20.3 cm) / CONCEPT From the cracking open of the stone cover to the vibrant interior, this book is
a sensory adventure cataloging both the typographic artistry and physical energy from the exhibition. Firebelly's third Typeforce
catalog explored new heights in fundamentals by uniting history, honored typographic traditions, and the discovery of new methods.
Simple mark making and hand-carved forms set the stage. Custom type, hand-tooled plates, and fluorescent video-blurred reflections
elevated the documentation. The production and paper effects used throughout this catalog were meant to inspire, challenge, and
encourage a stronger connection to ideas by way of print and paper.

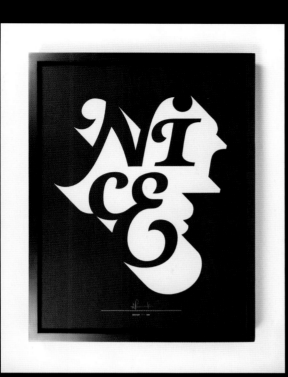

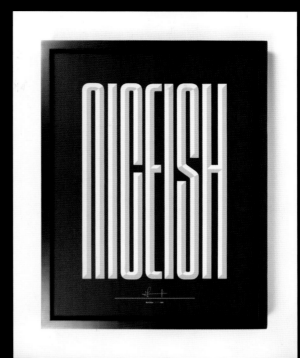

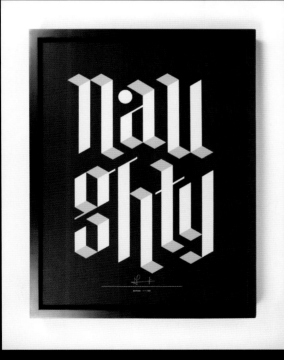

DESIGN Brian Gartside / DESIGN DIRECTOR Juan Carlos Pagan, New York / ART DIRECTION Michael Kushner / EXECUTIVE CREATIVE DIRECTOR
Menno Kluin / CHIEF CREATIVE OFFICER Matt Eastwood / GROUP CREATIVE DIRECTOR Andrew Mckechnie / LETTERING Brian Gartside /
COPYWRITER Daniel Paredes / PROJECT MANAGER Namita Howard / PRODUCTION MANAGER Kim Oetting / URL briangartsi.de /
AGENCY DDB New York / CLIENT DDB Global / PRINCIPAL TYPE handlettering / DIMENSIONS 18 × 24 in. (45.7 × 61 cm) / CONCEPT Two hundred
limited-edition prints were screen printed for each of the four posters. In lieu of a holiday card for DDB in 2013, we produced a series
of custom typographic posters to send to employees and clients. The inspiration for the series was Santa's "Naughty or Nice" list — but
that seemed a bit too black-and-white for the advertising industry, so we added some shades of gray with options such as Nice, Niceish,
Naughty, and Naughty as Hell.

TYPEFACE
DESIGN 2014
CHAIRMAN'S STATEMENT

When I started my career in Italy thirty years ago, it was extremely difficult to find any texts on how to design typefaces or on typography in general. Books on type were being printed only in the United States, and for an Italian self-taught apprentice of the art of type design it was like wandering thirstily through a desert land.

But now is the best time to be a student of type design in any country: There are actual schools that focus solely on type design! (You'll find the Royal Academy of Art in The Hague, Netherlands; the University of Reading in the United Kingdom; and Type@Cooper in New York City, just to name a few.) Books on typography have even made it onto the *New York Times* bestsellers list (for example, *Just My Type: A Book About Fonts*, by Simon Garfield). Typefaces are mentioned in mainstream movies as part of dialogues — and contrary to what Erik Spiekermann said years ago, today if you talk type at a party you'll find that people will engage in font conversations instead of shunning you for the type geek you are. This is a great achievement for the profession of the type designer. Type has become mainstream.

Nowhere is this more obvious than in the submissions of this year's competition. The work of the old-hand type designers has only gotten better and the new, novice designers are showing work of a quality that would have been unimaginable ten years ago. Congratulations and thank you to type designers new and old around the globe. I'd also like to thank the judges who selected the work with knowledgeable expertise and give a big thanks to Maxim Zhukov, who coordinated the work of the non-Latin experts to help us judge the ever increasing work coming from the non-Western world.

— Matteo Bologna

Matteo Bologna° is the founding partner and principal of Mucca Design, where he also serves as creative director.

Under his direction, the Mucca Design team has solved numerous design challenges and created uniquely successful work for a wide variety of global companies such as Shinsegae, Whole Foods, Victoria's Secret, Barnes & Noble, Rizzoli, Adobe Systems, and Target. With his team, Matteo designed the identities for a variety of now classic New York City culinary destinations such as Balthazar and Brooklyn Fare.

The work produced by the Mucca Design team has also been widely recognized by industry publications, competitions, and exhibitions, including *AIGA*, *Communication Arts*, *Eye*, *Graphis*, *HOW*, *Print*, the Type Directors Club, and the Art Directors Club.

Matteo is president of the Type Directors Club and a former board member of AIGA/NY. He frequently lectures about branding and typography around the world.

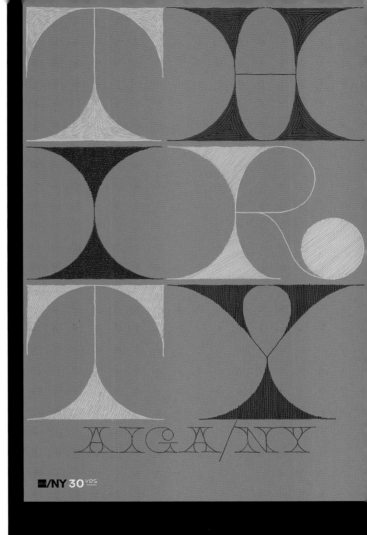

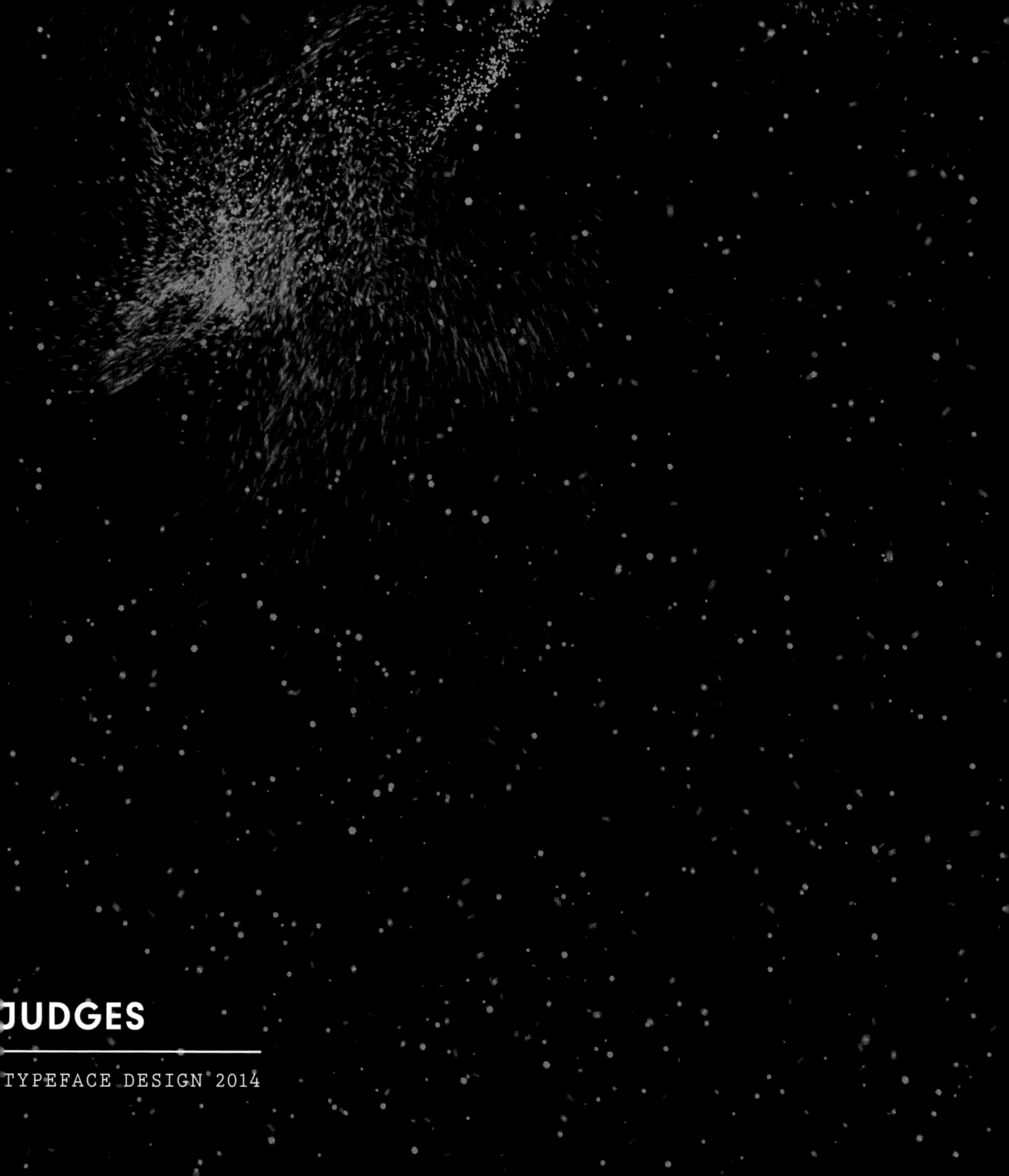

JUDGES

TYPEFACE DESIGN 2014

Andy Clymer° has worked for the past nine years as a typeface designer and developer at Hoefler & Co. (formerly Hoefler & Frere-Jones) in New York City. He teaches in the Type@Cooper program at The Cooper Union and has taught type design at the University of the Arts in Philadelphia.

Over the years of working with Jonathan Hoefler and Tobias Frere-Jones, Andy has had the opportunity to contribute to the design of several notable type families, including Archer, Ideal Sans, Vitesse, Forza, and Surveyor, and has produced custom work for clients such as The Art Institute of Chicago, The Nature Conservancy, and *Wired* magazine.

Before moving to New York, Andy earned a master's of design degree in type design from the Type & Media postgraduate course at the Koninklijke Academie van Beeldende Kunsten (Royal Academy of Art) in The Hague, Netherlands.

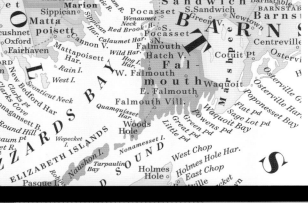

FOUR PONDS CONSERVATIO

Shop Pond, Freeman Pond, Upper Po
Basin comprise the eponymous Four
splendid area. With a total area of 28
terrific ride, with rolling hills and cha
well-marked for both hiking and ridir
start at the parking area, where trails
signed for the first hundred yards. Pr
the Pine Trail, where you'll see color
Eagle Trail (red), Pine Trail (black), T
Trail (blue), although all trails are sig

~Z R92 CDX-5

SEASONAL

EWMASTER'S
RESERVE
WINTER ALE

SIX 16 OZ (1 PINT) CANS

satisfying seaso
rich, Scottish me
Belgian aromatic
bready flavors to
full copper color,
smooth palate an
a brisk hopping
into balance.

10.8% alcohol by

line-height: 15px;
margin: 0 0 9px 8px

}

#maincontent .subhe
/* dynamic items */
font-weight: Bold;
font-size: 15px;
line-height: 19px;

}

#maincontent .overv

specials
served with rice, and choice of soup or salad

lotus root & duck pastry **7.95**
bbq beef short ribs **10.95**
crispy shrimp & mango rolls **7.95**

Hames, Margaret
Hitchcock, H. R. *World A*
Holland, Laurence B., ed.
Howard, Ebenezer *Garde*
Huxtable, Ada Louise *Pi*

J
Jacobs, Jane *The Death a*
Johnson, Philip *Architect*
Johnson, Carl, et al. *Stati*
Jordan, R. Furneaux, *The*
Jung, Friedrich *Examinati*

DO NOT LEAVE VEHICL
WHILE FUEL IS PUMPIN
PORTABLE CONTAINER
MUST BE FILLED ON TH

Our Philosophy

CITIZENSHIP is a concept as old
whether ancient city-states or r
resources, and the rise of enviro
comes the notion that we each
obligation to all of humanity, an
itself. Today there is a growing b
that the greatest development o

CRIMSON-CRESTED WOODPECKER
Campephilus melanoleucos

Wherever there are woodlands, there are wood
new world, from Panama to Argentina, the crin
of the largest woodpeckers in its habitat: regula
13-15 inches (33-38cm) in height, the crimson-cr

Ellen Lupton is senior
contemporary design at the
Cooper-Hewitt, National De
in New York City. Recent mu
include *Graphic Design — Nc*
an exhibition on national
2014, co-organized by Coop
the Walker Art Center. Ell
director of the Graphic De
at MICA (Maryland Institut
where she has written nume
design processes, includi°
Type, *Graphic Design Think*
Design: The New Basics. He
Type on Screen, is a colla
graduate students at MICA.

Making Things Work

Blue-collar mastery of physical skills is undervalued, and it brings satisfactions that white-collar office jobs do not.

BY FRANCIS FUKUYAMA

"SHOP CLASS AS SOULCRAFT" is a beautiful little book about human excellence and the way it is undervalued in contemporary America.

Matthew B. Crawford, who owns and operates a motorcycle repair shop in Richmond, Va., and serves as a fellow at the University of Virginia's Institute for Advanced Studies in Culture, notes that all across the United States, high school shop classes teaching mechanical arts like welding, woodworking or carpentry are closing down, to free up funds for computer labs. There is a legion of experts deni-

SHOP CLASS AS SOULCRAFT
An Inquiry Into the Value of Work.
By Matthew B. Crawford.
246 pp. The Penguin Press. $25.95.

grating manual trades like plumber, carpenter and electrician, warning that the United States labor force needs to be "upskilled" and retrained to face the challenges of a high-tech, global economy. Under this new ideology, everyone must attend college and prepare for life as a "symbolic analyst" or "knowledge worker," ready to add value through mental rather than physical labor.

There are two things wrong with this notion, according to Crawford. The first is that it radically undervalues blue-collar work that involves the manipulation of things rather than ideas. Expertise with things permits human beings to have agency over their lives — that is, their ability to exert some control over the myriad faucets, outlets and engines that they depend on from day to day. Instead of being able to top up your engine oil when it is low, you wait until an "idiot light" goes on

tions and planning meetings. None of this bears the worker's personal stamp; none of it can be definitively evaluated; and the kind of mastery or excellence available to the forklift driver or mechanic are elusive. Rather than achieving self-mastery by confronting a "hard discipline" like gardening or structural engineering or learning Russian, people are offered the fake autonomy of consumer choice, expressing

worked on a white-collar assembly line, writing abstracts of articles in scientific journals that he could not understand. Straight out of graduate school Crawford got a job as the executive director of an unnamed Washington "think tank," which he soon realized was being financed by oil companies to issue scientific studies questioning global warming. "I landed a job at the think tank because I had a pres-

simply by following rules, as a computer does; they require intuitive knowledge that comes from long experience and repeated encounters with difficulty and failure. In this world, self-esteem cannot be faked: if you can't get the valve cover off the engine, the customer won't pay you.

Highly educated people with high-status jobs — investment bankers, professors, lawyers — often believe that they could do anything their less-educated brethren can, if only they put their minds to it, because cognitive ability is the only ability that counts. The truth is that some would not have the physical and cognitive ability to do skilled blue-collar work, and that others could do it only if they invested 20 years of their life in learning a trade. "Shop Class as Soulcraft" makes this quite vivid by explaining in detail what is actually involved in rebuilding a Volkswagen engine: grinding down the gasket joining the intake ports to the cylinder heads, with a file, tracing the custom-fit gasket with an X-Acto knife, removing metal on the manifolds with a pneumatic die grinder so the passageways will mate perfectly. Small signs of galling and discoloration mean excessive heat buildup, caused by a previous owner's failure to lubricate; the slight bulging of a valve stem points to a root cause of wear that a novice mechanic would completely fail to perceive.

Crawford asserts that he is not writing a book about public policy. But he has a clear preference for a "progressive republican" order in which the moral ties binding workers to their work or entrepreneurs to their customers are not so readily sacrificed at the altar of efficiency and growth. He argues that there is something wrong with a global economy in which a Chinese worker sews together an Amish quilt with no direct connection with its final user, or understanding of its cultural meaning. Economic ties, like those between a

Jesse Ragan° is an independent typeface designer in Brooklyn. Over the past decade, he has created custom types and lettering for brands, publications, and cultural institutions. He co-founded and teaches for the Type@Cooper certificate program at Cooper Union, and he serves on the board of directors for AIGA/NY. Previously he was a staff designer at Hoefler & Frere-Jones and taught at Pratt Institute.

Jesse has collaborated on many retail typefaces, notably Gotham, Archer, Omnes, and Chronicle. Freelance clients include Pentagram, Landor, Reebok, *The New York Times*, Font Bureau, and House Industries. His work has been recognized by AIGA, the Type Directors Club, Brand New Awards, and the Museum of Modern Art. He holds a BFA from Rhode Island School of Design.

Fascination

Chic & Sweet

The Big Reveal

Quintessential Style

Stunning Everyday Kicks

ST BART's

NEW HEADLINE TYPE
Coffee & Crossword
GEOMETRIC
Ideal News
FIELD REPORT
Major Stories
SPACE EFFICIENCY
Rain or Sunshine
TODAY'S TOP STORIES
Futura & Her Friends

ABCDEFGHIJKLM
NOPQRSTUVWXYZ
abcdefghijklm
nopqrstuvwxyz
0123456789&
ÐŁØHÞÆŒ
ðłøħþæœß
.,:;...·•¡!¿?-–—
""''‚'«»‹›||()[]{}
*†‡™®©¶§@$£¥€ƒ¢
ɑo⁰%‰#+−×÷<>="''

Lincoln
TRENTON
Harrisburg
SAINT PAUL
Boston
ATLANTA
Montpelier
NASHVILLE
Raleigh
LANSING

Bauhaus University graduate Georg
Seifert (b. 1978 in Halle an der Saale,
Germany) is a type designer and a software
developer. His typeface families Graublau
Sans and Graublau Slab have become international bestsellers. He also designed
the signage and type for the new Berlin
Airport. He is most well known, however,
for the easy-to-use font editor Glyphs,
released in 2011. Georg lives and works
in Berlin.

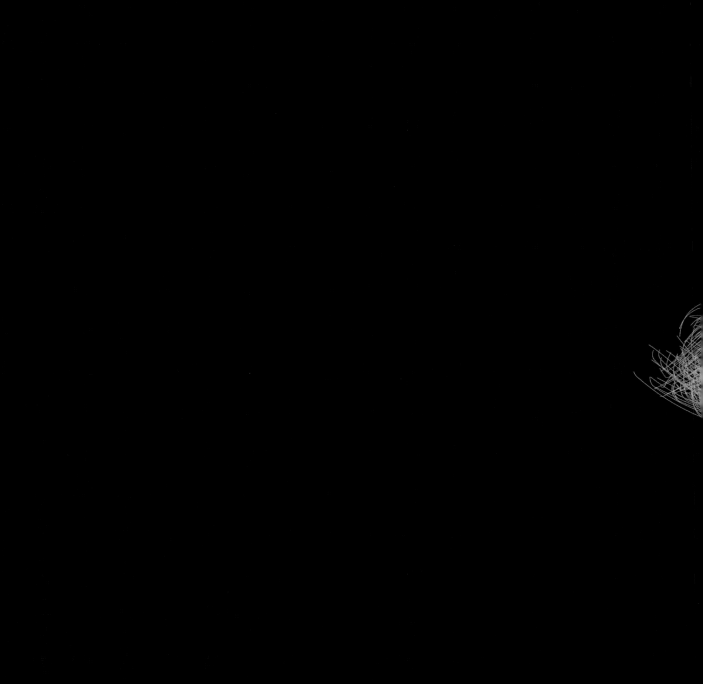

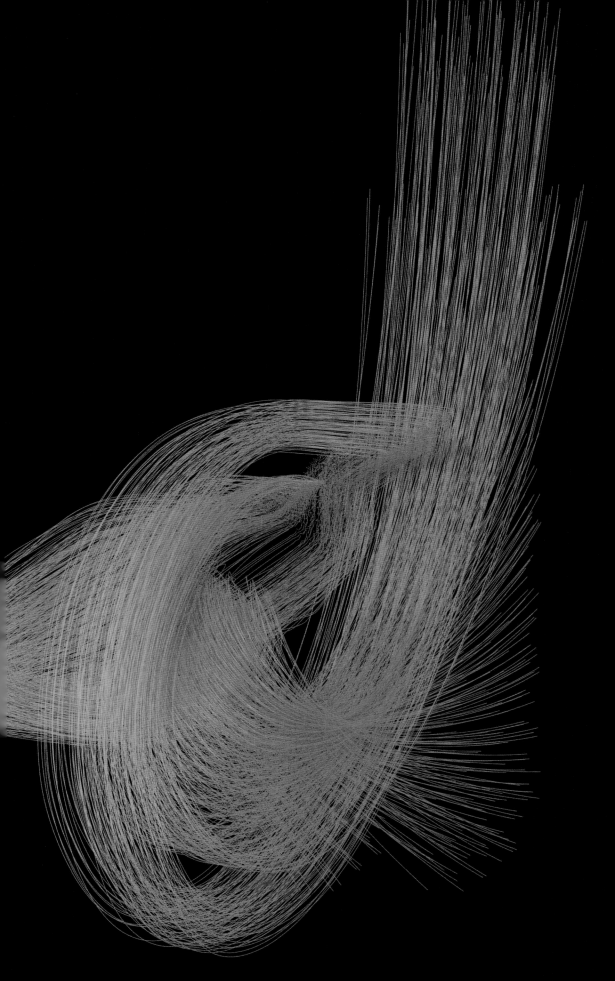

JUDGES' CHOICES

DESIGNER'S CONCEPT / Odesta is a decorative script typeface with detached strokes and pronounced ball terminals. It has seven weights with small capitals, swash capitals, plenty of ligatures, and initial and final forms for each of the lowercase letters.

The design of Odesta started as a custom lettering logo for a wedding photography service, but quickly transformed into a versatile full-fledged family of a wide range of weights. Despite its script nature, the typeface is highly modular. This gives the text set in Odesta nice rhythm and visual order while remaining engaging and expressive.

ANDY CLYMER'S STATEMENT / There has been a resurgence of interest recently in stenciled typefaces, but Odesta shouldn't be mistaken for a simple script that mimics a stenciled form. Instead, what I see in it is something that takes a detached approach for what I think is a smart design solution: Crafting a connected script as a typeface can sometimes require many dozens (or even hundreds) of alternate forms of letters and ligatures to actually function as a connected design. The solution that Ondrej Job appears to have found is this: Reducing the connecting stroke to a hairline that drops out before it makes its connection to the next letter still makes for a very believable appearance of a connected script without fussing around with alternate drawings of every character or the need for complex OpenType features.

Aside from its technical merits, the design is gorgeous. There are some incredibly beautiful forms, particularly in the oldstyle figures and in the heavier weights, and I love the combination of the hairlines and drilled circular terminals. Ondrej was able to capture a feeling that's casual and light in one moment but still has some formality from an engraving from either the 1870s or 1970s. Either way, I'm really looking forward to seeing it in use.

Atlantic Canary

Serinus Canaria

LINNAEUS

Systema Naturae

1758

NER'S CONCEPT / Sori is a result of the interest in new writing
The goal was to create an innovative and unique writing system that
elements from the Korean and Latin writing systems. Regarding the
phabet, the new system has to enable a syllable formation. As a
the syllables can be written in imaginary squares. This structure has
pted to the Latin alphabet and syllables. Each letter was put into
blocks relevant to the structure and construction of the syllable.
onants and vowels have a fixed position in each block. The blocks are
rom left to right and from top to bottom. The font has three styles
combined according to the number of letters of a syllable.

LUPTON'S STATEMENT / We saw many beautiful and accomplished
designs during our day of judging, from lovely scripts and striking
aces to workhorse text families. As a member of the committee who is
er rather than a type designer, I was drawn to projects that went an
p in communicating the designer's thought process and intellectual
sign competitions should foster new, experimental work as well as
ng successful commercial endeavors. With my choice, I wanted to
the ability of TDC to illuminate typographic endeavors that most
the community would not otherwise see. Among those submissions
ued a more experimental direction, the typeface Sori stood out to
s intellectual inventiveness. This fascinating typographic system
arrange Latin characters within a square grid in a manner analogous
nstruction of Korean hangul, a syllabic writing system. The Sori
nerates compact word marks that would not result from any other
Applied to a grid of international city names, the Sori type specimen
a new image of global typography. The designer communicated the
learly and vividly in the materials submitted and has made an unusual

TYPEFACE DESIGN Sebastian Moser, Stuttgart / PROGRAMMER Alexis Luengas / CONSULTANT Young-Hun Jung / SCHOOL School of Design of Pforzheim University / MEMBERS OF TYPEFACE FAMILY Regular Big, Regular Small, Light Condensed Big, Light Condensed Small, Extra Condensed Big, and Extra Condensed Small /

DESIGNER'S CONCEPT / The development of the Metro typeface began as a "design dare." First released in 1929, Metro was the wildly popular result of a challenge to create a new, versatile and distinctive sans serif typeface for Linotype typesetters. More than eighty years later, Toshi Omagari welcomed the opportunity to update this seminal design for digital imaging. The new typeface, Metro Nova, builds on the foundation of the original Metro, preparing it perfectly for today's taste and technology.

Because of duplexing requirements, characters in the original Metro started quite wide in the lightest weight and became progressively more condensed in heavier designs. Metro Nova, however, is not encumbered by these design restrictions. Omagari also gave Metro Nova a softer demeanor than its predecessor's.

JESSE RAGAN'S STATEMENT / Metro Nova demonstrates that a historical typeface can be reimagined for our time, while keeping its identity intact.

Mergenthaler Linotype debuted Metro in 1929 for its ubiquitous type casting system. To compete with the most popular new sans serif types, W.A. Dwiggins designed two Metro series. Metro No. 1's humanist structure and stress made it a quirky cousin to Gill Sans. Metro No. 2 dressed up the design with geometric shapes, looking a bit more like Futura. Linotype's first digital revival of Metro, a stiff interpretation of No. 2, left the face feeling stale—and left No. 1 in the dust.

In Toshi Omagari's digital revival, No. 1 is number one again. Its cheerful e's and outrageous two-story g's steal the scene. Dwiggins's flights of whimsy show even in the No. 2 alternates, which are accessible through OpenType features. Omagari has changed many aspects of the design to make the family useful today, but it is unmistakably Metro. The revisions and extensions celebrate rather than second-guess Dwiggins's original ideas. The family sparkles in text for print and screen (at moderate sizes), and its nuances make for elegant display settings. Here is a Metro that Dwiggins might have created in 2013, feeling as fresh and energetic as it must have in 1929.

Metro Nova sets an excellent example for future do-overs: "Novas," and "Nexts." I hope we'll see more old typefaces similarly liberated and living in the present.

metronova

Metro Nova is Toshi Omagari's restoration and reinvention of W. A. Dwiggins' classic Metro and Metro No.2. This versatile new sans-serif face works beautifully in a wide range of settings and sizes, from the page to the screen.

örþrifaráðs

Kałwągi

Sajitha

¡gracious!

$273.99

beauty

Rome

1936

Quantum

Martinsville

———— Be creative with Stylistic Alternates ————

DEFAULT STYLE

wrangler,

STYLISTIC SET 1
ALL ALTERNATES

wrangler,

STYLISTIC SETS 6 & 7
ALTERNATE 'e' AND 'g'

or wrangler?

TYPEFACE DESIGN Toshi Omagari, London / FOUNDRY Linotype Originals / MEMBERS OF TYPEFACE FAMILY Regular, Black, Black Italic, Bold, Bold Italic, Italic, Light, Light Italic, Medium, Medium Italic, Thin, Thin Italic, Xtra Black, Xtra Black Italic, Condensed, Condensed Black, Condensed Black Italic, Condensed Bold, Condensed Bold Italic, Condensed Italic, Condensed Light, Condensed Medium.

DESIGNER'S CONCEPT / "Azer" in Arabic means friendly, ready to assist
and lend a hand. This typeface combines simple lines with careful detailing
to create a serious but approachable look. The Arabic is a Naskh / Kufi
hybrid and retains a balance between calligraphic angular cuts and unadorned
construction. Azer is congenial without being sloppy, serious without
being conformist.

The fonts include Arabic, Farsi, Urdu, and Latin variants. Azer is
available in five weights, ranging from a delicate thin that is ideal for
refined headlines to a thick black that is perfect for chunky titles and
in-text emphasis.

GEORG SEIFERT'S STATEMENT / The typeface finds an interesting balance
of calligraphic and typographic elements. Because it doesn't have a strong
baseline, it can have nicer shapes and balance. The ascenders are even
thicker than the horizontals without completely reversing the contrast.
Together this gives a fresh appearance, and I can imagine the typeface in
all kinds of situations.

تَمُرُّ النُّجُومَ بِمَرحَلَةٍ تَكَوُّنٍ لِيَبْدَأَ فِيهَا تَفَاعُلُ نَوَوِيٌّ

تَحَوُّلَاتٍ فِي الْخَمْسِينَاتِ فِي بُنْيَتِهَا الْإِقْتِصَادِيَّةِ

زِيَارَة جَزِيرَة تَقَعُ عَلَى السَّاحِلِ الْغَرْبِيِّ لِأُورُوبَّا

الْفِكْرُ الْبَشَرِيُّ الإِنسَانِيُّ الْمَبْنِيُّ عَلَى الْمُسَاوَاةِ

تَشْكِيلُ اَلْحُرُوْفِ بِاللُّغَةِ اَلْعَرَبِيَّةِ والعَامِّيَّةِ

شوربة دجاج مع الأرز

الإنسانية في الأسرة

مستمتعة بالموسيقى

خربشات وتناقضات

لماذا لا يشعر بالفرح

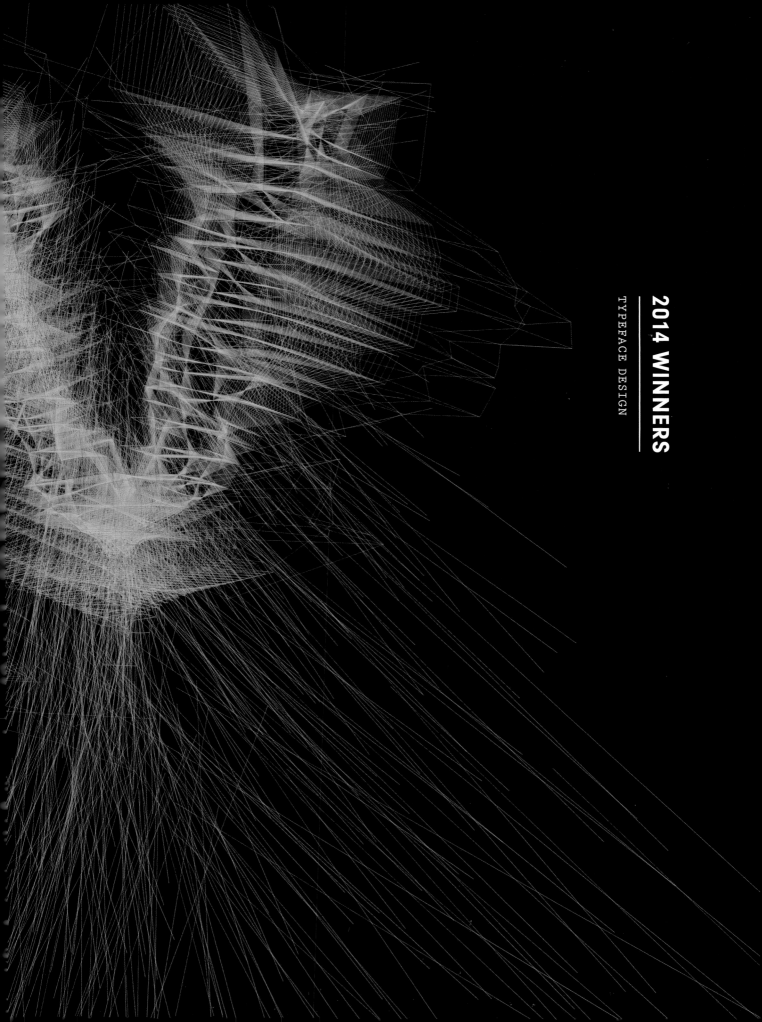

2014 WINNERS

TYPEFACE DESIGN

TYPEFACE DESIGN Weinzierl / FOUNDRY Monotype / CLIENT Crispin Porter + Bogusky / MEMBERS OF TYPEFACE FAMILY Pizza Press,
Pizza Press Antique, Pizza Press Antique Display, Pizza Press Fill, Pizza Press Inline, Pizza Press Ornaments, Pizza Press Outline,
Pizza Press Shadow / CONCEPT The Pizza Press family is a custom typeface created for one of the world's largest pizza companies,
Domino's Pizza. Designed collaboratively between Weinzierl and the creative team at the advertising agency Crispin Porter + Bogusky,
Pizza Press was developed as a series of modular fonts that can be layered to add flexibility, variety, and excitement. To develop this
chromatic typeface family, we used layering techniques to enable variety with colors and effects.

MEATZZA FEAST

BUFFALO CHICKEN

PACIFIC VEGGIE

FIERY HAWAIIAN

MEATBALL CHEESE

0123456789$

DOUBLE CRUST

ANCHOVIE & OLIVE

QUEEN CITY OF THE GREAT LAKES

20TH CENTURY LIMITED

NIAGARA

NEW YORK CENTRAL (J-1) #5270

401 EUCLID AVENUE

SPIRIT OF '76

BLATZ

ZOOPRAXISCOPE

1893 COLUMBIAN EXHIBITION

12TH STREET

MCSORLEY'S OLD ALE HOUSE

Amplify.

ABCDEFGHIJKLMNOPQRSTVWXYZ
abcdefghijklmnopqrstuvwxyz #$*†‡
1234567890.,:;..."""''',,,«~»$!¡?¿‹•›({[&]})

Amplify is reimagining the way teachers teach and students learn.

Amplify Light

Amplify enables teachers to manage whole classrooms and, simultaneously empower them to offer more personalized instruction, so that students become more active, engaged learners through technology.

Amplify Regular

Amplify enables teachers to manage whole classrooms and, simultaneously empower them to offer more personalized instruction, so that students become more active, engaged learners through technology.

Amplify Bold

Amplify enables teachers to manage whole classrooms and, simultaneously empower them to offer more personalized instruction, so that students become more active, engaged learners through technology.

Gigantic

and unconventionally reversed

confident

enough to break traditional conventions

Suitable

for bringing an extraordinary and impressive look

TYPEFACE DESIGN Maria Doreuli, Moscow / URL mariadoreuli.com / TWITTER @maria_doreuli / SCHOOL Type and Media. Royal Academy of Art, The Hague (Netherlands)/ PROFESSORS Erik van Blokland, Paul van der Laan, and Peter Verheul / MEMBERS OF TYPEFACE FAMILY Chimera Display Black, Chimera Display Bold, Chimera Display Bold Italic, Chimera Text, and Chimera Text Italic / CONCEPT Chimera is a reversed contrast typeface with a dynamic character that comes from the broad-nib tool. The type family consists of five styles drawn from scratch. Intended specifically for display use, the typeface includes two low-contrast text companions. The text styles are an extension of the display ones. They keep the same concept but are adjusted to be able to perform in smaller sizes. Although all the styles in the family are based on the same concept and share certain characteristics, they are not meant to be used together. Each one works individually, bringing its own unique style.

TYPEFACE DESIGN Xavier Dupré. / FOUNDRY Typofonderie / CONCEPT Referred to as Egyptian in the early years of the nineteenth century, today slab serifs are primarily used in display sizes but seldom used in body text. Mislab combines the strength of a slab serif with the lightness of a sans serif. Xavier Dupré has designed a brighter and more legible slab serif than most. This versatile typeface brings clarity to headlines and any applications, thanks to the thirty-two styles in three widths.

Antarctica

Asia *Africa*

EUROPE

North America

Mislab

Oceania

South America

Jordbruksavtalet

Overcompression

Particulièrement

Zusammenhang

Arquitectónicos

Immédiatement

Möglicherweise

Yhdeksäntoista

Alþjóðavæðing

Pengeøkonomi

Epigraphically

Manifestações

TYPEFACE DESIGN Miguel Reyes and Christian Schwartz, New York / FOUNDRY Commercial Type / URL commercialtype.com / TWITTER @commercialtype / MEMBERS OF TYPEFACE FAMILY Duplicate Ionic Thin, Thin Italic, Light, Light Italic, Regular, Regular Italic, Medium, Medium Italic, Bold, Bold Italic, Black, and Black Italic / CONCEPT Duplicate Ionic is one of three related families in the Duplicate collection. The bracketed serifs and ball terminals of the traditional Clarendon, also known as Ionic, emerged in Britain in the middle of the nineteenth century. Combining these structures with a contemporary interpretation of Antique Olive seems counterintuitive, but this unexpected marriage feels natural. As the Ionic genre has traditionally been popular for newspapers,

LA MANCHA

Campo de Montiel

1845–1726

Ingenious Gentleman

Golden Age

skinny horse 'Rocinante'

TYPEFACE DESIGN Frank Griesshammer, Santa Clara, California / FOUNDRY FontShop / MEMBERS OF TYPEFACE FAMILY Light, Medium, Extra Bold, Regular, Bold, and Black with Italics for each / CONCEPT FF Quixo was conceived by exploring pointed-pen calligraphy, deciding to take on the style in a more casual manner, and interpreting the model with different-sized brushes. Each of the weights is based on a different writing tool, just as in an analog workflow. Then, the original idea was re-evaluated and considered as the basis for a larger-scale project. The complete family was redrawn, the number of styles was increased, and many stylistic details were changed to be more functional than conceptual. In the final typeface, the visual influence of the writing tool is minimized in lighter weights but is increasingly prominent at the bold end of the spectrum. This concept led to a design that can show a playful side without looking goofy, but also provides the necessary precision for more functional applications.

Exquisite day

MENDOZA . CHUBUT . CLAROMECÓ . SAN JUAN

huechulafquen

Cronología del las culturas originarias del Noroeste

Lago Chimehuin

THE MOST IMPORTANT MEAL OF THE DAY IS THE ONE

En la Quiaca

Puna, fue fundada el 30 de Agosto de 1883 como

TYPEFACE DESIGN Dario M. Muhafara, Buenos Aires / FOUNDRY Tipo Type Foundry / URL tipo.net.ar / TWITTER @dmuhafara / CLIENT FutureBrand / CONCEPT The typeface was created as a country brand for Argentina. In the first stage, the logo was designed; then we expanded this to a six-weights family. The project was developed for FutureBrand. The idea was to find a logo with a look that was both contemporary and long-lasting. The versatility of this typographic family allows a wide variety of uses for different situations. From its sans serif origin and humanistic spirit, its kind and precise characteristics make it unique. The italics refer to calligraphic stroke to complete

A display typeface in roman and italic inspired by the work of twentieth-century book designer Oscar Ogg.

Telegram

Peaches,

Resin *Hop*

Metalic *Enoch.*

Xylophones *Dominante*

خوبصورت خوبصورت کتنا حیرت انگیز کتنا حیرت انگیز۔ شاندار شاندار افزودگی افزودگی ریسلی ریسلی سواد قصوراتی سواد چ قصوراتی بہترین بہترین عنیزحقیقی

ہائے میں مرگئی ایناٹیٹی برگر

ہر انسان کچھ بحیادی آزادیاں تے برابر دے اے حقوق اپنے نال لے کے ایس دنیا وچ آوندا اے جہیڑے لوہدے کولوں کوئی

دی گریٹ ملالہ چکن شوارما سپشل شوارما ۴۵ روپیہ

The great Malala chicken shawarma special shawarma 45 rupees

ایک مشرقی ذائقہ کے ساتھ نستعلیق وَإِنَّنَا نُسْتَعْلِقُ إِسْتِعْلَاقًا شَا مِلَّا

Nastaleeq with an Eastern flavor

وَہ بولوُں توُ غوُلغان

اَور بازارے لے آے اگر ٹوٹ گیا   ساغرِ جم سے ہم اجام سفال اچھا ہَے

DECO ⓓ type   linguistic experts & designers of computer typography   Mirjam Somers — Thomas Milo — Peter Somers

י וַיְהִי לְשִׁבְעַת הַיָּמִים וּמֵי הַמַּבּוּל הָיוּ עַל־הָאָרֶץ: יא בִּשְׁנַת
שֵׁשׁ־מֵאוֹת שָׁנָה לְחַיֵּי־נֹחַ בַּחֹדֶשׁ הַשֵּׁנִי בְּשִׁבְעָה־עָשָׂר יוֹם
לַחֹדֶשׁ בַּיּוֹם הַזֶּה נִבְקְעוּ כָּל־מַעְיְנוֹת תְּהוֹם רַבָּה וַאֲרֻבֹּת
הַשָּׁמַיִם נִפְתָּחוּ: יב וַיְהִי הַגֶּשֶׁם עַל־הָאָרֶץ אַרְבָּעִים יוֹם
וְאַרְבָּעִים לָיְלָה: יג בְּעֶצֶם הַיּוֹם הַזֶּה בָּא נֹחַ וְשֵׁם־וְחָם וָיֶפֶת
בְּנֵי־נֹחַ וְאֵשֶׁת נֹחַ וּשְׁלֹשֶׁת נְשֵׁי־בָנָיו אִתָּם אֶל־הַתֵּבָה: יד הֵמָּה
וְכָל־הַחַיָּה לְמִינָהּ וְכָל־הַבְּהֵמָה לְמִינָהּ וְכָל־הָרֶמֶשׂ הָרֹמֵשׂ
עַל־הָאָרֶץ לְמִינֵהוּ וְכָל־הָעוֹף לְמִינֵהוּ כֹּל צִפּוֹר כָּל־כָּנָף:

Hebrew Biblical text with vowels and cantilation marks
set in Venecia Hebrew Regular

א **בראשית.** אמר רבי יצחק: לא היה צריך להתחיל את התורה
אלא מ"החדש הזה לכם", שהיא מצוה ראשונה שנצטוו ישראל,
ומה טעם פתח בבראשית? משום "כח מעשיו הגיד לעמו לתת
להם נחלת גוים". שאם יאמרו אומות העולם לישראל: "לסטים
אתם שכבשתם ארצות שבעה גוים", הם אומרים להם: "כל
הארץ של הקב"ה היא, הוא בראה ונתנה לאשר ישר בעיניו,
ברצונו נתנה להם, וברצונו נטלה מהם ונתנה לנו": **בראשית
ברא.** אין המקרא הזה אומר אלא דרשני, כמ"ש רבותינו ז"ל:
בשביל התורה שנקראת "ראשית דרכו", ובשביל ישראל שנקראו
"ראשית תבואתה". ואם באת לפרשו כפשוטו, כך פרשהו:
"בראשית בריית שמים וארץ, והארץ היתה תהו ובהו וחשך,
ויאמר אלהים יהי אור". ולא בא המקרא להורות סדר הבריאה,
לומר שאלו קדמו, שאם בא להורות כך, היה לו לכתוב "בראשונה
ברא את השמים' וגו', שאין לך 'ראשית' במקרא שאינו דבוק
לתיבה של אחריו, כמו: "בראשית ממלכות יהויקים", "ראשית
ממלכתו", "ראשית דגנך". אף כאן אתה אומר "בראשית ברא

Commentary is set in Venecia Hebrew Semi-cursive
with Venecia Hebrew Bold call-outs

BIRDLAND

Baker

Coltrane.

CORNELIA STREET

BLUE NOTE

Scofield.

BARBES

THE VANGUARD

Rollins

Davis

SMOKE JAZZ CLUB

ornaments kindness

snowflakes cookies

Ohhh ✳

Bygones ✳ laughter

Frosty the Snowman

✳ Rudolph Holiday Cheer

sugar ✳ goodwill

plums 15 Type designers tweeting

presents silly putty

elf 13 Letterers a Lettering

A Partridge in a Pear Tree

即能見確少被爭代方銀説夫海麥需秋節走成
功以回會肉風高種強費多速我你登馬報發池春
愛飛必黑是表公刻看入然將名享國花食舟恨健
勝交采寶旨州雨毫慶終益魚放力戲濟九剛版嚴
情至醒藝環去孩政經轉無路泰邊點斗剛量學就
險埃尹衣參器播圖吃頓聯貴派君累私琴鑄騰
獲素爾參餐霧處贊營銀石森緒越鳳靠綠亂鳥风
驕啪曙眼噲畔出叁吳爭務号变备经鱼鸟风
㈱㊣0123456789？！：；。，、
あぁいぃうぅえぇおおアァイィウゥエェず

幟黑
MZhiHei

TYPEFACE DESIGN Kenneth Kwok, Hong Kong / FOUNDRY Monotype / URL fonts.com / TWITTER @Monotype / LANGUAGE Chinese / CONCEPT The Monotype ZhiHei (蒙納幟黑) typeface, an ultra bold design that supports both the Traditional and Simplified Chinese writing systems, was designed primarily for designers, advertising agencies, and creative professionals. Monotype ZhiHei offers a unique, modern feel and is characterized by stiff and clean lines with high-contrast stroke weights that help promote a strong message while still providing high legibility at large and medium sizes, which is critical for Chinese advertising markets.

TYPEFACE DESIGN John Meng, Beijing / STUDIO Meng Shenhui Graphic Design Studio / TWITTER @shenhui / CONCEPT Cloud Mountain Type
was inspired by Zhang Jiajie (the Chinese cloud-fog mountains) and ancient Chinese landscape painting. The typeface combines the
traditional Chinese cloud landscape with Western characters. When you stare at the details of the font, you can't even recognize the
letter "I," referencing the Chinese saying: "You cannot know the shape of a mountain when you stand on it."

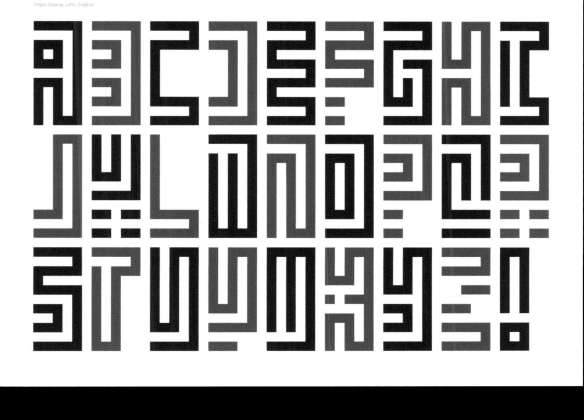

PARKING

PERMANENT PRESS

TIRES

LIGHTS & DARKS

SOAPS

LIQUID DETERGENT

SPIN CYCLE

POOLSIDE

COIN-OPS

THE HAWAIIAN

DINER

LIQUOR

BAR

BURGERS

SLATERY

MOTEL

FROMAGERIE

LOUNGE

ROSIE'S

AUTOS

TEATRO MUNICIPAL

Marcel

Et toi, mon aimée, c'est toujours
mes plus tendre baisers que cela réserve.

And for you, my beloved one,
I always save my most tender kisses.

The closing words of a letter from Marcel to his wife

— June 1944 —

TYPEFACE DESIGN Carolyn Porter, St. Paul, Minnesota / FOUNDRY P22 Type Foundry / URL porterfolioinc.com / TWITTER @porterfolio / CONCEPT Marcel Script is named in honor of Marcel Heuzé, a Frenchman conscripted into labor during World War II. During the months Marcel was in Germany, he wrote letters to his beloved wife and daughters back home in France. His letters began with affectionate greetings such as *Mes chères petites* (My little darlings) and were filled with the most beautiful expressions of love imaginable. Marcel's letters also contain rare first-person testimony of day-to-day survival within a labor camp. These letters were the source documents used to create a font that retains the expressive character of Marcel Heuzé's original handwriting.

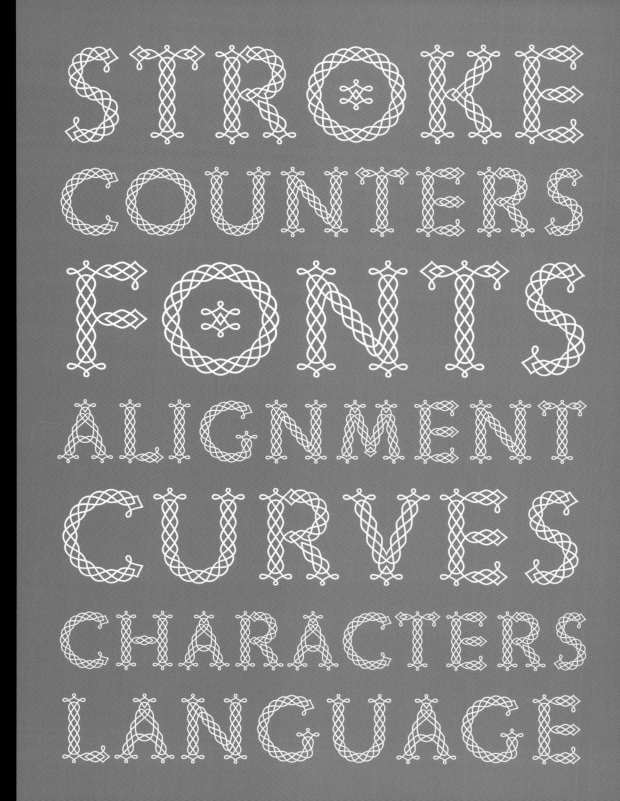

TYPEFACE DESIGN Jonathan Perez, Angoulême, France / FOUNDRY typographies.fr / URL typographies.fr / TWITTER @typographies_fr / CONCEPT Chapitre is based on the principle of the endless knot, a symbol used particularly in Hinduism and Buddhism. As its name implies, an endless knot has no beginning and no end. Although the construction of the letters is complex, special attention was given to achieving a high level of readability. Chapitre contains more than 250 glyphs and offers extensive language support. The typeface was designed to perform optimally when used between thirty and forty-five points.

Lalola

A SINGLE STYLE DISPLAY TYPEFACE

AaBbCcDdEe
FfGgHhIiJj
KkLlMmNn
OoPpQqRrSs
TtUtVvWw
XxYyZz

Musica Tradičního!
Jubedalt möirgav lõukoer hüppas tänaval
·>CITROEN EN IJS<·
Voix ambiguë d'un cœur
-Czekolada pączki-
Jlinkdama fechtuotojo špaga sublykčiojusi
Un Satèl·lit a la Lluna

Lalola (whose early version was released as 'Lola' by the Spanish
foundry Type-Ø-Tones in 1997) is a display typeface with strong
attitude. It was inspired by a lettering model found in a book by
Eugen Nerdinger and Lisa Beck. From a few letters of that model,
Lalola became an original design and a single font, comprising all
the necessary characters for languages based on the Latin alphabet.
You can 'say it loud' with Lalola, either in lower or uppercase,
yet with and a unique, distinctive friendly voice.

Designed by Laura Meseguer, 2013

Lalola SANS Lettering
CE Character Set
YES...WE'RE OPEN TYPE

TYPEFACE DESIGN Laura Meseguer, Barcelona / FOUNDRY Type-Ø-Tones / URL type-o-tones.com / TWITTER @typeotones /
CONCEPT Lalola is a display typeface with strong attitude. It was inspired by a lettering model found in a book by Eugen Nerdinger
and Lisa Beck. From a few letters of that model, Lalola became an original design and a single font, comprising all the necessary
characters for languages based on the Latin alphabet. You can "say it loud" with Lalola, either in lowercase or uppercase, yet with
wit and a unique, distinctive, friendly voice.

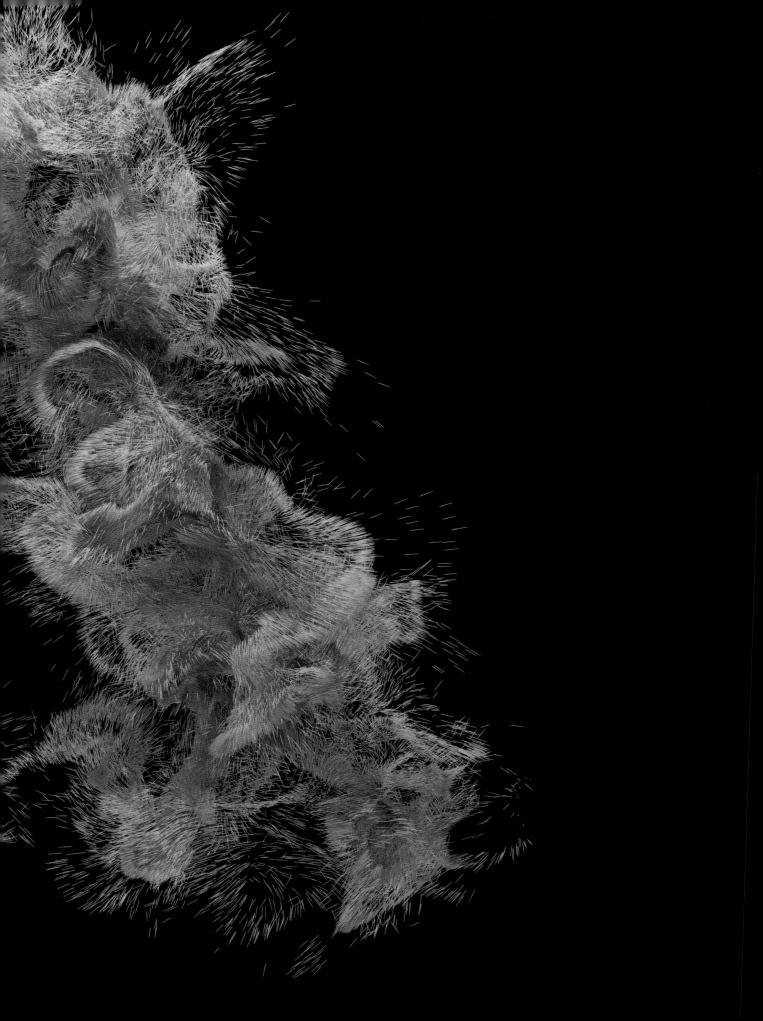

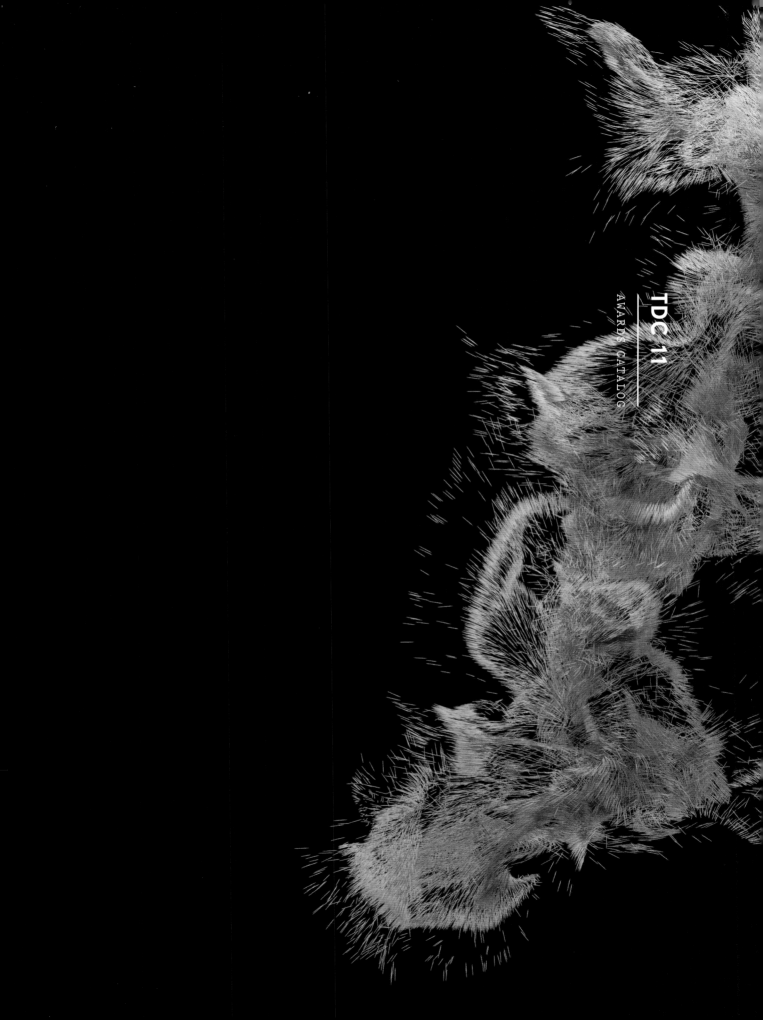

TDC 11

AWARDS CATALOG

TDC 11
AWARDS
CATALOG

The book in your hands is the thirty-fifth hardbound record of the winners of the annual TDC competitions. Before producing hardbound annuals, the Type Directors Club recorded its competition winners in more modest booklets, which were numbered separately. Although this book has the title *Typography 35*, the communication design competition it records is actually the club's sixtieth.

Since 2005, we have been reprinting the old, rare competition booklets within our annuals, to serve as inspiration for designers and as a resource for historians. Reproduced here is the 1965 TDC11 booklet. Among the winning works it shows are iconic designs by Milton Glaser, Herb Lubalin, Seymour Chwast, Elaine Lustig Cohen, Aaron Burns, George Tscherny, and Louis Dorfsman. The six competition judges are shown in white shirts and ties, intently analyzing entries. Three of them were "Mad Men," and many of the winning entries were advertisements, reminding us of the close connection between the young TDC and the advertising business in New York City. This was the age of clever slogans and bold headlines in advertising, and sometimes ads were purely typographic, such as the famous public service tagline "I quit school when I were sixteen," designed by Dick Lopez.

Both TDC11 and *Typography 35* serve as valuable records of the ongoing work of the Type Directors Club to support excellence in typography worldwide.

— The Board of Directors / *Type Directors Club*

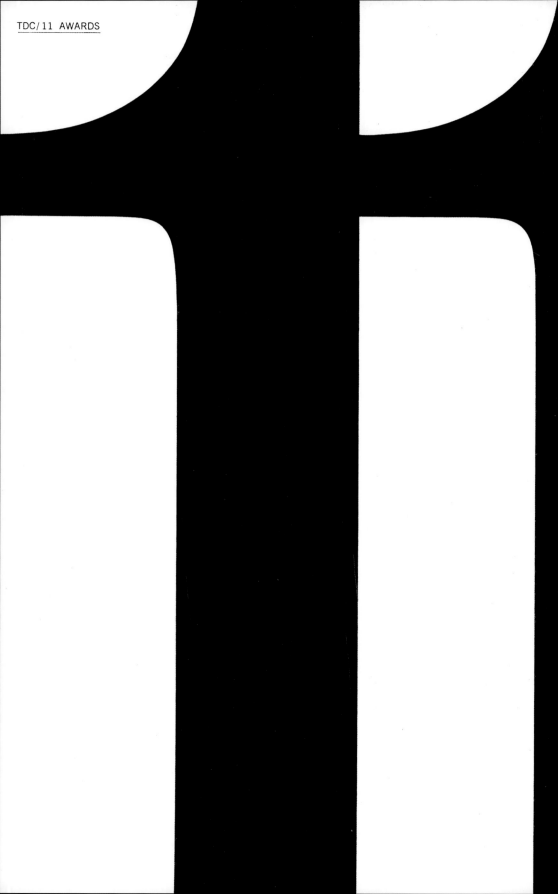

The 11th annual awards exhibition is sponsored by
the Type Directors Club of New York and will be held
at the Mead Library of Ideas, 200 Park Avenue,
New York City, May 5th to 28th, 1965.

The pieces selected for the exhibit are an excellent
sample of fine typographic application. The exhibit
shows that the designer is more and more concerned
with communicating an idea than with showing-off his
graphic technique. He is more often heard than
seen, and yet, all the qualities of craftsmanship and
excellent design are still there.

We thank every participant from United States,
Canada, England and Germany for contributing
to the exhibit and for helping us examine and document
the state of typography today.

Al Robinson, Chairman for the TDC/11 Committee.

MURRAY JACOBS
SAADYAH MAXIMON
DON FINCK

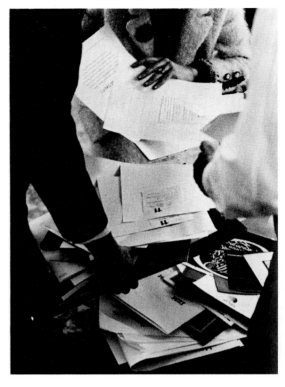

MURRAY JACOBS
MARTY SOLOMON
SAADYAH MAXIMON
DON FINCK

WILLIAM SEKULAR
GERRY ANDREOZZI
HERB LUBALIN

HERSCHEL WARTIK
MURRAY JACOBS, MARTY SOLOMON,
SAADYAH MAXIMON
DON FINCK

THE JURY:

GERRY ANDREOZZI: V.P.-Art Director—Gilbert Advertising
MURRAY JACOBS: V.P.-Art Director—Jacobs Gibson & Vogel, Inc.
HERB LUBALIN: President—Herb Lubalin, Inc.
SAADYAH MAXIMON: Typographic Consultant—Graphic Arts Typographers, Inc.
WILLIAM SEKULAR: Director of Typography—Benton & Bowles
MARTIN SOLOMON: Design and Typographic Consultant—Royal Typographers

2
Designer: Bill Wurtzel
Type Director: Bill Wurtzel
Typographer: E. J. Creedon
Client/Agency: Milford McDonald

3
Designer: Jacqueline S. Casey
Type Director: Jacqueline S. Casey
Typographer: Machine Composition Company
Client/Agency: M.I.T. Association of
Women Students

1
Designer: Martin Solomon
Type Director: Martin Solomon
Typographer: Royal Typographers
Client/Agency: Hy Abbott/Henry Sandbank

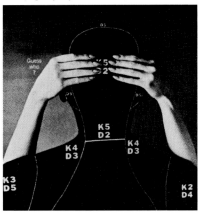

Designer: Mo Lebowitz
Type Director: Mo Lebowitz
Typographer: The Antique Press
Client/Agency: The Antique Press
5

Designer: Appelbaum and Curtis
Type Director: Appelbaum and Curtis
Typographer: Linocraft, Inc.
Client/Agency: E. P. Dutton & Company
Applebaum & Curtis
4

Designer: Reginald Troncone
Type Director: Reginald Troncone
Typographer: Graphic Arts Typographers, Inc.
Client/Agency: Chemical Engineering
Muller, Jordan & Herrick
6

7
Designer: Dick Lopez
Type Director: Dick Lopez
Typographer: Lettering Inc. and Aaron Burns
Client/Agency: Kinney Corporation,
Smith/Greenland Co., Inc.

9
Designer: Robert Paganucci
Type Director: Robert Paganucci
Typographer: Graphic Arts
Client/Agency: International Business
Machines Corporation

8
Designer: Mo Lebowitz
Type Director: Mo Lebowitz
Typographer: Royal Typographers/The Composing Room
Client/Agency: Standard Oil Co. (N.J.)
Needham, Harper & Steers

Designer: Roger Ferriter
Type Director: Milt Zudeck
Typographer: Ad Agency Service
Client/Agency: Coca Cola/McCann-Erickson
10

Designer: Mo Lebowitz
Type Director: Mo Lebowitz
Typographer: The Antique Press
11

12
Designer: Bob Farber—Norm Citron
Typographer: Royal Typographers, Inc.
Client/Agency: Royal Typographers, Inc.

13
Designer: James J. Broderick
Type Director: James J. Broderick
Typographer: Haber
Client/Agency:
Sybil Ives Inc.

14
Designer: John M. Fraioli
Type Director: Anthony J. Teano
Typographer: General Composition
Client/Agency: Hoffmann-LaRoche Inc.
Marsteller Inc. [1]

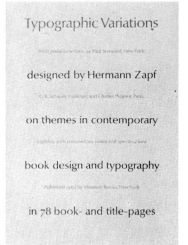

Designer: F. Newfeld
Type Director: F. Newfeld
Typographer: F. Newfeld
Client/Agency: McClelland & Stewart Ltd.
17

Designer: James Yates
Type Director: James Yates
Typographer: The Typographic Service Company
Client/Agency: Reilly Electrotype Company
15

Designer: Hermann Zapf
Typographer: Hermann Zapf
Client/Agency: Museum Books, Inc.
16

18
Designer: Herb Lubalin
Type Director: Herb Lubalin
Letterforms: Tom Carnase
Client/Agency: Bonder & Carnase Studio
Herb Lubalin Inc.

19
Designer: Herb Lubalin
Type Director: Herb Lubalin
Letterforms: Tom Carnase
Client/Agency: American Institute of Graphic Arts
Herb Lubalin Inc.

20
Designer: Leonard Jossel
Type Director: Leonard Jossel
Typographer: Riegert & Kennedy Inc.
Client/Agency: Venture Magazine

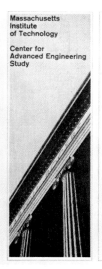

Designer: Ron Keller
Type Director: Ron Keller
Typographer: Ron Keller
Client/Agency: Ron Keller
21

Designer: Santo Pulise
Type Director: Santo Pulise
Typographer: Royal
'Client/Agency: L. Rose & Company, Ltd.
Erwin Wasey, Ruthrauff & Ryan Inc.
22

Designer: Ralph Coburn
Type Director: Ralph Coburn
Typographer: Machine Composition Company
Client/Agency: Center for Advanced Engineering
Study/MIT
23

24
Designer: Amil Gargano
Type Director: Amil Gargano
Typographer: Tri-Arts Press
Client/Agency: SAS/Carl Ally Inc.

25
Designer: Herb Lubalin
Type Director: Herb Lubalin
Letterforms: Tom Carnase
Typographer: Morgan Press
Client/Agency: Herb Lubalin Inc./Drum Litho

26
Designer: Sheldon Cotler
Type Director: Sheldon Cotler
Typographer: Typographic Service Inc.
Client/Agency: Time Magazine

Designer: Reginald Troncone
Type Director: Bernard Hirsch
Typographer: Graphic Arts Typographers, Inc.
Client/Agency: Sweet's Catalog Service
Muller, Jordan & Herrick
27

Designer: Al Robinson
Type Director: Al Robinson
Typographer: Composing Room
Client/Agency: Janet Robinson
28

Designer: Rodger Johnson
Type Director: Hector Huerta
Carlos Huerta
Typographer: Monsen
Typographers
Client/Agency: The Art Group
29

31
Designer: Erich Schulz-Anker
Type Director: Erich Schulz-Anker
Typographer: Erich Schulz-Anker
H. Heiderhoff
Client/Agency: D. Stempel, AG

30
Designer: Alex Tsao
Type Director: Alex Tsao
Typographer: Ad Compositers &
The Earl Hays Press
Client/Agency: Higby & Horsby Ltd.
Bernard Nagler Assoc.

32
Designer: Herbert Cytryn
Type Director: Herbert Cytryn
Typographer: Metro
Client/Agency: American Broadcasting Company

Designer: Tony Zamora
Type Director: Tom Carnase
Typographer: Graphic Arts
Client/Agency: New York Herald Tribune
34

Designer: Erich Schulz-Anker
Type Director: Erich Schulz-Anker
Typographer: Erich Schulz-Anker
Client/Agency: D. Stempel AG
35

Designer: Olaf Lev
Type Director: Olaf Lev
Typographer: Lettera Layoutsatz
Client/Agency: Gebr. Schmidt GmbH
33

37
Designer: Rosaline Hagler
Type Director: Ron Barger
Typographer: Haber
Client/Agency: Redbook Magazine

36
Designer: William Gilmore
Type Director: Jeremy John
Typographer: Thomas P. Henry Company
Client/Agency: Pitman-Moore
MacManus, John & Adams, Inc.

38
Designer: Elaine Lustig Cohen
Type Director: Elaine Lustig Cohen
Typographer: Cover—Aaron Burns Inc.;
Inside—Clarke & Way Inc.
Client/Agency: The Jewish Museum

Designer: Elaine Lustig Cohen
Type Director: Elaine Lustig Cohen
Typographer: Clarke & Way Inc.
Client/Agency: The Jewish Museum
40

Designer: Ron Barger
Type Director: Ron Barger
Typographer: Provident
Client/Agency: Redbook Magazine
41

Designer: Olaf Lev
Type Director: Fritz Hofrichter
Typographer: Lettera Layoutsatz
Client/Agency: Farbwerke Hoelst AG
39

43
Designer: Herb Lubalin
Type Director: Herb Lubalin
Typographer: Graphic Arts Typographers Inc.
Client/Agency: Strathmore Paper Company
Lampert

42
Designer: Stephen Ancona
Type Director: Ancona/Gianakos Inc.
Typographer: John Sagan
Client/Agency: Pellegrini/Ancona/Gianakos Inc.

44
Designer: Eiko Emori
Type Director: Eiko Embri
Typographer: Eiko Emori
Client/Agency: Yale University School of Art and Architecture

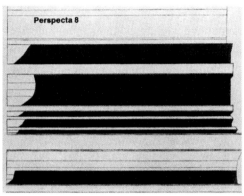

Designer: Seymour Chwast/Milton Glaser
Type Director: Tom Gorey
Typographer: Haber, Graphic Arts, etc.
Client/Agency: Champion Papers, Inc.
Needham, Louis & Brorby, Inc.
45

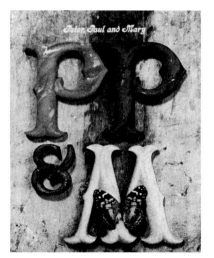

Designer: Milton Glaser
Type Director: Milton Glaser
Typographer: Metro
Client/Agency: Albert B. Grossman Management
Push Pin Studios
46

Designer: Sam Smidt
Type Director: Sam Smidt
Typographer: Spartan Typographers
Client/Agency: Stanford School Planning
Laboratory/Sam Smidt Graphic Designers
47

49
Designer: Harold Peter
Type Director: Harold Peter
Typographer: Harold Peter
Client/Agency: Hallmark, Kansas City

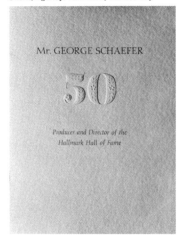

50
Designer: Louis Dorfsman/Sheila Green
Type Director: Louis Dorfsman
Typographer: T.P.I.
Client/Agency: CBS Television Network

51
Designer: Robert Pliskin
Type Director: William L. Sekuler
Typographer: Royal Typographers
Client/Agency: Benton & Bowles Inc.

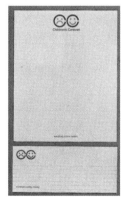

Designer: George A. Zariff
Type Director: George A. Zariff
Typographer: Southern New
England Typographic Service
Client/Agency: Children's Caravan
52

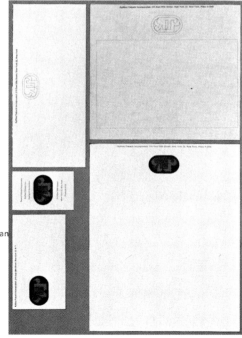

Designer: Reynold Ruffins/Simms Talack
Type Director: Reynold Ruffins/Simms Talack
Typographer: Empire Typographers Inc.
Client/Agcy: Ruffins/Talack
53

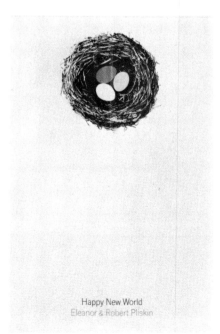

Happy New World
Eleanor & Robert Pliskin

Designer: Robert Pliskin
Type Director: William L. Sekuler
Client/Agency: Benton & Bowles, Inc.
54

55
Designer: Ken Saco/Curt Lowey/Arno Sternglass
Type Director: Ken Saco, Curt Lowey
Typographer: Rapid Typographers
Client/Agency: MGM Television/Ken Saco Assoc. Inc.

56
Designer: Olaf and Karin Leu
Type Director: Erich Schulz-Anker
Typographer: Leu
Client/Agency: D. Stempel AG

57
Designer: Mort Rubenstein/David November
Type Director: Mort Rubenstein
Typographer: Aaron Burns Inc.
Illustrator: Charles B. Slackman
Client/Agency: CBS Television Network

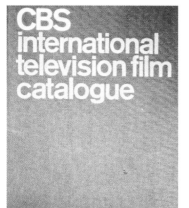

Designer: Peter Rauch
Type Director: Mort Rubenstein
Typographer: Composing Room Inc.
Client/Agency: CBS Films
58

Designer: William Wurtzel
Type Director: Mort Rubenstein
Letterforms: Verdun P. Cook
Typographer: Typography Place Inc.
Client/Agency: CBS Television
59

Designer: Fred Mackie
Type Director: Fred Mackie
Typographer: Graphic Arts Typographers Inc.
Client/Agency: Fifth Avenue Club
Graphic Arts Typographers Inc.
60

68
Designer: Milton Glaser
Type Director: Milton Glaser
Typographer: Metro Typographers
Client/Agency: K & F Productions/Push Pin Studios

67
Designer: Onofrio Paccione
Type Director: Sal Lodico
Typographer: Royal
Client/Agency: American Cancer Society/
Leber, Katz, Paccione

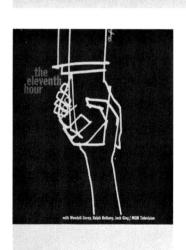

Designer: Dick Hess
Type Director: Dick Hess
Typographer: Franklin
Client/Agency: National Geographic/Van Brunt & Co.
70

Designer: Sy Schreckingin
Type Director: Ed Provost
Typographer: Tri Arts Press
Client/Agency: Schraffts/Marschalk Co.
71

Designer: Ken Saco/Curt Lowey/Arno Steinglass
Type Director: Ken Saco/Curt Lowey
Typographer: Boro Typographers
Client/Agency: MGM Television/
Ken Saco Assoc. Inc.
69

73
Designer: Al Bensusen
Type Director: Milt Zudeck/Lou Lepis
Typographer: Royal
Client/Agency: Minute Maid/McCann-Erickson Inc.

74
Designer: Amil Gargano
Type Director: Amil Gargano
Typographer: Tri-Arts Press
Client/Agency: Quality Importers Inc.—
Old Bushmills/Carl Ally Inc.

72
Designer: Fran Elfenbein
Type Director: Fran Elfenbein
Typographer: Typography Place Inc.
Client/Agency: World Telegram/
Warren, Muller & Dolobowsky

Designer: Tony Zamora
Type Director: Olie Olafson
Typographer: Graphic Arts
Client/Agency: New York Herald Tribune
75

Designer: Gennaro Andreozzi
Type Director: Gennaro Andreozzi
Typographer: Provident
Client/Agency: Guerlain/Gilbert Adv.
76

Designer: Bob Wilvers
Type Director: Bob Wilvers
Typographer: Tri-Arts Press
Client/Agency: Salada Foods Inc./Carl Ally Inc.
77

78
Designer: Herb Lubalin
Type Director: Herb Lubalin
Typography: Aaron Burns & Co. Inc.
Client/Agency: Stan Harris/Herb Lubalin Inc.

79
Designer: Roger Trlak
Type Director: Roger Trlak
Typographer: Monsen Typographers
Client/Agency: WBBM-TV/Martin-Trlak, Inc.

Designer: Lawrence Leblang
Type Director: Klaus F. Schmidt
Typographer: Chris Olsen/Eisenman & Enock
Client/Agency: Sports Illustrated/Young & Rubicam Inc.
82

Designer: Louis Dorfsman/Ed Lee
Type Director: Louis Dorfsman/Ed Lee
Typographer: Aaron Burns
Client/Agency: CBS News
80

Designer: Amil Gargano
Type Director: Amil Gargano
Typographer: Tri-Arts Press
Client/Agency: Quality Importers Inc.—
Old Bushmills/Carl Ally Inc.
81

83
Designer: Irwin Schonhorn
Type Director: Irwin Schonhorn
Typographer: Empire Type
Client/Agency: MBA Music Inc.

84
Designer: Ron Barrett
Type Director: Klaus F. Schmidt
Typographer: Kurt H. Volk/Morgan Press
Client/Agency: The American Wool Council/
Young & Rubicam Inc.

85
Designer: Ralph Pucci
Type Director: Ralph Pucci
Typographer: Haber
Client/Agency: S. A. Schonbrunn & Co. Inc./
Hicks & Greist, Inc.

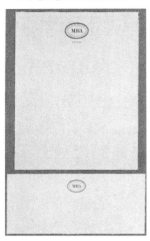

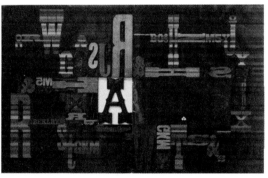

Designer: John Russell
Type Director: M. F. McGrew
Typographer: Woodtype: Charles McHugh, Text: Herbick & Held
Client/Agency: Alcoa/Ketchum, Macleod & Grove Inc.
86

Designer: Gennaro Andreozzi
Type Director: Gennaro Andreozzi
Typographer: Provident
Client/Agency: Gold Seal/Gilbert Adv.
87

Designer: Thomas F. Coleman
Type Director: Thomas F. Coleman
Typographer: Schmidt Printing
Client/Agency: IBM Design Center,
Rochester, Minnesota
88

89
Designer: Harry Jacobs
Type Director: Harry Jacobs
Typographer: Harry Jacobs
Client/Agency: Cargill, Wilson & Acree, Inc.

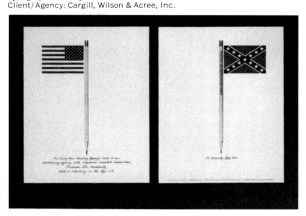

90
Designer: Muts Yasumura
Type Director: Klaus F. Schmidt
Typographer: Aaron Burns & Co./Chris Olsen
Client/Agency: Young & Rubicam Inc.

91
Designer: Lou Frimkess/
Advertising Designers
Type Director: Lou Frimkess/
Advertising Designers
Typographer: Advertising Designers Inc.
Client/Agency: Jeffries Banknote Co./
W. Dent Dowler Adv.

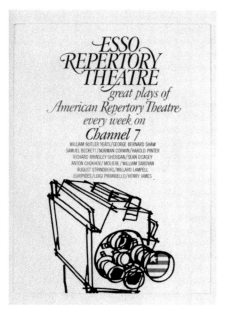

Designer: Mo Lebowitz
Type Director: Mo Lebowitz
Typographer: Royal Typographers/
The Composing Room
Client/Agency: Standard Oil Co./
Needham, Harper & Steers
92

Designer: Burt Klein
Type Director: Burt Klein
Typographer: Aaron Burns
Client/Agency: Smith/Greenland Co. Inc.
93

Designer: Bob Salpeter
Type Director: Bob Salpeter
Typographer: Diamant
Client/Agency: IBM World Trade Corp.
94

95
Designer: Martin Freidman
Type Director: Martin Friedman
Typographer: Empire Typographers
Client/Agency: Empire Typographers Inc.

96
Designer: Tony Zamora
Type Director: Beverly Zakarian
Typographer: Graphic Arts
Client/Agency: New York Herald Tribune

97
Designer: Tony Zamora
Type Director: Olie Olafson
Typographer: Graphic Arts
Client/Agency: New York Herald Tribune

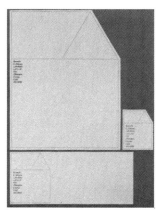

Designer: Hugh Michaelson
Type Director: Hugh Michaelson
Typographer: Cooper & Beatty Ltd.
Client/Agency: Toronto Star Limited
98

Designer: Rodger Johnson
Type Director: Rodger Johnson
Typographer: John F. Mawson Co.
Client/Agency: Kenneth C. Johnson
99

Designer: Rocco Campanelli
Type Director: Lou Lepis
Typographer: Tri-Arts Press
Client/Agency: Buick/McCann-Erickson Inc.
100

101
Designer: Bob Dolobowsky
Type Director: Bob Dolobowsky
Typographer: Superior
Client/Agency: Seneca/
Warren, Muller & Dolobowsky

102
Designer: Edward G. Foss
Type Director: Edward G. Foss
Typographer: Edward G. Foss
Client/Agency: University Press of Virginia

103
Designer: Abe Seltzer/Howard Menken
Type Director: Abe Seltzer/Howard Menken
Typographer: Royal
Client/Agency: Eaton Laboratories/
Robert E. Wilson Inc.

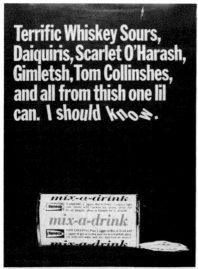

The new frozen concentrate from **Seneca** for people
who like to drink 'em...but hate to mix 'em.

Designer: Tom Chambers
Type Director: Victor Stein
Typographer: Tom Chambers/
Victor Stein
Client/Agency: The Type House
104

Designer: Tom Getsmar/Jack Hough
Type Director: Tom Getsmar
Typographer: Progressive
Client/Agency: Chermayeff & Getsmar
105

Designer: Herb Lubalin/Lou Dorfsman
Type Director: Herb Lubalin/Lou Dorfsman
Typographer: The Composing Room
Client/Agency: CBS News
106

Designer: Louis Dorfsman/
Sheila Green
Type Director: Louis Dorfsman/
Sheila Green
Typographer. Aaron Burns & Co.
Client/Agency: CBS News
107

108
Designer: John Graham
Typographer: Empire
Client/Agency: NBC

109
Designer: Roger Ferriter
Type Director: Roger Ferriter
Typographer: Roger Ferriter/Tri-Arts Press
Client/Agency: Roger Ferriter

110
Designer: William R. Farrell
Type Director: William R. Farrell
Typographer: Lino Craft Inc.
Client/Agency: IBM

Designer: Push Pin Studios, Milton Glaser
Type Director: Milton Glaser
Typographer: Graphic Arts Typographers Inc.
Client/Agency: Strathmore Paper Company/Lampert
111

Designer: Ralph Coburn
Type Director: Ralph Coburn
Typographer: Machine Composition Company
Client/Agency: M.I.T. Department of Physics
112

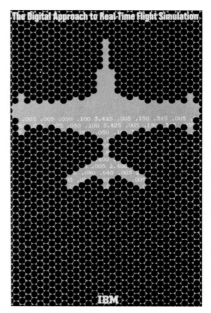

Designer: Clarence Lee
Type Director: Clarence Lee
Typographer: Clarence Lee
Client/Agency: IBM
113

114
Designer: Robert M. Jones
Type Director: Robert M. Jones
Typographer: Robert M. Jones
Client/Agency: Gladhand Press

We are hoping to see you at the Tenth Annual
Glad Hand Press Graphic Arts Festival and
Exhibition Saturday, August First, from Four p.m.
The occasion will be celebrated in the back-yard
at Seventy-Seven Rachelle Avenue, Stamford,
Connecticut. As is the custom there will be snacks
and booze. Clean sneakers and please, Ladies,
roll up your stockings, the Journal of CA will
be reporting and photographing the Gala.

115
Designer: Harvey Gabor
Type Director: Verdun Cook
Letterforms: Verdun P. Cook
Typographer: Typographic Craftsmen
Client/Agency: Redbook Magazine

116
Designer: William Wurtzel
Type Director: Mort Rubenstein
Letterforms: Verdun P. Cook
Client/Agency: CBS Television Network

Designer: Gennaro Andreozzi
Type Director: Gennaro Andreozzi
Typographer: A1
Client/Agency: London Fog/Gilbert Adv.
117

Designer: Harvey Gabor
Type Director: Verdun Cook
Letterforms: Verdun P. Cook
Typographer: Typographic Craftsmen
Client/Agency: Redbook Magazine
118

Designer: Louis Dorfsman
Type Director: Louis Dorfsman
Typographer: Aaron Burns & Co.
Client/Agency: CBS News
119

125
Designer: Lawrence Ratzkin
Type Director: Lydia Fruhauf
Typographer: Lawrence Ratzkin
Client/Agency: William Morrow & Co.

126
Designer: Lee Epstein
Type Director: Al Robinson
Typographer: Typo Craftsmen
Client/Agency: Volkswagen/Doyle Dane Bernbach

Designer: Tom Geismar/Jack Hough
Type Director: Tom Geismar
Typographer: Progressive
Client/Agency: Chermayeff & Geismar Assoc.
128

Designer: Bernie Zlotnick
Type Director: Bernie Zlotnick
Typographer: Aaron Burns & Co.
Client/Agency: School of Visual Arts/
Katz, Jacobs & Zlotnick
129

Designer: Lydia Fruhauf
Type Director: Lydia Fruhauf
Typographer: Lydia Fruhauf
Client/Agency: William Morrow & Co.
127

130
Designer: Peter Rauch
Type Director: Ted Andresakes
Typographer: Typography Place Inc.
Client/Agency: WCBS-TV

131
Designer: Richard Laurenzi
Type Director: James H. McWilliams
Typographer: Richard Laurenzi
Client/Agency: Philadelphia College of Art

132
Designer: Milton Glaser
Type Director: Milton Glaser
Typographer: Weltz Ad Service
Client/Agency: Push Pin Studios

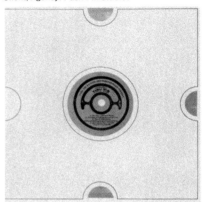

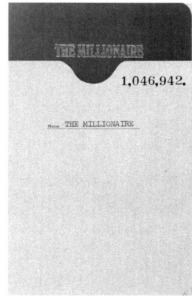

Designer: Robertson-Montgomery
Type Director: Robertson-Montgomery
Typographer: Spartan Typographers
Client/Agency: Polytron Company,
Richmond, California
133

Designer: Markus Low
Typographer: Empire Typographers
Client/Agency: Geigy Chemical Corporation
134

Designer: Peter Rauch
Type Director: Ted Andresakes
Letterforms: Tom Carnase
Typographer: Typography Place Inc.
Client/Agency: CBS Films
135

136
Designer: John Massey/Bob Lipman
Type Director: John Massey/Bob Lipman
Typographer: Frederic Ryder
Client/Agency: Container Corporation of
America/Center for Advanced Research
in Design

137
Designer: Mo Lebowitz
Type Director: Mo Lebowitz
Typographer: The Antique Press
Client/Agency: The Antique Press

138
Designer: Muts Yasumura
Type Director: Mario Fiore
Typographer: Chris Olsen
Client/Agency: Young & Rubicam Inc.

Designer: James Cross/Don Handel
Type Director: James Cross
Typographer: Creative Type
Client/Agency: California Chamber Symphony/
James Cross Design Office
141

Designer: John Graham/Herb Reade
Type Director: John Graham/Herb Reade
Typographer: Empire
Client/Agency: NBC
140

Designer: Ivan Chermayeff
Type Director: Ivan Chermayeff
Typographer: Clarke & Way
Client/Agency: Chermayeff & Geismar
139

142
Designer: Herb Lubalin/Alan Peckolick cvr.
Type Director: Herb Lubalin/
Alan Peckolick cvr.
Client/Agency: Fact Magazine Inc.

143
Designer: Herb Lubalin
Type Director: Herb Lubalin
Client/Agency: Fact Magazine Inc./
Herb Lubalin Inc.

144
Designer: Herb Lubalin
Type Director: Herb Lubalin
Client/Agency: Fact Magazine Inc./
Herb Lubalin Inc.

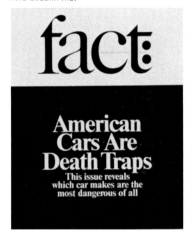

Type Director: Mo Lebowitz
Typographer: The Antique Press
Client/Agency: The Antique Press
145

Designer: Charles Haftel
Type Director: Charles Haftel
Typographer: Franklin Typographers
Client/Agency: Franklin Typographers
146

Designer: Roger Ferriter
Type Director: Milt Zudeck
Typographer: Tri-Arts Press
Client/Agency: John Hancock/
McCann-Erickson
147

148
Designer: Herb Lubalin
Type Director: Herb Lubalin
Client/Agency: Fact Magazine Inc./
Herb Lubalin Inc.

149
Designer: Herb Lubalin
Type Director: Herb Lubalin
Client/Agency: Fact Magazine Inc./
Herb Lubalin Inc.

150
Designer: Herb Lubalin
Type Director: Herb Lubalin
Client/Agency: Fact Magazine Inc./
Herb Lubalin Inc.

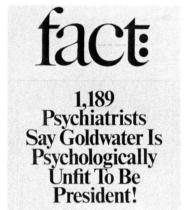

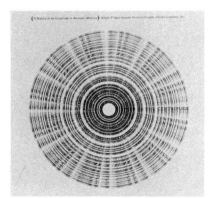

Designer: Lewis Van der beken
Type Director: Lewis Van der beken
Typographer: Typographic Service Co.
Client/Agency: Douglas Aircraft Company
Missile & Space Systems Division
152

Designer: John Baeder
Type Director: John Baeder
Typographer: Chuck Robertson/Tin Horn Press
Client/Agency: John Baeder
153

Designer: Frank Kirk
Typographer: Franklin Typo
Client/Agency: Rob Roy/J. Trahey
151

156
Designer: Eileen Platt
Type Director: Eileen Platt
Typographer: Composing Room
Client/Agency: Borg Fabrics/
Douglas Simon Adv. Inc.

154
Type Director: Bradford Boston
Type Director: Bradford Boston/Advertising Designers
Typographer: Advertising Designers Inc.
Client/Agency: Beckman Instruments Inc./Advertising Designers

155
Designer: Onofrio Paccione
Type Director: Sal Lodico
Typographer: Royal
Client/Agency: LKP/Leber Katz Paccione

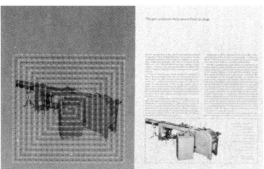

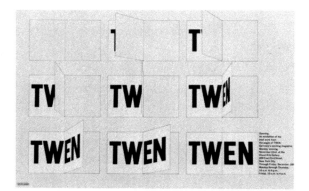

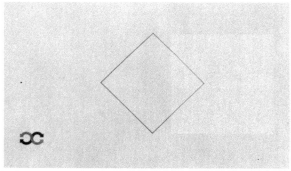

Designer: Milton Glaser
Type Director: Milton Glaser
Typographer: Metro
Client/Agency: School of Visual Arts/Push Pin Studios
157

Designer: George Rosenfeld
Type Director: George Rosenfeld
Typographer: Empire
Client/Agency: American Telephone & Telegraph/Documenta Inc.
158

159
Designer: Carl Brett
Type Director: Carl Brett
Typographer: Howarth & Smith Monotype Ltd.
Client/Agency: Typographic Designers of
Canada

160
Designer: Ted Andresakes
Type Director: Ted Andresakes
Typographer: Typography Place Inc.
Client/Agency: CBS Television Stations
National Sales

161
Designer: John Massey
Type Director: John Massey
Typographer: Beck Engraving Company
Client/Agency: Container Corporation of America/
Center for Advanced Research in Design

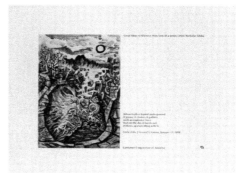

Designer: Harvey Gabor
Type Director: Verdun Cook
Typographer: Typographic Craftsmen
Client/Agency: Redbook Magazine
162

Designer: Allan Buitekant
Type Director: Irmari Weinstein-Nacht
Typographer: Provident
Client/Agency: Chemstrand/
Doyle Dane & Bernbach
163

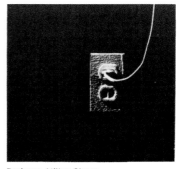

Designer: Milton Glaser
Type Director: Milton Glaser
Typographer: Metro
Client/Agency: Krasner Gallery/
Push Pin Studios
164

165
Designer: Hugh Michaelson
Type Director: Hugh Michaelson
Typographer: Cooper & Beatty Ltd.
Client/Agency: Toronto Star Ltd.

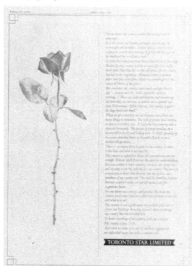

166
Designer: Louis Dorfsman/Ed Lee
Type Director: Louis Dorfsman/Ed Lee
Typographer: T.P.I.
Client/Agency: CBS News

167
Designer: Herb Lubalin
Type Director: Herb Lubalin
Typographer: Aaron Burns & Co. Inc./
John Pistilli (type face)
Client/Agency: Visual Graphic Corporation/
Herb Lubalin Inc.

Designer: Elton Robinson
Type Director: Elton Robinson
Typographer: John Pistilli
Client/Agency: Horizon Magazine/American Heritage Pub. Co. Inc.
168

Designer: Charles Kintzing
Type Director: William L. Sekuler
Typographer: Typographic Service Co.
Client/Agency: IBM/Benton & Bowles
169

170
Designer: Burt Purmell
Type Director: Burt Purmell
Typographer: Provident
Client/Agency: Berlitz/Gilbert Adv.

171
Designer: Verdun Cook
Type Director: Verdun Cook
Typographer: Typographic Craftsmen
Client/Agency: Redbook Magazine

Designer: Milton Glaser
Type Director: Milton Glaser
Typographer: Metro
Client/Agency: Viking Press/Push Pin Studios
172

Designer: Verdun Cook
Type Director: Verdun Cook
Typographer: Typographic Craftsmen
Client/Agency: Redbook Magazine
173

174
Designer: John Alcorn
Type Director: Larry Ottino
Typographer: Morgan Press
Client/Agency: Ad Agencies/Headliners

175
Designer: Larry Ottino (promotion)/
John Alcorn (catalog)
Type Director: Larry Ottino
Typographer: Headliners International
Client/Agency: Ad Agencies/Headliners

176
Designer: Milton Glaser
Type Director: Milton Glaser
Typographer: Metro
Client/Agency: Holt, Rinehart & Winston/
Push Pin Studios

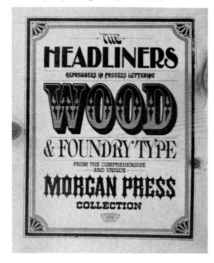

Designer: Theo Welti
Typographer: Empire
Client/Agency: Geigy Chemical Corp.
177

Designer: Sheldon J. Streisand
Type Director: Sheldon J. Streisand
Typographer: Sheldon J. Streisand/U.S. Post Office
Client/Agency: The Streisand Family
178

Designer: Carl Brett
Type Director: Carl Brett
Typographer: Howarth & Smith Monotype Ltd.
Client/Agency: Howarth & Smith Monotype Ltd.
179

180
Designer: Carl Brett
Type Director: Carl Brett
Typographer: Howarth & Smith Monotype Ltd.
Client/Agency: Howarth & Smith Monotype Ltd.

181
Designer: Verdun P. Cook
Type Director: Verdun P. Cook
Typographer: Typographic Craftsmen Inc.
Client/Agency: Art Direction Magazine

182
Designer: Jay Novak
Type Director: Jay Novak
Typographer: Vernon Simpson
Client/Agency: Northrop Corp.

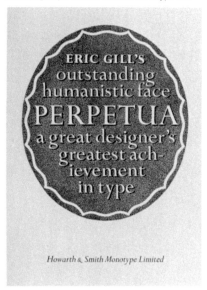

Designer: Graduate Class, Design Program
Type Director: George Sadek
Typographer: Graduate Class, Design Program
Client/Agency: Indiana University
184

Designer: Herb Lubalin/Lou Dorfsman
Type Director: Herb Lubalin/Lou Dorfsman
Typographer: Aaron Burns
Client/Agency: CBS News/
Herb Lubalin Inc.
185

Designer: Herb Levitt
Type Director: Mort Rubenstein
Typographer: Typography Place Inc.
Client/Agency: CBS Films
183

186
Designer: Bernard Gilwit
Type Director: Irmari Weinstein-Nacht
Typographer: Ad Agency
Client/Agency: Bulova/Doyle Dane Bernbach

187
Designer: William Cadge
Type Director: Verdun Cook
Letterforms: Verdun P. Cook
Typographer: Typographic Craftsmen
Client/Agency: Redbook Magazine

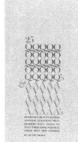

Designer: Page Graphics
Type Director: Page Graphics
Typographer: Empire
Client/Agency: Weiskopf & Pickworth,
Consulting Engineers/Page Graphics
188

Designer: J. Supliva/Assoc. Adv. & Des.
Type Director: J. Supliva
Client/Agency: Canada Dry/
Assoc. Adv. & Design
189

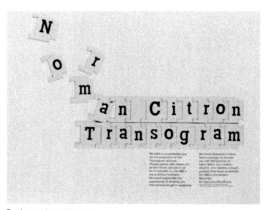

Designer: Larry Ottino
Type Director: Larry Ottino
Typographer: Ad Agencies Service Co.
Client/Agency: Ad Agencies/Headliners
190

191
Designer: Bill Tobias
Type Director: Robert M. Runyan
Typographer: Keith Axelson/Monsen
Client/Agency: General Precision/
Robert M. Runyon & Assoc.

192
Designer: Werner Pfeiffer
Type Director: Werner Pfeiffer
Typographer: Druckspeigel
Client/Agency: Pratt Institute

193
Designer: Herb Lubalin
Type Director: Herb Lubalin
Typographer: Aaron Burns & Company/John Pistilli (type face)
Client/Agency: Visual Graphic Corp./Herb Lubalin Inc.

Designer: Bob Dolobowsky
Type Director: Bob Dolobowsky
Typographer: Superior
Client/Agency: Lippes Bakeries Inc./Warren, Muller & Dolobowsky
195

Designer: William Wurtzel
Type Director: Mort Rubenstein
Typographer: Typography Place Inc.
Client/Agency: CBS Television Network
196

Designer: Peter Rauch
Type Director: Ted Andresakes
Typographer: Typography Place, Inc.
Client/Agency: CBS Television Stations,
National Sales
194

198
Designer: George Tscherny
Type Director: George Tscherny
Typographer: Haber
Client/Agency: The Aluminum Association

199
Designer: Elton S. Robinson
Type Director: Elton S. Robinson
Typographer: Case-Hoyt Corporation
Client/Agency: Morgan Guaranty Trust
Company of New York

197
Designer: Aaron Burns
Type Director: Aaron Burns
Typographer: Aaron Burns & Co. Inc.
Client/Agency: Aaron Burns & Co. Inc.

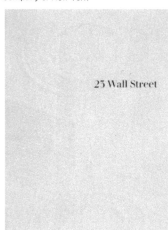

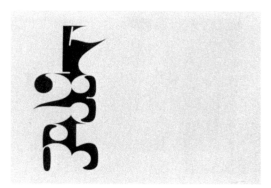

Designer: Robert Ross
Type Director: Robert Ross
Typographer: Rochester Monotype
Client/Agency: Printing Week Committee/Rumrill Co.
201

Designer: William Wurtzel
Type Director: Mort Rubenstein
Typographer: Typography Place Inc.
Client/Agency: CBS
200

Designer: Dick Hess
Type Director: Dick Hess
Typographer: Franklin
Client/Agency: National Geographic/
Van Brunt & Co.
202

203
Designer: Bill Tobias
Type Director: Robert M. Runyan
Typographer: Monsen
Client/Agency: General Precision/
Robert M. Runyon & Assoc.

204
Designer: Archie Apkarian
Type Director: Archie Apkarian
Typographer: Adcraft
Client/Agency: Union-Bag Camp
Paper Corp.

205
Designer: Michael Schacht
Type Director: Michael Schacht
Typographer: Gould
Client/Agency: Mead Papers/Library of Ideas

206
Designer: Lawrence Needleman
Typographer: J. F. Mawson Co.
Client/Agency: Neutrogen Corp.

Designer: Amil Gragano
Type Director: Amil Gargano
Typographer: Tri-Arts Press
Client/Agency: SAS/Carl Ally Inc.
207

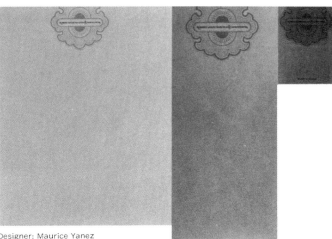

Designer: Maurice Yanez
Type Director: Robert M. Runyan
Typographer: Keith Axelson
Client/Agency: Robert Miles Runyan & Assoc.
208

209
Designer: Herb Lubalin
Type Director: Herb Lubalin
Letterforms: Tom Carnase
Client/Agency: Anthony Hyde, Jr./Herb Lubalin Inc.

210
Designer: Harvey Gabor
Type Director: Harvey Gabor
Typographer: Franklin
Client/Agency: The Society of Illustrators

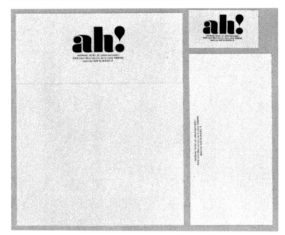

Designer: Peter Rauch
Type Director: Ted Andresakes
Typographer: Tri-Arts Press
Client/Agency: Merle Jones/CBS Television Studios
211

Designer: Reynold Ruffins/Simms Talack
Type Director: Reynold Ruffins/Simms Talack
Typographer: Empire
Client/Agency: New Vision Display Inc./Ruffins/Talack Inc.
212

213
Designer: Bernie Zlotnick
Type Director: Bernie Zlotnick
Typographer: Aaron Burns & Co.
Client/Agency: Pioneer-Moss/Katz, Jacobs & Zlotnick

214
Designer: Edward Nussbaum
Type Director: Edward Nussbaum
Typographer: Rapid Typographers
Client/Agency: Edward Nussbaum

216
Designer: Michael Schacht
Type Director: Michael Schacht
Typographer: Royal Typographers
Client/Agency: Mead Papers/Library of Ideas

215
Designer: Seymour Chwast/Milton Glaser
Type Director: Seymour Chwast/Milton Glaser
Typographer: Graphic Arts
Client/Agency: H. M. Storms Co./Push Pin Studios

"I quit school
when I were sixteen."

Designer: Dick Lopez
Type Director: Dick Lopez
Typographer: Graphic Arts
Client/Agency: Smith/Greenland Co., Inc.
218

217
Designer: Don Finck
Type Director: Don Finck
Typographer: Don Finck
Client/Agency: Melissa Kamille

Grateful acknowledgments are made to the following people for their contributions to the success of this exhibition: Tony Perrusi and his staff at Advertising Agency Typographers.
Michael Schacht and the staff of the Mead Library of Ideas, Mead Corporation.

TYPE DIRECTOR CLUB MEMBERSHIP/1965

ROBERT DAVID ADAMS	NICHOLAS A. COSTANTINO	AUSTIN GRANDJEAN	GILLIS L. LONG	GERARD J. O'NEILL
ROBERT J. ALDAG	FREEMAN CRAW	JAMES HALPIN	MELVIN LOOS	A. LARRY OTTINO
KELVIN J. ARDEN	JAMES A. CROSS	HOLLIS W. HOLLAND	JOHN H. LORD	DR. G. W. OVINK
JOSEPH S. ARMELLINO	THOMAS L. DARTNELL	ROBERT M. JONES	HERB LUBALIN	JOSEPH A. PASTORE
LEONARD F. BAHR	EUGENE DE LOPATECKI	R. RANDOLPH KARCH	EDGAR J. MALECKI	EUGENE P. PATTBERG
ARNOLD BANK	O. ALFRED DICKMAN	FREDERICK A. KELLAR	SOL MALKOFF	MICHAEL N. PELLEGRINO
EDWARD E. BENGUIAT	LOUIS DORFSMAN	LAWRENCE KESSLER	SAADYAH MAXIMON	JOHN A. PFRIENDER
PAUL A. BENNETT	CIEMAN DRIMER	WILBUR KING	JAMES H. McWILLIAMS	JAN VAN DER PLOEG
TED BERGMAN	CLAUDE ENDERS	ZOLTAN KISS	EGON MERKER	GEORGE A. PODORSON
AMOS G. BETHKE	EUGENE M. ETTENBERG	EMIL J. KLUMPP	FRANK MERRIMAN	FRANK E. POWERS
PIETER BRATTINGA	ROBERT FARBER	EDWIN B. KOLSBY	LAWRENCE J. MEYER	ERNST REICHL
JOHN H. BRIGHT	SIDNEY FEINBERG	RAY KOMAI	HERBERT M. MEYERS	ANDREW ROBERTS
BERNARD BRUSSEL-SMITH	ROGER G. FERRITER	RAY KONRAD	R. HUNTER MIDDLETON	AL ROBINSON
WILLIAM BUNDZAK	BRUCE FITZGERALD	BERNARD KRESS	FRANCIS MONACO	ROBERT ROCHE
AARON BURNS	GLENN FOSS	MORRIS LEBOWITZ	LLOYD BROOKS MORGAN	RICHARD VICTOR ROCHETTE
WILL BURTIN	VINCENT GIANNONE	ARTHUR B. LEE	TOBIAS MOSS	EDWARD RONDTHALER
TRAVIS CLIETT	LOU GLASSHEIM	ACY R. LEHMAN	LOUIS A. MUSTO	HERBERT M. ROSENTHAL
MAHLON A. CLINE	ARTHUR GLAZER	LOUIS LEPIS	ALEXANDER NESBITT	FRANK ROSSI
MARTIN CONNELL	WILLIAM P. GLEASON	CLIFTON LINE	OSCAR OGG	GUSTAVE L. SAELENS
VERDUN P. COOK	EDWARD M. GOTTSCHALL	WALLY LITTMAN	ROBERT J. O'DELL	LOU SARDELLA

JOHN N. SCHAEDLER
KLAUS F. SCHMIDT
JAMES M. SECREST
WILLIAM L. SEKULER
ARNOLD SHAW
JAN SJODAHL
MARTIN SOLOMON
JAMES SOMERVILLE
WALTER STANTON
HERBERT STOLTZ
OTTO STORCH
HERB STRASSER
WILLIAM A. STREEVER
ROBERT SUTTER
DAVID B. TASLER
WILLIAM TAUBIN
ANTHONY J. TEANO
BRADBURY THOMPSON
M. JOSEPH TRAUTWEIN
ABRAHAM A. VERSH

MEYER WAGMAN
BEATRICE WARDE
HERSCHEL WARTIK
STEVENS L. WATTS
JOSEPH F. WEILER
IRVING WERBIN
HOWARD WILCOX
HAL ZAMBONI
HERMANN ZAPF
ZEKE ZINER
MILTON K. ZUDECK

COMMITTEE FOR TDC/11

AL ROBINSON: Chairman
HERSCHEL WARTIK: Jury Chairman
VERDUN COOK: Design / LEN FURY, Associate
ARNOLD SHAW: Film Strip Design
AL ROBINSON: Direct Mail Design
JOE PASTORE: Exhibit Design
ARTHUR LEE: Exhibit Tour
DON FINCK: Entries
BOB CURRAN: Exhibit Liaison
JERRY SINGLETON: Executive Secretary

OFFICERS OF THE TYPE DIRECTORS CLUB

FRANK E. POWERS: Chairman, Board of Governors
MILTON K. ZUDECK: President
HERSHAL WARTIK: Vice President
TED BERGMAN: Treasurer
LLOYD BROOKS MORGAN: Corresponding Secretary
EDGAR J. MALECKI: Recording Secretary
FRANCIS L. MONACO: Member at Large
JERRY SINGLETON: Executive Secretary

CREDITS

Photographs: BOB NACHT
Copy Photographs: FINLEY-PHOTO
Typography: TYPOGRAPHIC CRAFTSMEN, INC.
Printing: PUBLICATION PRESS
Paper: MEAD PAPER COMPANY

OBJECTIVES OF THE TYPE DIRECTOR CLUB:

To raise the standards of typography and related fields of the graphic arts.
To provide the means for inspiration, stimulation, and research in typography and related graphic arts fields.
To aid in the completion and dissemination of knowledge concerning the use of type and related materials.
To cooperate with other organizations having similar aims and purposes.

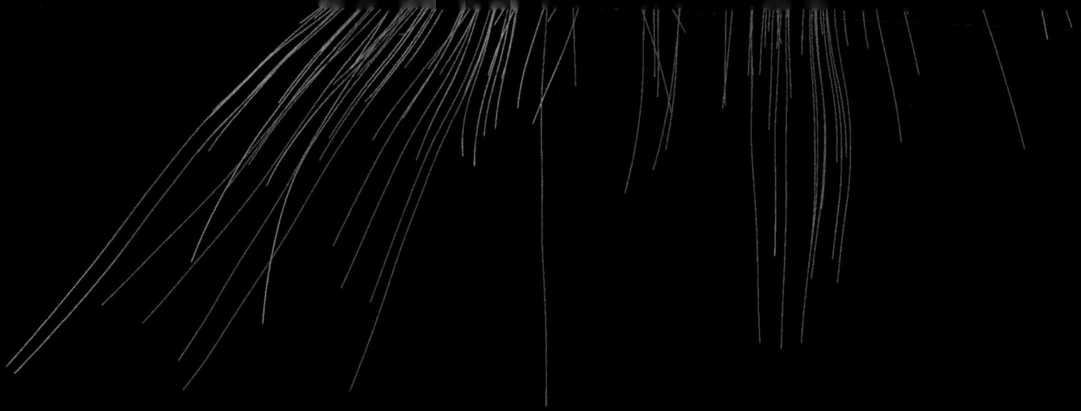

APPENDIX

TDC OFFICERS
MEMBERS
TYPE INDEX
GENERAL INDEX

James Montalbano
2002 / 2003

Gary Munch
2004 / 2005

Alex W. White
2006 / 2007

Charles Nix
2008 / 2009

Diego Vainesman
2010 / 2011

Graham Clifford
2012 / 2013

Matteo Bologna
2014

TDC MEDAL RECIPIENTS

Hermann Zapf
1967

R. Hunter Middleton
1968

Frank Powers
1971

Dr. Robert Leslie
1972

Edward Rondthaler
1975

Arnold Bank
1979

Georg Trump
1982

Paul Standard
1983

Herb Lubalin
1984 (posthumously)

Paul Rand
1984

Aaron Burns
1985

Bradbury Thompson
1986

Adrian Frutiger
1987

Freeman Craw
1988

Ed Benguiat
1989

Gene Federico
1991

Lou Dorfsman
1995

Matthew Carter
1997

Rolling Stone magazine
1997

Colin Brignall
2000

Günter Gerhard Lange
2000

Martin Solomon
2003

Paula Scher
2006

Mike Parker
2011

Erik Spiekermann
2011

Gerrit Noordzij
2013

SPECIAL CITATIONS
TO TDC MEMBERS

Edward Gottschall
1955

Freeman Craw
1968

James Secrest
1974

Olaf Leu
1984 / 1990

William Streever
1984

Klaus F. Schmidt
1985

John Luke
1987

Jack Odette
1989

2014 TDC SCHOLARSHIP
RECIPIENTS

Christina Bull
Pratt Institute

Sedrick Chisom
*The Cooper Union
School of Art*

Maryann George
*Parsons The New
School for Design*

Shannon McLean
*Fashion Institute
of Technology*

Rocio Peralta Santana
*BAU, Centre Universitari
Disseny, Barcelona, Spain*

Lindsay Soto
School of Visual Arts

Abbie Winters
*Virginia Commonwealth
University*

2013 STUDENT
AWARD WINNERS

Best in Show / $1,000
Jeongho Park
*Seoul / Minneapolis
College of Art
and Design*

Second Place / $500
Kevin Kremer
Miriam Rieger
Corinna Rusker
Mediadesign
Hochschule München

Third Place / $300
Benny Lämmel
Nadine Mayer
Lars Reiners
Lea Roth
Mediadesign
Hochschule München

INTERNATIONAL
LIAISON CHAIRPERSONS

ENGLAND
John Bateson
Bateson Studio
5 Astrop Mews
London W6 7HR
john@batesonstudio.com

FRANCE
Bastien Hermand
ECV, École Communication
Visuelle
1, rue du Dahomey
75011 PARIS
b.hermand@ecv.fr

GERMANY
Bertram Schmidt-
Friderichs
Verlag Hermann Schmidt
Mainz
GmbH & Co.
Robert Koch Strasse 8
Postfach 42 07 28
55129 Mainz Hechtsheim
bsf@typografie.de

JAPAN
Zempaku Suzuki
Japan Typography
Association
Sanukin Bldg., 5th Floor
1-7-10 Nihonbashi-honcho
Chuo-ku, Tokyo 104-0041
office@typo.or.jp

MEXICO
Prof. Felix Beltran
Apartado de Correos
M 10733 Mexico 06000
felixbeltran@infinitum.
com.mx

RUSSIA
Maxim Zhukov
3636 Greystone Ave,
Apt.4C
Bronx, NY 10463-2059
Zhukov@verizon.net

SOUTH AMERICA
Diego Vainesman
181 East 93 Street,
Apt. 4E, New York, NY 10128
diego@40N47design.com

SPAIN
Christian Giribets
Bau, Escola Superior
de Disseny
Pujades 118
08005 Barcelona
christian@baued.es

VIETNAM
Richard Moore
21 Bond Street
New York, NY 10012
RichardM@RmooreA.com

TYPE DIRECTORS CLUB
347 West 36 Street
Suite 603
New York, NY 10018
212-633-8943
FAX: 212-633-8944
E-mail: director@tdc.org
www.tdc.org

TDC MEMBERSHIP

A /

kHyal™ — 2010
Christine Aaron — 2012a
Priyanka Agrawal — 2012s
Yunus Ak — 2014c
Seth Akkerman — 2008
Zahra Al-Harazi — 2012
Zainab Al-Mashat — 2013s
Salem Al-Qassimi — 2014
Anna-Lynn Albrink-Witt — 2014c
Lee Aldridge — 1996
Robert Alpe — 2011
Daniel Alt — 2014s
Gail Anderson — 2013
Jack Anderson — 1996
Lück Andreas — 2006
Christopher Andreola — 2003
Alexandra Andrews — 2014s
John Anstey — 2013
Flavio Arnizant de Zorzi — 2013s
Robyn Attaway — 2002
Bob Aufuldish — 2006
Nomar Augusto — 2013
Caio Avelino — 2012s

Ana Benaroya — 2015
Ed Benguiat — 1964***
Antonino Benincasa — 2013
Anna Berkenbusch — 1989
Sam Berlow — 2009
Kara Angeli Bermejo — 2013s

B /

Roberto Bernasconi — 2014
Ana Gomez Bernaus — 2014
John D. Berry — 1996
Peter Bertolami — 1969***
Maxwell Beucler — 2011
Gail Bichler — 2013
Michael Bierut — 2010
Klaus Bietz — 1993
Henrik Birkvig — 1996
Heribert Birnbach — 2007
Debra Bishop — 2008
R. P. Bissland — 2004
Roger Black — 1980
Thierry Blancpain — 2014
Marc Blaustein — 2001
Susan Block — 1989***
Halvor Bodin — 2012

Christopher Cannon — 2006
Francesco Canovaro — 2009
Wilson Capellan — 2007
David Caplan — 2012
Marco Aurelio Cardenas — 2014
Mauro Carichini — 2014
Paul Carlos — 2008
Tanner Carlson — 2014c
Scott Carslake — 2001
David Carpenter — 2014
Michael Carsten — 2008
Matthew Carter — 1988***
Amber Caae — 2013s
James Castanzo — 2008
Ken Cato — 1988
Jackson Cavanaugh — 2010
Len Cheeseman — 2009
Frank Chavanon — 2014
Scott Dadich — 2008
Chusheng Chen — 2014s
I-Ying (Annie) Chen — 2012s

Andrew Collette — 2013s
Thomas Colligan — 2013s
Nancy Sharon Collins — 2006
Cherise Conrick — 2009
Nick Cooke — 2001
Ricardo Cordoba — 2009
Kristenelle Coronado — 2012s
Madeleine Corson — 1996
Lynette Cortez — 2013
James Craig — 2004
Freeman Craw* — 1947
Michael Crawford — 2013s
Kathleen Creighton — 2008
Andreas Croonenbroeck — 2006
Ray Cruz — 1999
Jacob Cummings — 2012s
John Curry — 2009
Rick Cusick — 1989
Ken Cutts — 2012

D /

Marie D'Ovidio — 2012s
Karen Charatan — 2010
Si Daniels — 2009
Charles Daoud — 2013
Susan Darbyshire — 1987

Tess Donohoe — 2012
Megan Doty — 2014c
Cynthia Dualher — 2012s
Lauren Draper — 2013
Ned Drew — 2011
Christian Drury — 2007
Christopher Dubber — 1985***
Christian Ducruet — 2012
Joseph P. Duffy III — 2003
Laurie Duggins — 2013s
Denis Dulude — 2004
Christopher Dunn — 2010
Andrea Duquette — 2009
Adonis Durado — 2013
Alexandra Dusky — 2013s
Simon Dwelly — 1998

E /

Thalia Echevarria — 2012
Ryon Edwards — 2013
Jodi Edwards — 2013
Anthony Elder — 2011
Nicholas Eldridge — 2009
Emily Elkins — 2013
Garry Emery — 1993

Louise Fortin — 2007
Dirk Fowler — 2003
Alessandro Franchini — 1996
George Frederick — 2012
Carol Freed — 1987
Russell Freedman — 2011
Phil Luciano Frezzo — 2013s
Ryan Pescatore Frisk — 2004
Adrian Frutiger — 1967**
Amy Fuller — 2013
Leigh Furby — 2012c
Dirk Fütterer — 2008

G /

Sara Gable — 2012
Evan Gaffney — 2009
Louis Gagnon — 2002
Pam Galvani — 2014s
Marc Gameroff — 2014
Courtney Garvin — 2013
Christof Gassner — 1990
David Gatti — 1981***
Alex George — 2010
Stephanie Ghozali — 2014c
Pepe Gimeno — 2001
Laura Giraudo — 2013c

Katarzna Gruda — 2009
Artur Marek Gulbicki — 2011
Nora Gummert-Hauser — 2005
Tushar Gupte — 2014
Peter Gyllan — 1997

H /

Faris Habayeb — 2012
Andy Hadel — 2010
Annette Haefelinger — 2013
Michael Hagemann — 2012
Diane Haigh — 2012
Bobby Haiqalsyah — 2013
Elizabeth Haldeman — 2002
Emily Hale — 2014
Allan Haley — 1978
Debra Hall — 1996
Jonathan Halpern — 2012s
Carrie Hamilton — 2013
Lorain Hamilton — 2013s
Dawn Hancock — 2003
Egil Haraldsen — 2000
Kat Hargrave — 2013a
Jillian Harris — 2012
Knut Hartmann — 1985

Kit Hinrichs — 2002
Jessica Hische — 2010
Genevieve Hitchings — 2010
Sarah Ho — 2012
Mark Ho-Kane — 2012
Sissy Emmons Hobizal — 2012
Henry Hobson — 2012
Fritz Hofrichter — 1980***
Alyce Hoggan — 1987
Michael Hoinkes — 2006
Richard Holberg — 2012
Karen Horton — 2007
Kevin Horvath — 1987
Debra Morton Hoyt — 2014
Christian Hruschka — 2005
Karen Huang — 2012
Wei Huang — 2013s
John Hudson — 2004
Aimee Hughes — 2008
Keith C. Humphrey — 2008
Grant Hutchison — 2013s

I /

Albert Ignacio — 2011s
Yuko Ishizaki — 2009
Alexander Isley — 2012

Kayre Axe 2013s
Atif Azam 2013s
Sarah Azpeitia 2012s
Eran Bacharach 2011
Min Bae 2014lc
Shinho Bae 2014lc
Furuzan Melis Bagatir 2013s
Hyejung Bahk 2012s
Linus Luka Bahun 2014s
Leah Bailey 2012
Peter Bain 1986
Michelle Bajurny 2014s
Allison Ball 2011lc
Rachel Balma 2014s
Jesus Barrientos 2013
Maria Bartolome 2012a
Priyanka Batra 2012
Mark Batty 2007s
Autumn Baxter 2011s
Jennifer Beatty 2013lc
Allan Beaver 2010
Katja Becker 2008
Misha Beletsky 2007
Jeff Bellantoni 2012
Amy Belledin 2013
Felix Beltran 1988***

Matteo Bologna 2003
Scott Boms 2012
Jason Booher 2011
Denise Bosler 2012
Clare Bottenhorn 2013
Maury Botton 2008
Matthew Bouloutian 2013s
Chris Bowden 2012s
Miriam Bowring 2013
Sarah Bradford 2012
John Breakey 2006
Orin Brecht 2013
Valeriya Brodnikova 2014s
Ed Brodsky 1980***
Caleb Brown 2013s
Craig Brown 2013
Paul Buckley 2004
Anthony Buza 2007
Michael Bundscherer 2007s
Bill Bundzak 1964***
Steve Byers 2010
Raymond Byron 2013

C /
Ronn Campisi 1988
Marta Galaz 2013
Cancio 2014

Joshua Chen 2008
Yue Chen 2012
Zhengda Chen 2011s
David Cheung, Jr. 1998
Sherlene Chew 2014lc
Todd Childers 2013
Patricia Childers 2011
Taylor Childers 2013s
Meagan Choi 2010
YonJoo Choi 2013lc
Angira Chokshi 2014lc
Viresh Chopra 2006
Champagne Choquer 2013lc
Sunmin Chung 2012s
Zuri Chung 2014
Stanley Church 1997
Francesco Ciavelli 2013
Nicholas Cintron 2003s
Scott Citron 2007
Susan Clark 2013
Thomas Clayton 2012
Graham Clifford 1998
Marc Clormann 2014
Doug Clouse 2009
Steven Clunis 2014s
Andy Clymer 2013
Ed Colker 1983***

Jo Davison 2007
Josanne DeNatale 1986
Arnaud de Vicq de Cumptich 2013
Roberto de Vicq de Cumptich 2005
Bridget Dearborn 2011
Ken DeLago 2008
Olivier Delhaye 2006
Liz DeLuna 2005
Andrea DeMarco 2013s
Richard R. Dendy 2000
Mark Denton 2001
Mona Desai 2014
Jennifer Devenny 2013s
James DeVries 2012s
Cara Di Edwardo 2009
Tony Di Spigna 2010
Di Vincenzo 2013
Chank Diesel 2000
Claude A. Dieterich 1984***
Kirsten Dietz 2013
Rachel Digerness 2003s
Joseph DiGioia 2011
Catherine Dimalla 1999
Matthew Dimas 2013
Elisabetta DiStefano 2007s

Manja Emran 2013
Marc Engenhart 2006
Kristen Engles 2014s
Joseph Michael Essex 1978
Knut Ettling 2005
Florence Everett 1989***
Jesse Ewing 2011

F /
Korissa Faiman 2009
John Fairley 2014
Michael Falco 2013lc
David Farey 1993***
Cate Ferman 2014
Jamie Fernandez 2014
Ryan Fernandez 2014
Matt Ferranto 2004
Vicente Gil Filho 2002
Louise Fili 2004
Anne Fink 2013
George Finlay 2002
Kathleen Fitzgerald 2013
Kristine Fitzgerald 1990
Megan Flood 2012
Linda Florio 2009
Jeremie Fontana 2013

Lou Glassheim 1947*
Howard Glener 1977***
Mike Gmitter 2013s
Mario Godbout 2002
Marti Gold 2013
Abby Goldstein 2010
Todd Goldstein 2013s
Deborah Gonet 2005
Paul Gonzalez 2014
Robert Gonzalez 2011s
Roberta Monique Gonzalez 2013
Eber Gordon 2010
Grace Gordon 2013s
Edward Gottschall 1952***
Jonathan Gouthier 2009
Diana Graham 1984
Melissa Green 2013s
Pamela Green 2010
Sarah Greene 2012s
Joan Greenfield 2006
Robson Grieve 2010
Amelia Grohman 2014
Jodan Grove 2014s

Lukas Hartmann 2003
Luke Hayman 2006
Oliver Haynold 2009
Amy Hayson 2012
Bonnie Hazelton 1975***
Amy Hecht 2001
Jonas Hecksher 2012
Aimee Hedman 2014s
Eric Heiman 2002
Karl Heine 2010
Elizabeth Heinzen 2013
Anja Patricia Helm 2010
Cristobal Henestrosa 2010
Oliver Henn 2009
John Paul Hennessey 2014
Nitzan Hermon 2012s
Luis Herrera 2014lc
Christine Herrin 2012s
Aymeric Herry 2013
Klaus Hesse 1995
Jason Heuer 2011
Fons M. Hickmann 1996
Jay Higgins 1988
Clemens Hilger 2008
Bill Hilson 2007

J /
Donald Jackson 1978**
Alex Jacque 2014s
Torsten Jahnke 2002
Russell James 2014
Mark Jamra 1999
Etienne Jardel 2006
Alin Camara Jardim 2011
Whittline Blanc Jean-Palillant 2013s
Jesus Jimenez 2013
Becky Johnson 2010lc
Elizabeth Johnson 2011s
Regan Johnson 2013
Marilyn Jones 2013
Patra Jongjitirat 2014lc
Alison Joseph 2014s
Giovanni Jubert 2004
Leo Jung 2012

K /
Marie Kacmarek 2014
Edward Kahler 2010
John Kallio 1996
George Kalofolias 2013s
Bill Kaminski 2013s
Wenkang Kan 2013lc

Jee Yubg Kang 2014lc
Boril Karaivanov 2014
Basia Karpiel 2013s
Diti Katona 2006
Quinn Keaveney 2012s
Richard Kegler 2012
Scott Kellum 2012
Paula Kelly 2010
Saskia Ketz 2012
Helen Keyes 2011
Satohiro Kikutake 2002
EunJee Kim 2013
Florence Kim 2014
Hayim Kim 2013s
Jee Kim 2013
Julie Kim 2013lc
Minah Kim 2014
Susie Kim 2014s
Rick King 1993
Sean King 2007
Katsuhiro Kinoshita 2002
Khuplunmang Kipgen 2013s
Dmitriy Kirsanov 2010
Nathalie Kirsheh 2004
Keith Kitz 2011s
Susanne Klaar 2011

L /
Gerry L'Orange 1991***
Ginger LaBella 2013
Raymond F. Laccetti 1987***
Nicole Lafave 2012s
Karen LaMonica 2012
Carl Landegger 2013s
John Langdon 1993
Sebastian Lange 2014
Brian LaRossa 2011
Amanda Lawrence 2006
Dongkyu Lee 2014lc
Jaedon Lee 2013s
Lillian Lee 2014
Sophy Lee 2012
Elizabeth Leeper 2012s
Pum Lefebure 2006
Edward Leida 2013
David Lemon 1995
Kimberly Leon 2014
Gerry Leonidas 2007
Mat Letellier 2010
Olaf Leu 1966***
Joshua Levi 2010
Edward Levine 2011
Esther Li 2012s
Xiaozhu Li 2012lc

Annica Lydenberg 2012
Peter Lytwyniuk 2011

M /
Bruno Maag 2013
Callum MacGregor 2009
Stephen MacKley 2011
Donatella Madrigal 2012s
Danusch Mahmoudi 2001
Avril Makula 2010
Reesa Mallen 2013s
Julie Manescau 2014lc
Anastasios Maragiannis 2012s
Courtney Marchese 2013
Alane Marco 2013s
Marilyn Marcus 1979***
Bernardo Margulis 2010
Nicolas Markwald 2006
Bobby Martin 2011
Alvin Martinez 2014
Frank Martinez 2013
Shigeru Masaki 2006
Jakob Maser 2006
Sophie Masure 2013
Vijay Mathews 2012
Mary Mathieux 2012

Javier Miguelez 2013s
Rony Mikhael 2013
Abbott Miller 2010
Brian Miller 2006
Noah Miller 2013
John Milligan 1978***
Debbie Millman 2012
Dexter Miranda 2012s
Michael Miranda 1984
Susan L. Mitchell 1998
Melissa Miyamoto-Mills 2013lc
Amanda Molnar 2010s
Sakol Mongkolkasetarin 1995
James Montalbano 1993
Chemi Montes 2014
Aaron Moodie 2012
Christine Moog 2011
Ahyoung Moon 2013s
Richard Earl Moore 1982
Tyler Moore 2012
Wael Morcos 2013
Richard Morgan 2014
Minoru Morita 2013lc
Daniel Morris 2014
Katherine Mueller 2014lc

Michelle Nix 2008
Hyun-Jung Noh 2010
Dirk Nolte 2012
Gertrud Nolte 2001s
Heidi North 2013
Alexa Nosal 1987***
Thomas Notarangelo 2010
Yves Nottebrock 2011
Beth Novitsky 2013
Jan Olaf Nygren 2014

O /
Gemma O'Brien 2014
Francesa O'Malley 2008
Tomo Ogino 2012
Gaku Ohsugi 2003
Blake Olmstead 2013
Ivan Ontra 2012
Robert Overholtzer 1994

P /
Michael Pacey 2001
Eduardo Palma 2013s
Ross Palumbo 2013c
Marisa Pane 2013lc
Lauren Panepinto 2010
Amy Papaelias 2008

Niberca Polo 2009s
Albert-Jan Pool 2000
Jean François Porchez 2013
James Propp 1997
Lars Pryds 2006
Kiran Puri 2013s
David Pybas 2013

Q /
Alan Qualtrough 2014s
Chuck Queener 2010
Vitor Quelhas 2011s

R /
Kellie Rados 2014lc
Jochen Raedeker 2000
Jesse Ragan 2009
Erwin Raith 1967***
Bjorn Ramberg 2013
Sal Randazzo 2000
Steven Rank 2011
Gautam Rao 2013
Patti Ratchford 2012
Kyle Reed 2013
Byron Regej 2013
Reed Reibstein 2012
James Reyman 2005

S /
Filiz Sahin 2013s
Mamoun Sakkal 2004
Martin Salazar 2013
Richard Salcer 2014
Karla Saldana 2013
Ilja Sallacz 2012s
Ina Saltz 1999
Rodrigo Sanchez 1996
Nikko-Ryan Santillan 2012s
Johanna Savad 2014s
Nathan Savage 2012
DC Scarpelli 2001
Sonia Scarr 2012
Nina Scerbo 2012
Hartmut Schaarschmidt 2006
Hanno Schabacker 2014
Anja-D Schacht-Kremler 2014s
H.D. Schellnack 2013
Paula Scher 2009
Emily Scherer-Steinberg 2010
Robbin Schiff 2013
Peter Schlief 2013
Hermann J. Schlieper 1987***
Evan Schlomann 2011s

Daphna Shalev 2012s
Susanna Shannon 2013
Paul Shaw 1987
Benjamin Shaykin 2012
Andrew Sheffield 2013
Nick Sherman 2009
David Shields 2007
Jeemin Shim 1996
Kyuha Shim 2010
Dina Shirin 2014s
Philip Shore, Jr. 1992***
David Short 2014
William Shum 2013s
Dipti Siddamsettiwar 2013s
Christopher Sieboda 2014
Etta Siegel 2014
Nicholas Siegrist 2001
Scott Simmons 2014s
Anthony Simone 1994
Mark Simonson 2011s
Dominque Singer 2012
Fred Smeijers 2012
Elizabeth Carey Smith 2013
Robbie Smith 2010
Richard Smith 2013
Steve Snider 2004

Amanda Klein 2011
Arne Alexander Klett 2005
Akira Kobayashi 2007
Claus Koch 2004
Florian Koch 2009
Boris Kochan 1960****
Masayoshi Kodaira 2002
Markus Koll 2007
Jonathon Kosla 2014s
Thomas Kowallik 2010
Hannah Kramer 2011s
Dmitry Krasny 2009
Markus Kraus 1997
Willem Krauss 2012
Stephanie Kreber 2001
Ingo Krepinsky 2013
Bernhard J. Kress 1963****
Gregor Krisztian 2005
Stefan Krömer 2013
Jan Kruse 2006
Henrik Kubel 2010
John Kudos 2010
Ken Kunde 2011
Christian Gregg Kunnert 1997
Dominik Kyeck 2002

Yue Li 2013s
Maxine Lin 2013s
Armin Lindauer 2007
Domenic Lippa 1999
Jason Little 1996
Wally Littman 2013
Ingsu Liu 2002
Sascha Lobe 2002
Ralf Lobeck 2007
Karolina Loboda 2014
Sharyn Belkin Locke 2014
Uwe Loesch 1996
Oliver Lohrengel 2004
Amy Lombardi 2013
Kirsten Long 2012
Adriana Longoria 2012c
Jay Loo 2014
Jamie Lopez 2013c
John Howland Lord 1947**
Chercy Lott 2008
Arline Lowe 2009
Christopher Lozos 2010
Luke Lucas 2012
Jessica Lucivero 2013c
Ken Lunde 2011

Steve Matteson 2006
Scott Matz 2011
Ted Mauseth 2001
Andreas Maxbauer 1995
Larry Mayorga 2009
Cheryl McBride 2009
Nick McBurney 2011s
Mark McCormick 2010
Rod McDonald 1995
Elizabeth McKinnell 2014
Shannon McLean 2012s
David McLeod 2014
Alexa McNae 2011
Marc A. Meadows 2013
Samuel Medina 2012s
Arturo H. Medrano 2013s
Roland Mehler 1992
Niyati Mehta 2013s
Maurice Meilleur 2013s
Matt Meiners 2012s
Uwe Melichar 2000
Myra Mendoza 2013
Shenhui Meng 2014lc
Frédéric Metz 1985***
Dina Michi 2013s
Jeremy Mickel 2009
Michael Mierzejwski 2012lc

Lars Müller 1997
Joachim Müller-Lancé 1995
Gary Munch 1997
N. Silas Munro 2011
Kara Murphy 2006
Jerry King Musser 1988
Louis A. Musto 1965***
Steven Mykolyn 2003

N /

Miki Nagao 2009s
Marc Nahas 2012
Andrea Nalerio 2008s
Cayetano Navarrete 1996
Ralph Navarro 2013
Jamie Neely 2013
Eduardo Nemeth 2011
Titus Nemeth 2010s
Helmut Ness 1999
Nina Neusitzer 2003
Ulli Neutzling 2009
Christina Newhard 2012
Jon Newman 2013
Joe Newton 2009
Vincent Ng 2004
Stefan Nitzche 2014
Charles Nix 2000

Jaewon Park 2013s
Jeongho Park 2013s
Juhyun Park 2001
Nari Park 1997
Sari Park 2011
Jonathan Parker 2006
Jim Parkinson 1988
Karen Parry 1994
Donald Partyka 2008
John Passfiume 2009
Dennis Pasternak 2010
Mauro Pastore 2006
Neil Patel 2006
Gudrun Pawelke 2011
Alan Peckolick 1996
Andre Pennycooke 2008
David Perrin 2013s
Sonia Persad 2011
Giorgio Pesce 2013s
Caitlyn Phillips 1999
Max Phillips 2000
Amanda Phingbodhipakkiya 2009
Stefano Picco 2003
Clive Piercy 1996
Massimo Pitis 2004
Deana Pnea 2013s
J.H.M. Pohlen 2006

Dan Rhatigan 2013
Kimberly Rhee 2013
Douglas Riccardi 2010
Claudia Riedel 2004
Helge Dirk Rieder 2003
Oliver Rios 2012
Phillip Ritzenberg 1997
Chad Roberts 2001
Duncan Robertson 2014s
Julie Robins 2013s
Katherine Robinson 2011s
Sofija Rockomanovic 2013s
Thomas Rockwell 2014
Allison Rodde 2012s
Jeff Rogers 2012
Stuart Rogers 2010
Salvador Romero 1993***
Kurt Roscoe 1993
Nancy Harris Rouemy 2007
Theo Rosendorf 2013
Linda Rubes 2013
Erkki Ruuhinen 1986
Carol-Anne Ryce-Paul 2001
Michael Rylander 1993

Holger Schmidhuber 1999
Hermann Schmidt 1983***
Klaus Schmidt 1959***
Bertram Schmidt-Friedrichs 1989
Thomas Schmitz 2009
Elnar Schnaare 2011
Guido Schneider 2003
Werner Schneider 1987
Wanja Schnurpel 2011
Hannah Schreiner 2012s
Markus Schroeppel 2003
Holger Schubert 2006
Eileen Hedy Schultz 1985
Eckehart Schumacher-Gebler 1985***
Robert Schumann 2007
Jennifer Sciafani 2013lc
Mary Scott 2012
Peter Scott 2002
Josh Scruggs 2014
Leslie Segal 2003
Hyunju Seo 2013s
Chris Sergio 2011
Thomas Serres 2004
Michelle Shain 2012

Jan Solpera 1985***
Patrick Sommer 2012s
Brian Sooy 1998
Allen Spector 2012lc
Erik Spiekermann 1988
Kirsli Spinks 2013
Erik Spooner 2014
Maximilano Sproviero 2012
Sunny Stafford 2013
Frank Stahlberg 2000
Rolf Staudt 1984***
Carissa Stein 2014s
Olaf Stein 1996
Olivia Sterling 2013s
Charles Stewart 1992
Roland Stieger 2009
Michael Stinson 2005
E Stocks 2014
Clifford Stoltze 2003
Sumner Stone 2011
DJ Stout 2010
Julie Strawson 2013
Charlotte Strick 2010
Ilene Strizver 1988
Hansjorg Stulle 1987***
Olen Subchuk 2014s
Sean Suchara 2012s

Neil Summerour 2008
Derek Sussner 2005
Zempaku Suzuki 1992
Don Swanson 2007
Paul Sych 2009
Lila Symons 2010

T /
Robin Tagliasacchi 2012s
Yukichi Takada 1995
Yoshimaru Takahashi 1996
Kei Takimoto 2011
Katsumi Tamura 2003
Jef Tan 2011
Siena Tan 2012s
Trisha Wen Yuan Tan 2011s
Matthew Tapia 2012
Judy Tashji 2011s
Jack Tauss 1975***
Pat Taylor 1985***S
Will Taylor 2014lc
Anthony J. Teano 1962***
Marcel Teine 2003
Yuliya Temeryazantseva 2014s

Eric Thoelke 2010
Drue Thomas 2014s
Louis-Charles Tiar 2014
Eric Tilley 1995
Colin Tillyer 1997
James Tocco 2012

U /
Andreas Uebele 2002
Dana Uher 2013lc
Thomas Uhlein 2013
Isabel Urbina 2011

V /
Diego Vainesman 1991
Scott Valins 2009
Patrick Vallée 1999
Emma Van Deun 2012s
Arlo Vance 2014
Jeffrey Vanlerberghe 2005
Leonardo Vasquez 2010
Massiel Vasquez 2013s
Rozina Vavetsi 2011
Meryl Vedros 2010s
Juan Villanueva 2013s
Nastassia Virata 2013
Frank Viva 2010
Jonas Voegeli 2013
Heidi Voelker 2014s

Oscar Von Hauske 2013
Mark Von Ulrich 2009
Danila Vorobiev 2013
Amanda Voss 2013lc
Angela Voulangas 2009

W /
Frank Wagner 1994
Jonathan Wagner 2014lc
Oliver Wagner 2001
Paul Wagner 2011
Tad Wagner 2012
Allan R. Wahler 1998
Jurek Wajdowicz 1980****
Sergio Waksman 1996
Andrej Waldegg 2013
Garth Walker 2005
Darcy Wang 2010
Michelle Wang 2013s
Craig Ward 2013s
Tiffany Wardle 2011
Katsunori Watanabe 2001
Michele Waters 2011
Cardon Webb 2009
Harald Weber 1999

Claus F. Weidmueller 1997
Sylvia Weimer 2001
Terrance Weinzierl 2012
Ari Weiss 2014lc
Craig Welsh 2010
Sharon Werner 2004
Shawn Weston 2012
Alex W. White 1993
Christopher Wiehl 2003
Michael Wiemeyer 2013
Andrew Wilcox 2014
Richard Wilde 1993
Luke Wilhelmi 2011
James Williams 1988****
Pamela Williams 2013
Steve Williams 2005
Brielle Wilson 2013lc
Grant Windridge 2000
Conny J. Winter 1985
KC Witherell 2014
Delve Withrington 1997
Lisa Wolfman 2012
David Wolske 2012

Fred Woodward 1995
Cheng Huan Wu 2014
Chia-Fang Wu 2013lc
Carolyn Wurtzel 2013lc

X /
Wendy Xu 2011

Y /
Jiaxi Yang 2014lc
Henry Sene Yee 2006
Kylene Yen 2013s
Helen Yentus 2014
Bumham Yu 2013s
Garson Yu 2005
Yah-Leng Yu 2014

Z /
Tony Zafirakos 2013s
Hermann Zapf 1952**
David Zauhar 2001
Haoqian Zhang 2014s
Zipeng Zhu 2010s
Maxim Zhukov 1996***
Ron Zisman 2011s
Roy Zucca 1969****

CORPORATE MEMBERS
Diwan Software Limited 2003
École de Visuelle Communications 2011
Grand Central Publishing 2005
School of Visual Arts, New York 2007
Sullivan 2012

TYPE INDEX

TDC 35 GENERAL INDEX

ABOUT TYPOGRAPHY 35

For the past sixty years, the Type Directors Club has encouraged the graphic arts community to achieve excellence in typography through its annual competition.

Typography 35 is the TDC's newest annual volume devoted exclusively to typography; the book presents the finest work in this field from 2013. Selected from more than 2,000 international submissions to the sixtieth Type Directors Club competition, the 209 winning designs are models of excellence and institution in contemporary type design. This year's selection encompasses a wide range of categories, including books, magazines, corporate identities, logotypes, stationary, annual reports, video and web graphics, and posters.

In addition, this year's volume features the results of the club's seventeenth annual type design competition, TDC2014. Each winning entry is displayed in full color and is accompanied by the complete information about the designer, client, typography and more. This edition also includes a special index listing the principal typefaces used and the names of their designers. The Judges' Choice sections feature the winning entries that have been singled out as each judge's personal favorite; these pieces are accompanied not only by the judges' comments but also by statements from the designers about the creative process involved in developing each piece. These components-along with this year's chairs, Gail Anderson and Matteo Bologna-exemplify the enormous vitality of the typography profession today.

ABOUT COLLINS

Collins is a brand agency focused on accelerating business growth through design thinking.

The agency believes the distinctions between digital, design, content, social, marketing, retail, experiential, and other disciplines are no longer tenable. Everything is converging. Collins' multidisciplinary team and approach creates blended solutions that deliver results to clients and memorable experiences to the public. As a result, the agency's portfolio is wildly diverse: brand identity systems, retail environments, music videos, experiential marketing, interactive spaces, e-commerce platforms, packaging systems, events, global advertising campaigns, exhibit design, content development, digital product innovation, software development, and much more.

Clients include, among others, Coca-Cola, Target, Spotify, Microsoft, American Express, Al Gore, Blackrock, Morgan Stanley, NBC, CNN, Hershey's, Optimum, EOS, and Babyganics.

This diverse portfolio of work has won awards for design craft, brand experience innovation, digital experience innovation, new media innovation, brand strategy, business efficacy, typographic excellence, and social media strategy.

collins1.com